Mexico's Fortress Monasteries

Teposcolula

Mexico's Fortress Monasteries

Richard Perry
with illustrations by the author

To the memory of my mother
Kathleen Mary Perry

Illustrations and design by Richard D. Perry

Printed in the United States of America

Library of Congress Catalog Card # 91-77484
ISBN 0-9620811-1-6

Published by Espadaña Press
P.O. Box 31067
Santa Barbara, California 93130

Cover illustration: San Miguel Huejotzingo

CONTENTS

MEXICO
Molango
Metztitlan
Ixmiquilpan
HIDALGO
Actopan
Tula
Atotonilco El Grande
Epazoyucan
Tepeapulco
Acolman
TLAXCALA
Tlatelolco
MEXICO CITY
Tlaxcala
Xochimilco
Huejotzingo
Tlalmanalco
Calpan
Cholula
Tepoztlan
Yecapixtla
Cuerna vaca
Oaxtepec
Tecamachalco
Huaquechula
MORELOS
PUEBLA
Coixtlahuaca
OAXACA
Teposcolula
Yanhuitlan
Santo Domingo de Oaxaca
Cuilapan
Tlacochahuaya

LIST OF MONASTERIES

Atlatlahucan, southwest posa

PREFACE

Today, five hundred years after the first Europeans set foot in the Americas, is an appropriate time to reflect on the momentous, and still controversial consequences of that encounter. This reexamination of our turbulent beginnings presents an opportunity to become better acquainted with the monuments of this formative period of the discovery and colonization of the New World. I hope that this book contributes to this exploration of our American past.

Among the kaleidoscope of new and exotic sights that dazzled me on my first journey through Mexico 25 years ago, the great fortress monasteries still stand out in my mind's eye. Craggy and ruinous, often neglected or abandoned, like medieval castles they seemed to dominate every town and village.

The Spiritual Conquest of Mexico is an epic story. Whatever our view of its conduct or its consequences, this rapid conversion to Christianity of the vast population of the Americas by a handful of friars, amazes us even today.

The imposing monasteries, built in the 16th century by Indians under the friars' supervision, are the most tangible monuments to this epic undertaking. Ignored or disparaged in the past, these early buildings are now the focus of a growing concern for their historical, cultural, and above all, the artistic heritage that they represent.

Although much work remains to be done, many magnificent monasteries once on the brink of oblivion have been rescued in recent years. Their treasures have been revealed and restored, and for the first time in centuries are now accessible to visitors through a network of paved roads.

Information on the monasteries remains scanty. Recent studies are few, and no general guide in English exists. This book attempts to fill that gap. It is a personal guide in words and pictures that I hope will convey to the reader a sense of my own pleasure and concern in exploring these unique monuments—buildings that not only mirror a crucial period in the history of the Americas, but continue to play a central role in the life of the Mexican people today.

There are hundreds of such monuments all across Mexico, from the frontier missions in the north, to the remote churches of tropical southern Mexico. The little known missions of the Yucatan peninsula have their own regional flavor, which we described in an earlier guide, *Maya Missions*.

The focus of the present book is the network of monasteries built in central Mexico and Oaxaca—the main theater of the Spiritual Conquest. Within this region, I have concentrated on the major monuments—those of outstanding artistic and historical interest—while not neglecting to mention the smaller monasteries of special note in each vicinity.

I should like to acknowledge the help of Ross Parmenter, who kindly read and made valuable comments on Oaxaca. Above all, I owe a special debt to my wife Rosalind, who visited all the monasteries with me and helped research and edit the material. Only with her unfailing support has this book been possible.

Finally, I hope that, with the help of this guide, the exploration of these fascinating buildings will be as rewarding for you as it has been for me.

The Emperor Charles V and his son, Philip II of Spain. (1547 woodcut)

INTRODUCTION

On June 24, 1524, twelve ragged friars arrived at Mexico City, the new capital of colonial New Spain, then rising from the ruins of Aztec Tenochtitlan. Exhausted, they had walked barefoot all the way from the Gulf coast of Mexico, over 250 miles to the east.

Awaiting them on the causeway into the island city was Hernando Cortés, the conqueror of Mexico, at the head of a grand retinue of high-ranking Spaniards and splendidly attired native nobles. To the astonishment of the Indian lords, the Spaniards, including the great Cortés himself, promptly fell to their knees in front of the travel-worn friars. With the arrival of these humble missionaries, the Spiritual Conquest of Mexico had begun.

Of all the events surrounding the discovery and colonization of the Americas, Cortés' astonishing campaign of conquest is undoubtedly the most dramatic. From its shaky beginnings in the turbulent frontier colony of Cuba to the final overthrow of the glittering Aztec empire, then in full flower, Cortés' odyssey was filled with moments of wonder, valour, and despair.

More than a simple story of conquest, this was a classic confrontation of two cultures. It marked the birth of a new nation and a new race, and was in every sense the beginning of a New World.

Landing near Veracruz in 1519, Cortés literally burned his boats before setting out on the long and arduous journey to the Aztec imperial capital, turning aside all attempts, by bribery, diplomacy or force of arms, to deter him.

With the help of native allies from Tlaxcala, longtime adversaries of the Aztecs, Cortés eventually arrived in Tenochtitlan, boldly seizing the Emperor Montezuma and holding him to ransom for gold and treasure. When the Emperor suddenly died of wounds received in a fracas, the infuriated Aztecs drove the Spaniards from the city, in a bloody retreat known as La Noche Triste, "the mournful night." But aided once again by their Tlaxcalan friends, the Spaniards were able to regroup and re-equip their army.

In 1521 they launched a second bloody assault on Tenochtitlan. This time, the defenders, led by their courageous new emperor, Cuauhtemoc, were routed and their imperial capital razed to the ground.

The military conquest was only the first step in the pacification of Mexico. Colonization quickly followed and, equally important to the Spaniards, the conversion of the Indians to Catholicism.

THE SPIRITUAL CONQUEST

In 1492, the pope had granted the Spanish monarchs sweeping authority to convert nonbelievers in the newly discovered lands of the Indies. As the acknowledged champions of the Catholic faith, the Spanish kings were eager to claim this host of new souls for the Church. In fact, bringing its indigenous peoples to Christ became the rationale for the conquest of the New World.

Although certainly peaceful compared with Cortés' swift and violent campaign, the Spiritual Conquest of Mexico was equally militant in its way, with equally far-reaching and profound effects.

The immense task of converting and evangelizing the Indians was too important, Cortés felt, to be left to the worldly Spanish priesthood of the time. He persuaded the monarch, Emperor Charles V, that this was a job for the "regular" clergy, the friars of the Mendicant Orders—the Franciscans, the Dominicans and the Augustinians—who lived humbly according to a *regula*, or Rule.

These friars claimed a long missionary tradition. The Franciscan and Dominican Orders especially, founded during the religious and social turmoil of the early 13th century, sought to restore the vitality of primitive Christianity among a European populace dismayed by the worldliness and corruption of the medieval Church. By embracing poverty and preaching to the masses, in imitation of Christ and the Apostles, they hoped to inspire a universal renewal of faith.

The 14th and 15th centuries were apocalyptic times. War was endemic, and disease and famine raged. The traditional authority of the Catholic Church was being challenged, its fabric torn by schism and beset with heresy. The friars became convinced that they were living in the Final Days before the Second Coming of Christ and believed the Last Judgment was at hand.

The Reconquest of Spain from the Moors, completed in the same year as Columbus' discovery of the Americas, had been an intense stimulus to Spanish missionary fervor.

Radical reformers arose, known as Observants—strict observers of the austere Rules of the Mendicant Orders—who believed themselves specially chosen to carry out God's work of spiritual revitalization by preaching and by example. Reinvigorated by rigorous internal reforms and toughened by long years of converting the Moors, the friars were well prepared for the Spiritual Conquest of the populous New World.

For many of them, the discovery of the New World signaled a new age. In the millenarian tradition, it was seen as the culmination of a centuries-old religious quest, promising the imminent fulfillment of biblical prophecies. These foretold that all the peoples of the world would be brought to Christianity, and the Holy City of Jerusalem permanently liberated from the infidel.

Of the three missionary Orders, the Franciscans were the first to set foot in Mexico, soon followed by the Dominicans. The Augustinians arrived last, reaching Mexico almost a decade later.

The Franciscans

In 1524, the first Franciscans landed in Mexico, twelve in number to symbolize their apostolic role in the missionary enterprise ahead. The Twelve, as they were called, were led by Fray Martín de Valencia, head of the Observant Province of San Gabriel de Extremadura in Spain.

These early friars were men of vision. For them the New World, with its pagan masses awaiting conversion, presented an opportunity to establish ideal Christian communities of friars and Indians. Here, on pristine Mexican soil far removed from the corruption of the Old World, they would build the New Jerusalem.

The utopian zeal of the Twelve was reinforced by the humanist views of many Spanish officials, notably Juan de Zumárraga, an Observant Franciscan who was appointed the first archbishop of New Spain, and the viceroy, Antonio de Mendoza.

By the *Omnimoda*, a papal decree of 1522, the friars were granted broad parochial powers, not only to administer the sacraments but also to organize religious life in the mission towns and expedite the evangelization of the Indians.

Missions sprang up everywhere. The Franciscans concentrated their efforts in the most populous areas near the capital. In 1524 alone, they founded four major monasteries in the Valleys of Mexico and Puebla, including the great monastery of Huejotzingo. By the late 1530s, Franciscan houses ringed the capital, from Tlalmanalco and the Pueblan missions in the east to Toluca and Morelia in the west; from Tula and Tepeapulco in the north to Xochimilco and Cuernavaca in the south.

The Dominicans

The Order of Preachers, as the Dominicans were known, prided themselves on their ability to convert even the most intractable unbeliever by impassioned preaching of the Word of God.

The Dominicans arrived in Mexico in 1526, only two years after the Franciscans, led by

Fray Domingo de Betanzos, also an Observant friar and a dedicated religious reformer. But their early evangelical efforts were ineffective, plagued by illness and dwindling numbers. By 1527, when the Dominican missionary campaign finally got under way, much of central Mexico was already under Franciscan control.

Although they built a few monastic houses in the vicinity of the capital, notably at Coyoacan and Azcapotzalco, the Dominicans directed their main thrust to the south. From their monastery at Oaxtepec, in the present state of Morelos, they founded a chain of missions that extended through Puebla into Oaxaca, where they built their most magnificent monasteries, and eventually reached as far south as Chiapas and even Guatemala.

The Augustinians

By the 16th century, the Augustinians—originally a contemplative order of ascetic hermits—had become active utopian reformers. Like the Franciscans, they saw the New World as an earthly paradise free of sin, a Garden of Eden in which they hoped to create the City of God.

They were the most militant and apocalyptic of the missionaries, viewing the task of conversion in terms of a cosmic battle with Satan for Indian souls.

By the time the Augustinians reached Mexico in 1533, the others were well entrenched. Led by Fray Francisco de la Cruz, the "Venerable One," the first friars were forced to limit their missionary activities to areas not already claimed by the Franciscans and Dominicans.

From their priory at Acolman, northeast of the Mexico City, they established a network of missions that stretched north into present-day Hidalgo and included such grand monasteries as Actopan, Ixmiquilpan and Metztitlán. To the south, they built a cluster of fortress monasteries around their principal priory at Yecapixtla, in the hill country of what is today northern Morelos.

The Mission Towns

The friars ventured fearlessly into pacified and unpacified areas alike. Often they were the first Europeans to arrive and the only ones to stay. They conducted mass baptisms of the Indians, sometimes thousands in a day—a conversion on a scale unprecedented in the history of Christianity.

The mainstay of the Spiritual Conquest was the mission town. To ease the task of evangelization, the friars gathered the Indians from several communities, sometimes by force, into larger centers. Mission buildings, often flimsy temporary quarters, were hastily erected.

The independence of the early mission towns was initially encouraged by the Spanish Crown, in the interests of social peace among the Indians and the fulfillment of the missionary imperative. Many of these early communities developed into large *repúblicas de Indios*—virtually autonomous Indian communities, under the benevolent but firm supervision of the friars.

By the mid-16th century, many of the primitive early missions—in many cases makeshift thatched structures of wood and adobe—were being replaced by permanent monasteries, massive stone structures erected by armies of Indian laborers. A sustained building campaign, begun in the 1540s, continued virtually unchecked until, by the end of the century, more than one hundred monasteries stood in towns and villages across Mexico.

Ironically, in the final decades of the 1500s, at a time when all the great monasteries had at last been completed, the utopian world of the friars threatened to collapse. To their dismay, the resurgence of pre-Conquest religious practices revealed that the great conversion had been only superficial. In what the embattled friars saw as divine judgment, epidemics were taking a terrible toll of the Indian population. To many, it seemed that the long awaited Last Days were at hand.

By this time, the aging pioneers of the Spiritual Conquest found themselves in bitter conflict with their less zealous successors. These included the worldly, Mexican-born clergy who now viewed the humanist, pro-Indian friars as dangerous radicals. Plans for a native priesthood were abandoned.

At this time too, the Crown moved decisively to limit the influence of the missionary Orders—now viewed as a rival source of power and, in light of the orthodoxy of the Counter-Reformation, potential heretics. Complaints about the burden placed on the native population by monastery construction, often perceived as grandiose and extravagant by colonial officials, were echoed by the secular Catholic hierarchy, who resented the friars' usurpation of their traditional privileges.

By 1600, the Spiritual Conquest was over. As the native population shrank, the ranks of European settlers and mixed-race *mestizos* swelled in town and country. In the face of bitter protests from the Mendicants and Indians alike, most monasteries were gradually integrated into the established Catholic Church. Friars were eventually replaced by episcopal clergy.

But the friars' imposing monasteries, built by the converts, still stand to this day—living monuments to the visionary experiment of the Spiritual Conquest.

ART AND ARCHITECTURE

The history of American art has been the history of the continuous transformations and metamorphoses undergone by European forms as they have taken root on our continent. The first example of this process is the art of 16th century New Spain... a sublime example.

Octavio Paz

Mendicant monasteries in Europe had always reflected the preoccupation of the Orders with their divine mission. Instead of an inward-looking community of monks, the friars were missionaries whose place was in the real world, converting the heathen, preaching and ministering to the populace.

The traditional layout of the monastery, or more accurately, the friary, reflected this role. Function was more important than form. Mendicant churches were designed as public preaching halls rather than as secluded monastic temples.

Traditional communal dormitories gave way to individual cells, where each friar could meditate alone to prepare himself for the missionary task. Lay people and parishioners were even admitted to the cloister, which had originally been closed to the public, as the name implies. Infirmaries and schools became essential components of the conventual complex.

Poverty and humility were the friars' watchwords in their daily lives. In their monasteries, too, they strove to avoid luxury and embrace the virtues of simplicity. Architecture was subordinate to pictorial decoration, especially murals, whose aims were didactic rather than esthetic. The friars reached out to the community, often using outdoor areas and public squares for catechizing and preaching.

In Mexico, the architecture of the Spiritual Conquest built upon these traditions and introduced several innovations dictated by the special needs of the evangelical task.

Isolated in an unknown land, limited in their architectural knowledge and hampered by the constraints of time and primitive construction methods, the practical friars were forced to improvise, relying on their own energies and talents. Marshalling the abundant local building materials and native labor, they created one of the most distinctive bodies of architecture in the New World.

The Fortress Monastery

Frequently built on the platforms of pre Conquest pyramids and constructed with the stones from demolished temples, the monasteries were clearly intended to impress the Indians with the power of Christianity.

Most 16th century monasteries can be instantly recognized by their imposing "fortress" appearance. Built on a massive scale with plain stone walls, they are heavily buttressed and decorated with battlements.

The Open-Air Church

Faced with overwhelming numbers of new converts, the friars responded by inventing the open-air church. Although in Europe, medieval preachers had often used the churchyard for sermons and plays, its sacramental use and integration as the atrium of the monastery was a New World innovation.

The open-air church was a concept already familiar to native congregations. They were used to participating in religious ceremonies—from dancing to human sacrifice—performed in the outdoor precincts of the prehispanic temple. In many cases, the new monastery atrium now physically occupied these sacred places—a factor that encouraged Indian acceptance of the new religion.

The Atrium

The atrium was, in effect, the nave of the open-air church. Usually of spacious dimensions, it was enclosed by high walls and fitted with arched gateways and four corner chapels, or *posas*. Processional pathways outlined the perimeter and a carved cross stood in the center. The friars preached there and led the parishioners and religious fraternities in ceremonial processions. On feast days, it was the scene of colorful religious dramas.

Embellished with military-style merlons, the walled atrium was an essential component of the fortress style, designed to emphasize the ascendancy of the new Catholic religion over the ancient gods.

Some have interpreted the crenelated atrium, its corner chapels bristling with battlements, as a conscious attempt by the early friars to recreate in their New World monasteries the physical appearance of the biblical New Jerusalem, giving tangible expression to their utopian and millenarian hopes.

The Open Chapel

A second innovation of the Mexican monastery was the open chapel. As the atrium was the nave of the outdoor church, the open chapel was its sanctuary.

In the early years of the Spiritual Conquest, the open chapel was the main focus of religious activity. Although usually modest, sometimes it was large and elaborate, as at Cholula, Cuernavaca or Teposcolula. Generally attached to the monastery, the chapel was sometimes a separate building—often the result of its being the first part of the monastery to be built. From its raised steps or balcony, the friars celebrated mass, administered the sacraments and preached to the multitudes of Indians assembled in the atrium below.

The Convento

The other essential component of the monastery was the *convento*, or friars' living quarters. These 16th century *conventos* should not be confused with the closed convents of nuns which were established in large numbers during the 17th and 18th centuries in Mexico.

After the open chapel, the *convento* was usually the first part of the monastery to be built and rapidly became the social and political heart of every mission town. Here were located the school and the infirmary. Under the friars' paternal guidance, the Indians came to the *convento* for help in religious, personal, and even civic matters.

Architecturally, the *conventos* were workaday places, in most cases spacious but strictly functional buildings. Nevertheless, the cloisters of many monasteries were constructed with finely cut stone, and the walls of even the smallest *convento* were invariably embellished with large-scale murals.

The Church

As time went on, the churches assumed greater importance in the life of the monastery. After the period of mass conversion passed, they came to be seen as places for honoring the *santos*, or community saints—a tradition that continues to this day.

Because of their grand scale and military aspect, the churches became dominant local landmarks. Although many fortress churches served as redoubts in troubled times, they were not intended primarily as military citadels. Their formidable appearance was primarily the result of their massive construction on commanding sites. Crenelations, merlons and turrets provided a simple method of enlivening plain walls and facades, while reinforcing the concept of the church militant.

Not all the architectural trappings of the monasteries were so elementary. The doorways and window frames of many monastic churches, even the earliest and most primitive, displayed a dazzling variety of carved decoration.

Stylistically, this eclectic detailing defied precise labeling. The forms were predominantly European in origin. Northern Gothic features were frequently combined with elements from Italian Renaissance architecture, filtered through Iberian variants of these styles, such as Isabelline and Plateresque. There was a powerful Moorish, or *mudéjar*, influence, and motifs from Portuguese Manueline, Flemish Mannerism and Andalusian Baroque added further piquancy to the blend.

This potentially discordant mixture of Old World styles, however, was unified and transformed into a uniquely American art by the sensibility and traditional stonecarving skills of the Indian stonemasons who usually executed the work. Known by the Aztec term *tequitqui*, signifying "art of the conquered," the indigenous sculptural tradition stressed densely patterned ornament in flat, sharply undercut relief—a technique developed to dramatize the contrasts in surface forms beneath the brilliant tropical sun.

From fine facade reliefs and statuary to carved crosses and rude baptismal fonts, all 16th century sculpture exhibits this concern with texture and pattern. Thus energized and integrated, surface ornament itself is transformed into a dynamic expressive force—an artistic tradition that thrives in modern Mexican art and architecture.

Inside the churches, Gothic vaults, often of majestic proportions and intricately patterned with tracery, cover the naves. Outstanding rib vaults can be seen at Oaxtepec and the monasteries of Puebla and Oaxaca. Similar vaults, normally on a lesser scale although no less complex, frequently cover the cloister walks and occasionally crown the open chapel, as at Huaquechula and Teposcolula.

Many early churches had pitched wooden beamed roofs, some carved and decorated, and occasionally inlaid with elaborate geometric and *mudéjar* designs. Little of this *artesonado* work, as it is known in Mexico, has survived, although exceptional 16th century examples may still be admired at Yanhuitlan and San Francisco de Tlaxcala.

The Murals

Large scale wall painting has a long history in Mexico, from pre-Conquest times to its spectacular revival in this century. Colorful murals covered the stuccoed walls of prehispanic temples, portraying the ancient gods, myths and scenes of warfare.

Building on this native tradition as well as European custom, religious frescoes were the principal form of early monastic decoration. Sixteenth century murals were derived from prints, woodcuts and the illustrations that decorated the friars' devotional books—small, two-dimensional black-and-white images that blossomed into vast visionary murals that brightened every church and cloister.

These striking murals were painted by itinerant bands of *tlacuilos*, indigenous artists instructed in Christian iconography and artistic canons by the missionary schools but also aware of their older pictorial heritage, which was still visible in the fading friezes of the ancient temples.

Thematically, the murals generally illustrated episodes from the Old and New Testaments. Some, notably the spectacular, multi-colored open chapel murals at Actopan, depicted apocalyptic scenes from Revelation. The main emphasis, however, especially in the abundant frescoes of the *conventos*, was on devotional cycles documenting the Life and Passion of Christ. As with the architecture, they were executed in an amalgam of European styles, subtly transformed by the distinctive touch of the native artist.

The narrative paintings were invariably bordered by fantastic friezes drawn from Renaissance grotesque designs, decorative panels of patterned foliage inhabited by fantastic masks and a bestiary of fabulous creatures. Here, the creative impulse of the native *tlacuilo* was allowed greater freedom and found fuller expression. Sometimes, prehispanic motifs got past the vigilant friars and occasionally dominated the entire design, as in the lively battle friezes of Ixmiquilpan.

Most of the murals were didactic, and location reflected function in their placement within the monastery. Some themes were suitable for public areas while others were deemed more appropriate for the more secluded sections of the *convento*. The murals of the church and the monastery entrance, or *portería*, were directed at lay viewers—primarily Indian neophytes—and illustrated the fundamentals of the Christian Faith, the Church and the Mendicant Orders. The frescoes of the sacristy and the cloister, which were more devotional in character, were generally accessible only to the friars and privileged visitors.

Although, at the end of the 16th century, most of the murals were covered over, many outstanding examples have survived, some only recently come to light beneath layers of whitewash. Not only do these early murals constitute a unique art form, but they are also authentic historical documents, offering unique insight into the era of the Spiritual Conquest.

The Altarpieces

As the frescoes were whitewashed, wooden altarpieces took their place inside the churches. Starting modestly in the late 1500s, these *retablos* grew grander as the colonial period progressed, eventually gracing almost every church and monastery in New Spain. Sadly, vandalism and neglect over the centuries have exacted a heavy toll, but the surviving altarpieces constitute a unique and important part of the Mexican cultural and artistic heritage

Produced in the workshops of master craftsmen, who were attracted to Mexico from all over Europe, these elaborately carved and gilded architectural structures carried skyward tier after tier of huge glowing canvases and larger-than-life statues of saints and apostles.

Like the murals that preceded them, these towering altarpieces were designed to instruct as well as inspire the congregation. Their complex iconography, often dictated by the doctrinal orthodoxy of the Counter-Reformation, sought to glorify the history of the Church, its teachings and its hierarchy, as well as the pivotal role played by the Mendicant Orders.

Although magnificent altarpieces are also found in the great cathedrals and parish churches, the monasteries were pioneering patrons of the *retablo*-maker's art, and they alone house the handful of 16th century works that survive. Drastically reduced in numbers and frequently in bad condition, these altarpieces still retain their power. Restored examples, like those at Huejotzingo and Xochimilco, are awe-inspiring in their splendor and spiritual force.

Today, one of the enduring qualities of these churches of the Spiritual Conquest is that they are full of life. Instead of dusty museums or dead monuments to the past, they remain active places of worship, still providing a vital focus for community life in Mexico's towns and villages.

The creative impulse of the Mexican people continues to find expression in the religious folk art that brightens even the darkest recess of every church. Happily, parochial as well government-sponsored efforts at repair and restoration continue, despite hard times. Each year, more of this irreplaceable artistic and cultural heritage is being preserved for later generations and the fortunate visitor.

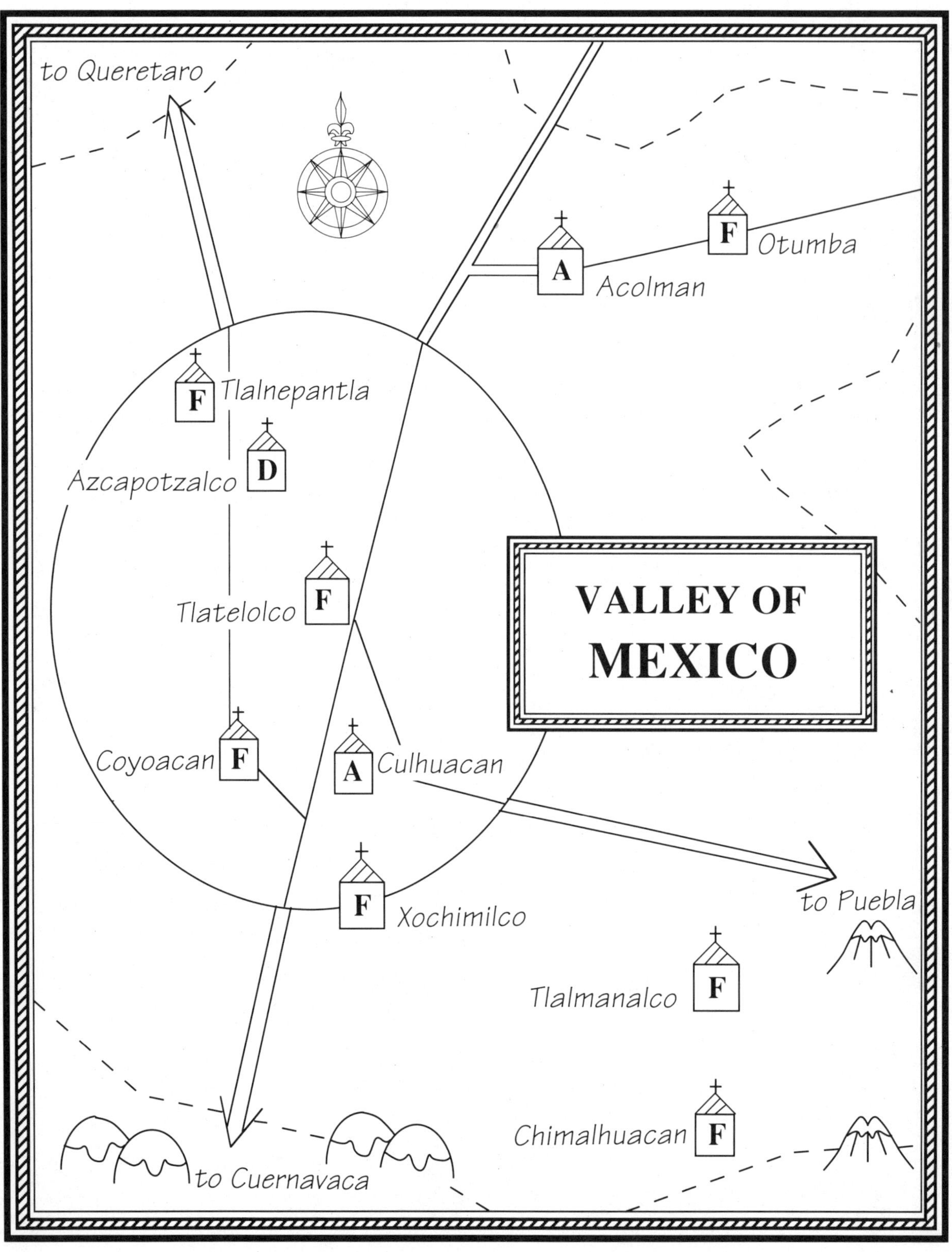
VALLEY OF MEXICO
to Queretaro
Otumba
F
A
Acolman
F
Tlalnepantla
D
Azcapotzalco
F
Tlatelolco
F
Coyoacan
A
Culhuacan
F
Xochimilco
to Puebla
F
Tlalmanalco
F
Chimalhuacan
to Cuernavaca

Chapter One

Cradle of the Conquest

The Valley of Mexico

The former beauty of this magical highland valley—the snow-capped volcanoes etched sharply in the clear mountain air and its ancient temples reflected in shimmering lakes—is difficult to visualize in the smoggy environs of modern Mexico City.

After the Conquest, the Spaniards razed Tenochtitlan, the spectacular island capital of the Aztecs, and built colonial Mexico City on its ruins. The canals were filled in and the lakes gradually drained. Palaces and churches rose upon the foundations of demolished temples.

Before evangelizing the hinterland, the missionary orders established their mother houses in the new capital: the Franciscans at San Francisco, the Augustinians at San Agustín and the Dom-inicans at Santo Domingo. Sadly, these splendid monasteries are now shadows of their former selves. Their once spacious precincts and ornamented cloisters have been lost to later encroachment. Only the sculpted church facades still emit a faded glow against the drab cityscape.

Fortunately, most of the monasteries in the lakeside towns and villages that ringed the colonial city still endure. Although some have been altered over the centuries and many are threatened by urban sprawl, many 16th century buildings remain.

We begin by visiting the only metropolitan monastery to survive largely intact, **Santiago Tlatelolco**, located in what used to be the principal Indian quarter, or *barrio*, of the colonial capital. Its brooding church, built upon the ruins of a major Aztec temple, now forms the centerpiece of the Plaza of the Three Cultures north of the Zócalo, Mexico City's main square. We also look at the nearby monasteries of **Azcapotzalco** and **Tlalnepantla**, located in the industrial northwestern suburbs of the city.

Next, we journey to **Xochimilco**, on the southern fringes of the city, a historic lakeside town whose center is dominated by the grand monastery of San Bernardino, noted for its unique 16th century altarpiece. While in the southern suburbs, we can compare the contrasting basilican churches at the monasteries of **Culhuacan** and **Coyoacan**.

Beyond Xochimilco to the east, in the shadow of the volcano Ixtaccihuatl, stands the Franciscan monastery of **Tlalmanalco**, famous for its carved open chapel. We also pay a visit to the little Dominican monastery of neighboring **Chimalhuacan**—a personal favorite of the author.

Finally, on the north rim of the valley, close to the pyramids of Teotihuacan, we arrive at the spectacular frescoed priory of **Acolman**, whose sculpted facade was the model for numerous other Augustinian monasteries in Mexico.

Our last stop is at the primitive Franciscan monastery of **Otumba**, just up the road in the direction of Hidalgo.

Tlatelolco, the Burning of the Temple

TLATELOLCO

Round Mound of Earth

Early in the morning of September 17, 1985, the startled residents of Mexico City were awoken by a terrifying earthquake—a catastrophe that took thousands of lives and left the metropolis in shambles.

Among the many scenes of devastation, few were as dramatic as that confronting rescue workers in Tlatelolco, a historic section of the city just north of the center. At its heart, the Plaza of Three Cultures—a showcase of modern urban planning with apartments, offices, schools and hospitals—lay in ruins. Only the venerable monastery of Santiago Tlatelolco, planted firmly on the foundations of an Aztec temple, had survived the prolonged and violent tremors. Now it stood unscathed amid the rubble and twisted girders of the fallen highrise buildings on every side.

The proud and ancient *barrio* of Tlatelolco is no stranger to violence and destruction. Even before the Aztecs arrived, the powerful lords of Tlatelolco ruled much of the Valley of Mexico from their island fastness in Lake Texcoco. Unwisely, they permitted the Aztecs to settle there and build their imperial capital of Tenochtitlan. Eventually, the Tlatelolcans were reduced to subjection by the people to whom they had given sanctuary.

When the Spaniards arrived in 1519, the Aztec emperor Montezuma insisted that Cortés accompany him to the Temple of Huitzilopochtli, the bloodthirsty Aztec war god, located in Tlatelolco. Conducted to the inner sanctum atop a lofty pyramid, Cortés rashly suggested that it would be an ideal site for a Christian shrine—a proposal that did not sit well with the emperor.

From the summit, the awed Spaniards looked down across the vast market spread out below, the commercial hub of the far-flung Aztec empire and the largest *tianguis* in the Americas. Bernal Diaz, the chronicler of the Conquest, expressed the Spaniards' wonderment:

On reaching the marketplace we were astounded at the swarm of people buying and selling, and the quantities of merchandise. Every kind was kept separate and in its fixed place... dealers in gold, silver and precious stones; feathers, cloaks and slaves... skins of lions and tigers... young ducks and little dogs... pottery of all kinds, honey, cochineal... chocolate merchants, sellers of salt and makers of flint knives. If I describe everything in detail, I shall never be done. Some of our soldiers, who had been in Constantinople, Rome and all over, said that they had never seen a market so large, so well laid out, and so full of people.

Tlatelolco, west front

Although the bustling marketplace has long since disappeared, a panoramic mural in Mexico City's National Palace, by the artist Diego Rivera, has recreated this colorful scene for posterity.

During the apocalyptic last days of the Spanish siege of Tenochtitlan, Tlatelolco was fiercely contested. Cuauhtemoc, the youthful prince of Tlatelolco and successor to Montezuma, fought tenaciously to defended his fief.

The great temple was set afire and bodies piled up in the lake. Cortés himself narrowly escaped death, snatched from the bloodstained waters, the Spaniards claimed, by the miraculous intervention of Santiago (St. James the Apostle), the militant patron saint of Spain.

The Church

With the razing of the Aztec city, Cortés' proposal for a Christian shrine in Tlatelolco became a reality. Bernal Diaz again:

> *After we had conquered that great and strong city, we decided to build a church to our patron and guide Santiago in place of the temple. A major part of the site was taken for the purpose. When the ground was excavated to lay a foundation, gold, silver, pearls and other precious stones were found in huge quantities, which treasure was preserved for the building of the church.*

Nothing now remains of this first church, which was reputedly decorated with a giant mural depicting Cortés being saved by Santiago on his white charger. By the end of the 16th century, the building was crumbling, and the Franciscan engineer and historian Fray Juan de Torquemada was commissioned to build a new church—the one we see today. In his chronicle, *Monarchia Indiana*, he writes with scant humility:

I built a vaulted church for the monastery of Santiago... among the most notable in Christendom, without having any teachers to instruct me, but all by myself.

Despite his disclaimer of architectural knowledge, Father Torquemada's church was innovative. Its soaring verticality contrasted with the traditional stolidity of earlier monastic churches and palaces throughout the city. In fact, the design became a model for the many lofty colonial churches that rose all across Mexico in later years.

The fabric of the church is red and black *tezontle,* the same volcanic stone used for the temples upon which it stands. The coarse, dark stone provides a stark counterpoint to the smooth white doorways carved from fine-grained *chiluca* limestone—a striking architectural effect also adopted in many other colonial buildings in Mexico City.

Flaring bastions at the base of the towers flank the grandiose west porch. Although now bereft of the statuary that once filled its niches, the sophisticated Mannerist portal set the metropolitan style for doorways in the early 1600s, and is elaborately dressed out with triumphal arches and baroque scrolls in the upper tiers. The ornamental Cross of Santiago is still visible in the crowning parapet of the facade.

The north doorway is less pretentious but more interesting, with greater clarity and coherence of design. The humble statue of St. Francis is isolated in an ornate niche above the doorway. At its apex, a sculpted eagle perches on a *chimalli*, or Aztec war shield, emblazoned with the Stigmata—the Five Wounds of Christ—a universal emblem of the Franciscans in Mexico. The triumph of the church militant over the old order could hardly be more explicit.

During the anti-clerical excesses of the 19th century, the church was vandalized and stripped of its furnishings. Today, the newly renovated interior is grandly austere. Aside from a few small windows of red and blue stained glass, the only illumination of the cavernous nave emanates from the dome. Light streams down from the cupola, throwing into dramatic relief the enormous stucco figures of the Four Evangelists, who gesture heavenward in ecstasy from the supporting pendentives.

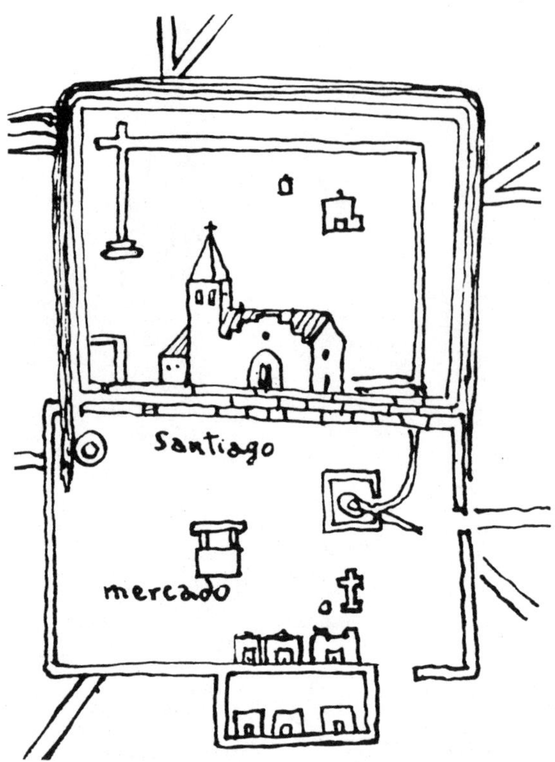

Tlatelolco in 1550

Santiago Mataindios

The focus of Father Torquemada's church was its great altarpiece. Completed about 1610 in the same style as the main retablo at Xochimilco, it too featured paintings by Baltazar de Echave Orío, the pre-eminent artist of the period.

Justly celebrated in colonial times, the altarpiece also fell victim to 19th century vandalism. The only remaining fragment is the central relief of Santiago Mataindios (St. James the Indian-Killer), which has been restored and is now displayed in the apse against a gilded backdrop.

This painted wooden tableau is one of the

Santiago Mataindios

most interesting and instructive pieces of early colonial sculpture in Mexico. The militant saint wears a plumed helmet and sits astride his white warhorse, brandishing a sword above a scene of fearful carnage. On the left, Spanish troops dressed as Roman soldiers engage Indian warriors, many maimed and bloody, with their severed limbs around them. Even Santiago's horse bites the vanquished natives, and tramples them beneath his ironshod hooves. Although the Indians wear feathered headdresses and carry flint swords, their features are those of classical Greeks.

Whether attributable to the lively hand of the Indian woodcarver, Miguel Mauricio, or to the angular composition of the woodcut on which it was based, the style of this animated composition transcends the sedate classical canons of the time and seems to anticipate the energy of the Baroque.

The ferocity and violence of the scene, equating the Spanish Conquest with the triumph of imperial Rome over Greece, may seem at variance with Franciscan ideals of brotherhood and reconciliation. But this emphasis reflects the uncompromising militance of the Spanish church during the Counter-Reformation.

By contrast, the towering mural of St. Christopher above the north door symbolizes the spiritual pacification of the New World. As he comes into focus in the half light of the nave, the colossal saint strides through the river, bearing the diminutive figure of Christ on his shoulder. Bringing Christ across the waters, he offers a peaceful alternative to the brutal image of conquest represented by Santiago Mataindios.

The other artifact of note in the church is the simple stone font in which Juan Diego was baptized. This humble Indian, to whom the Virgin of Guadalupe first appeared, is shown in a side altar, holding up his *tilma* or native cloak, full of blooming roses.

The Convento

Behind its unprepossessing orange walls, the restored *convento* has its own claim to history. Here was the site of the first and only native seminary ever to be established in New Spain.

The College of Santa Cruz was founded here in 1536, with the blessing of Viceroy Mendoza and Archbishop Zumárraga. Eminent Franciscan teachers and scholars instructed the sons of the native nobility in Christian doctrine, in preparation for the priesthood. Although plans for an Indian clergy were later abandoned, the institution continued to flourish—ironically, as a college for privileged white Spaniards, taught by native *maestros*!

The handsome entrance is akin to the north doorway of the church, classically framed with finely detailed capitals and cornices. The ample cloister is also a model of architectural sobriety, with plain arcades and doorways. Remnants of wall frescoes, monograms and grotesque friezes add a touch of color to the gray walks.

Founded in the aftermath of war and destruction, Santiago Tlatelolco has suffered all the tribulations of Mexican history. Emblazoned with the conflicting emblems of violence and spirituality, pride and humility, the monastery is a monument to Mexico's painful journey from the ancient, through the colonial and into the modern world.

Almost buried in the workaday suburbs of Mexico City, northwest of Tlatelolco, are two early monasteries: **Azcapotzalco** and **Tlalnepantla**. Both can be seen en route to the museum of Spanish colonial art at **Tepotzotlan**, located in an impressive former Jesuit seminary just outside the city in the direction of Querétaro.

AZCAPOTZALCO

Among the Beehives

Tucked away in the corner of a tree-shaded plaza, the Dominican monastery of St. James and St. Philip holds many attractions for the visitor. Its handsome church is full of colonial art and the 16th century cloister has great charm.

Imperial Azcapotzalco was the capital of the Tepanecs, a warrior people who dominated the Valley of Mexico before the rise of the Aztecs. This charming lakeside town retained its political and economic importance until late in colonial times, only to be engulfed in recent years by the expanding megalopolis.

The church is mostly 17th century with some 18th century additions. As at Tlatelolco, the rustic stonework of the facade provides a perfect foil for the elegant baroque porch. Carved from gray limestone, the doorway is a tapestry of extravagant scrolling, angular strapwork and curvetted cornices, dripping with stalactite-like *pinjante* pendants—a distinctive hallmark of 18th century architectural decoration.

Gilded altarpieces along the nave showcase many fine colonial works of art, including paintings by such well-known Mexican artists as Juan Correa and the prolific Cristóbal de Villalpando, whose Rubens-esque canvases ornament the *retablo* of St. Rose of Lima, on the south side of the church.

On the north side, the opulent Rosary Chapel—a common adjunct to many Dominican churches—is a study in extravagance. Above the entry arch, the Virgin of the Rosary extends her cloak to shelter a group of cowled friars.

Rays of sunlight from the high dome of the chapel illuminate the gilded *retablo*—a dazzling confection in the *anastilo*, or "style-less", manner of the late Mexican Baroque, in which the underlying structure is all but submerged beneath a profusion of luxuriant carving.

The Convento

The faded outline of a mural depicting the arrival of the Dominicans in the New World can still be traced on the walls of the arcaded *portería*.

Beyond lies an intimate cloister of archaic simplicity. Primitive Ionic capitals embossed with rosettes—an emblem commonly associated with the Dominican Order—adorn the broad arcades, and bands of rosettes also frame the corner niches. On the north side, a pair of intricately crafted wooden *artesonado* ceilings lend color and texture to the somber beamed walk.

Vestiges of early murals also add interest to the cloister. Decorative painted door frames are linked by grotesque friezes, where garlanded cherubs gambol in a world of fruit, flowers and chimerical beasts.

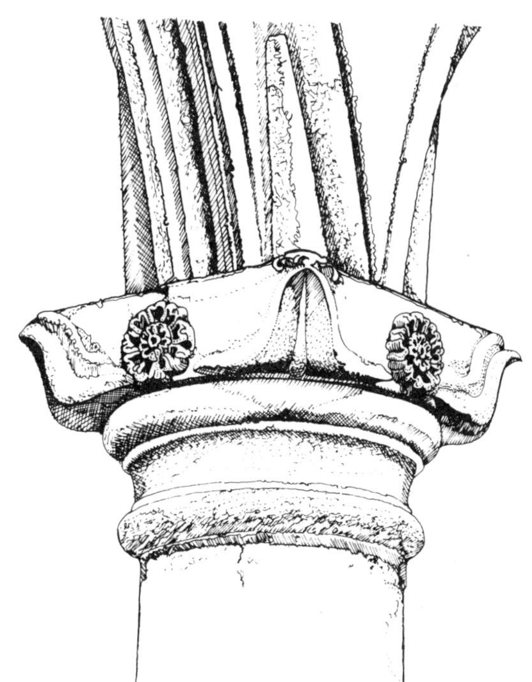

Azcapotzalco, cloister capital

Tlalnepantla, St. Bartholomew

TLALNEPANTLA
Middle Ground

After the Conquest, the Franciscans built a monastery on the boundary between two Indian communities long divided by political, cultural and linguistic differences. In an effort to reconcile the rivals, the Franciscans founded the new mission town of Tlalnepantla as a "middle ground" between the two groups: the Otomí of Teocalhuacan and the Nahua speakers of Tenayuca.

The enterprise succeeded in a manner unforeseen by the friars, for as the original Indian communities declined, colonial Tlalnepantla grew and flourished.

Known locally as the Cathedral, because of its imposing north tower, the monastery church of San Lorenzo was rebuilt in the 17th century following a disastrous fire which destroyed the beautiful wooden roof and damaged the main altarpiece.

Nevertheless, a unique 16th century sculptural record of the founding of the monastery has been preserved above the north doorway of the church. Two small reliefs flank the tiny statue of the Virgin. On the right is a medallion of St. Lawrence, the patron of the monastery, beneath which is inscribed the name of Teocalhuacan (Place of the Large Temple) in Roman letters. On the left, carved under a primitive image of St. Paul, is a row of battlements above a frieze of disks—a glyph that signifies "Walled City," the Aztec place name for Tenayuca.

A dedicatory inscription mentioning the two towns appears on the pediment overhead, with the date 1587. The carved disk flanked by hovering angels represents the Host, which, with the monstrance above, tells us that the church is dedicated to Corpus Christi.

The former atrium is now a landscaped garden. At its center stands the original red sandstone cross, its arms and shaft carved with the Instruments of the Passion. Facing the garden, a handsome arcaded loggia of seven bays stretches across the entire front of the *convento*. Behind the center arch, emphasized by its broad supporting piers, lies the recessed sanctuary of the former *portería* chapel. Perhaps such a long arcade was necessary to accommodate the two rival Indian groups on ceremonial occasions, one on either side of the altar.

The cloister recalls the one at Azcapotzalco—an airy, stone-flagged patio enclosed by simple Tuscan arcades. In the secluded sacristy, under the watchful gaze of a gallery of battered *santos*, rests an ancient baptismal font. Rimmed by the Franciscan knotted cord, it is also engraved with the worn glyph of Tenayuca, another reminder of the complex history of Tlalnepantla.

Xochimilco, west front

XOCHIMILCO
In the Flower Fields

During the Spanish Conquest, a resistant Xochimilco was burned to the ground by a vengeful Cortés, "truly a sorrowful sight to see," as he himself later admitted.

But because of its vital role as provisioner to the capital—most of the flowers and produce from its productive lakeside gardens were shipped by canoe to the Mexico City markets—Xochimilco recovered and flourished during the colonial period.

Fray Martín de Valencia, the leader of the Franciscan Twelve, personally founded the first mission here in 1525, dedicating it to San Bernardino of Siena, the popular 15th century Franciscan preacher and reformer. By 1550, much of the present monastery was built—a tribute to the skill and dedication of Xochimilco's famous artisans: stonemasons, woodcarvers and metalworkers.

In the 16th century, the monastery was famous for its vast atrium, called "the largest in the Indies". According to an eye-witness account, on the feast of Corpus Christi, in the year 1540, thousands of Indians from the surrounding villages converged here to watch the Dance of Eagles and Jaguars, a spectacular prehispanic ritual performed to the sound of the flute and the *teponaxtle*, the native drum.

Although reduced in scale, the atrium remains impressive to this day. Beyond the handsome wrought-iron gates of the western entrance, a broad cobbled terrace descends between grassy banks to the church.

The Church

The rugged stonework of the church is a study in textures—courses of rough volcanic stone embedded in smooth white mortar. The rectangular west front is capped with toothlike merlons inset with disks of black basalt taken from an Aztec temple. In a reversal of the usual pattern, the portal is carved from dark red *tezontle*, which stands out against the lighter facade.

When the facade was rebuilt following an earthquake, the elegant Mannerist west doorway, dated 1590 by the frieze inscription, must have been the height of architectural chic. Nevertheless, its sophisticated classical lines are disarmingly subverted by the rustic scrolls, bunches of grapes and folksy angels flanking the choir window.

The extraordinary north doorway, executed

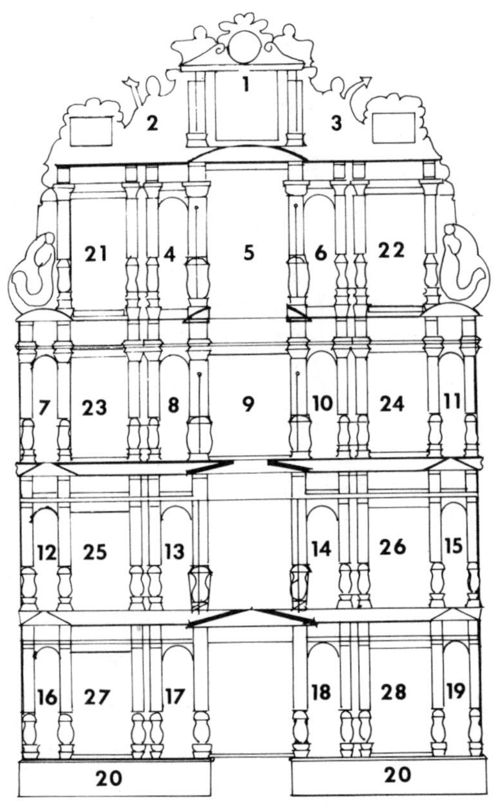

THE XOCHIMILCO ALTARPIECE

The Sculptures

1. God
2. Faith
3. Hope
4. St. Catherine
5. La Purísima
6. St. Clare
7. St. Lawrence
8. St. Michael
9. San Bernardino
10. John the Baptist
11. St. Stephen
12. Louis of Toulouse
13. St. Dominic
14. St. Francis
15. St Anthony
16. St. Ambrose
17. Pope Gregory
18. St. Jerome
19. St. Augustine
20. The Apostles

The Paintings

21. Ascension of Christ
22. Ascension of the Virgin
23. Resurrection
24. Christ in the Temple
25. Circumcision
26. Three Kings
27. Annunciation
28. Adoration of the Shepherds

some 40 years earlier, is quite different. This exuberantly carved work of the early Mexican Plateresque combines a rich vocabulary of eclectic forms. Banded Gothic colonettes and panels of rosettes frame the doorway, which is fringed by the Franciscan knotted cord.

But the decorative heart of the design is the lunette above the doorframe. A spiral ribbon molding encloses festoons of thistles and acanthus foliage as well as an outsize cartouche of the Five Wounds, surrounded by the crown of salvation.

Another pair of medieval angels flanks the empty niche above, looking much more at home here than in the west doorway. Two eagles (or doves ?) perch on either side of the upper pediment. The eroded basalt relief of the Hapsburg double eagle at the apex would not look out of place adorning some Aztec palace.

The Altarpieces

Although the church houses a choice collection of colonial art and artifacts, the undisputed masterpiece is the main *retablo* behind the high altar. Recently restored to pristine condition, this altarpiece was created in the final years of the 16th century and is considered the crowning achievement of late Renaissance altarpiece design in the Americas.

Drawing on the talents of the finest artists and craftsmen of the day, it is a stunning synthesis of painting, carving and gilding, The elegant frame, richly carved and lavishly gilded, rises in four main tiers towards the vault of the apse. Fluted columns, delicately ornamented with saints and friars, support classical capitals, cornices and pediments—all finished in refined detail.

Paintings and sculpted figures alternate in the seven vertical columns, or *calles*. In the center *calle,* framed by Atlantean pilasters, the main relief depicts San Bernardino protecting friars and Indians alike beneath his ample cloak.

Above him stands the image of La Purísima, newly resplendent in opulently textured *estofado* drapery. *Estofado* was a technique of imitating cloth on statuary by incising surface paint to reveal the gilding underneath, a method perfected by colonial *retablo* makers in Mexico. Formerly covered by a somber veil of black paint, she is still revered locally as the Virgen Viuda, or mourning Lady of Sorrows.

Luxuriously attired Franciscan saints and

church dignitaries in stately classical poses occupy the sculpted niches. Two exceptional figures stand beside San Bernardino. John the Baptist, on the right, is an expressive figure of extraordinary power and beauty, while the virile Archangel Michael, on the left, seems poised to stride forth from his niche to defeat the forces of darkness. Both images possess a freedom of movement and gesture that breaks free of the restrictive mold of the other figures, heralding the exuberance of the baroque era.

God the Father, youthful and bearded, gestures from the pediment at the top of the *retablo,* flanked by the reclining statues of Faith and Hope. Hope clutches a huge anchor, looking for all the world like a ship's figurehead.

Relief busts of rawboned Apostles fill the *predella,* or base panel of the altarpiece. Clutching the tools of their trade, these are clearly portraits of working men, perhaps the artisans who crafted the *retablo.*

Eight large paintings depict familiar episodes in the lives of Christ and the Virgin Mary, from the Annunciation and the Nativity on the first tier to the Ascension of Christ and the Assumption of the Virgin in the top tier. They are the work of Balthasar de Echave Orío, a Spanish artist who came to Mexico from Seville in the 1580s. A pioneer of the Mexican school, he founded one of the most successful and long-lived painting dynasties in the New World.

These panels are his only known complete cycle of paintings, all the more remarkable for having survived intact in their original location. They follow the prevailing Mannerist style of the period. In spite of the eccentric composition of some panels and the occasionally uncertain draftsmanship, the figures are sedate and aristocratic. Their serene, almost doll-like features are suffused with light—emphasizing their spirituality—just as their sumptuous draperies underscore their worldly dignity. Echave Orío was a master colorist, and the paintings are alive with rich warm tones accented with vivid greens and lilacs.

Several late 17th century altarpieces line the nave, all of similar design. The most notable of these is the *retablo* of the Crucifixion with its dramatic canvas of Purgatory by the baroque painter Cristóbal de Villalpando. The Virgin of Carmen in the center, flanked by St. Francis and St. Dominic, plucks suffering souls from the flames.

Xochimilco, John the Baptist

Xochimilco, arch of north doorway

Carved and painted religious objects of high quality are found in every corner of the church. The wooden choir stalls beside the altar, for example, are beautifully carved with reliefs of the Twelve Apostles. Executed by an unknown master, these are among the few Mexican colonial choir stalls to remain in place.

The marble statue of St. Sebastian, mounted in the Churrigueresque altarpiece on the north side, was brought from Spain in 1570 by Fray Jerónimo de Mendieta, the Franciscan chronicler, when he was Guardian of Xochimilco. The idealized Renaissance pose and serene expression of the semi-nude saint betray no hint of the drama or agony of his martyrdom.

The gigantic mural of St. Christopher above the north door is reminiscent of the figure at Tlatelolco. By the west entrance, you may be startled by the blackened stone death's heads embedded in the wall over the holy water stoups—macabre pre-Conquest relics unexpectedly preserved in the fabric of this Franciscan monastery.

The Convento

The dim outline of a 16th century mural appears inside the *portería*, showing Indian neophytes gathered to receive the sacraments of baptism and marriage. Reputedly, the mural included a portrait of Mendieta himself.

Simplicity is the keynote of the spacious cloister. Long Tuscan arcades are joined at the corners by complex piers carved with scrolls and cherubs—a welcome ornamental touch. A few tantalizing fragments of friezes and inscriptions cling to the walls, reminding us that these plain corridors were once aglow with murals.

Today Xochimilco is under siege. Threatened by the sprawl and traffic of Mexico City, its fertile farmlands and scenic waterways shrinking, this once beautiful Indian town is in danger of losing its distinctive character.

"slotted scroll" capital

Two Basilican Churches

Two other 16th century monasteries, at **Culhuacan** and **Coyoacan**, in the southern suburbs of Mexico City not far from Xochimilco, are distinguished by their basilican churches.

In prehispanic times the two towns were great rivals, facing each other across a narrow strait between the ancient lakes of Texcoco and Chalco. Coyoacan, on the west bank, was a strategic garrison town. Originally an outpost of the Tepanec empire, centered in Azcapotzalco, Coyoacan later guarded the main causeway to Aztec Tenochtitlan.

Culhuacan, on the right bank, had a more illustrious history. It was the seat of the Culhua, the oldest and most aristocratic lineage in the valley, who claimed direct descent from the Toltec kings of ancient Tula. The Culhua later intermarried with the Aztecs, helping to legitimize the upstart newcomers. Located close to the sacred Cerro de Estrella, site of the important New Fire Ceremony, Culhuacan retained its ceremonial prestige into colonial times.

The Franciscans evangelized both towns immediately after the Conquest, but it fell to the other orders to establish permanent monasteries—the Dominicans in Coyoacan and the Augustinians in Culhuacan.

COYOACAN

Place of the Coyote People

Of the two communities, Coyoacan has more successfully resisted the encroachment of Mexico City. A village within the city, this leafy suburb has been home to many luminaries, including Cortés himself and, in this century, the muralist Diego Rivera and the Russian revolutionary, Leon Trotsky.

The Atrium

The vast precincts of the monastery are spread in a carpet of gardens and plazas across the town center. The former atrium is now the Jardín de Hidalgo, a landscaped park with tall trees and bubbling fountains, still entered through the 16th century western gateway.

This double archway is sculpted with naive angels, fruits and foliage. Rosaries around the angels' necks and *fleur-de-lis* crosses indicate the Dominican origin of the gateway. The arms of the atrium cross in front of the church are carved with the Instruments of the Passion and also terminate in *fleurs-de-lis.*

The Church

The rectangular churchfront is anchored by a massive tower on the north and the *convento* to the south.

The triumphal arch of the portal lends a classical authority to the architecturally undistinguished facade. The frieze is inscribed with the resounding Latin legend, "This is none other than the House of God and the Gate of Heaven." An ornate relief of the Lamb of God stands above the doorway, flanked by sacred monograms and the Dominican cross.

The broad facade was designed as a frontispiece for the aisled basilican church—one of a handful built in 16th century Mexico. The classic basilican form, common among early Christian churches, had a long uninterrupted nave, flanked by lower side aisles and terminating in a narrow apse at the east end.

Originally, the nave at Coyoacan was covered with an attractive wood-beamed roof and was separated from the aisles by robust arcades of square piers. Alas, the arcades were removed in the 1920s and replaced with the florid mock-rococo interior of iron and concrete that greets us today. Ironically, this "improvement" was instigated by the normally conservative Franciscans—the original founders of Coyoacan—when they reclaimed the monastery after the Mexican Revolution.

The only authentic colonial survival inside the church is the late baroque *retablo* of the Virgin of the Rosary, in the Rosary Chapel on the north side of the church. Like its counterpart at Azcapotzalco, this lavishly carved and gilded *anastilo* altarpiece gleams with the Dominican insignia.

The Convento

The eight bays of the *portería* make it one of the longest arcades in Mexico. The capitals have slotted scrolls in the popular Ionic style we saw at Azcapotzalco, although no two are carved exactly alike. The portico also served as an open chapel. The flattened archway of its sanctuary is cut into the rear wall and the cave-like interior still shows remnants of early murals.

The Mystery Arch of Coyoacan

The most intriguing architectural feature of the monastery is the enigmatic carved doorway on the north side of the church. Apparently unrelated to any other decorative element in the monastery, its motifs are skillfully modeled in a style strongly reminiscent of the open chapel at nearby Tlalmanalco.

The origins and function of this doorway have excited much speculation. Currently it is the entrance to the old cemetery, but earlier in this century it served as the northern gateway to the atrium. Before that, old engravings show it in yet another location, with its surmounting *alfiz* still intact.

Its elaborate carving suggests a more important role—perhaps the facade of a long-lost *posa* or of the open chapel. It may have even framed the original north doorway of the church—removed in the 18th century to make way for the Rosary Chapel.

Whatever its origin, it remains one of the most accomplished works of 16th century sculpture in Mexico.

Frescoes on the north wall of the *portería* illustrate apocalyptic scenes such as the Torments of the Damned and the Fall of Man—popular mural themes in the turbulent 1570s, when they were painted. Grotesque friezes border the murals, bursting with birds, urns and twisting foliage.

Plain but pleasing Tuscan colonnades line the spacious cloister. Unlike the church, the walks have retained their beamed roofs. Attached to the beams on the south side are two remarkable *artesonado* ceilings, similar to those at Azcapotzalco but even more colorful, with lively painted panels of the signs of the zodiac and the Instruments of the Passion. They include cartoon-like scenes of John the Baptist, separated from his head, and Dominican emblems, including a little dog sitting on a book and rosary-bedecked cherubs holding baskets of flaming hearts.

A niche in the southeast corner frames the lone surviving cloister mural—a striking Crucifixion scene whose emaciated Christ speaks eloquently of the powerful religious emotions that moved the early friars.

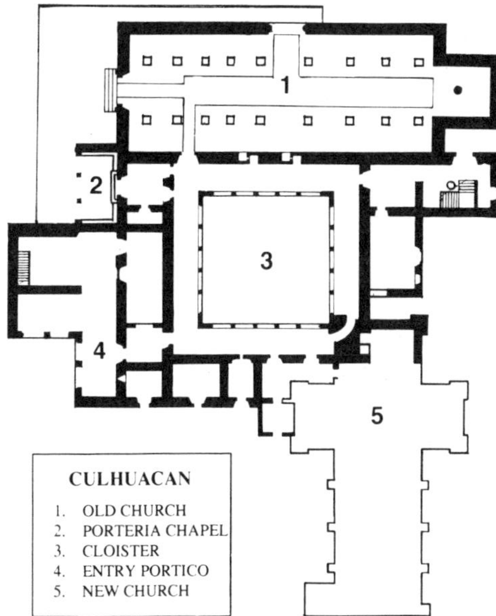

CULHUACAN

Hunchback Mountain

The rugged monastery at Culhuacan offers a dramatic contrast to urbane Coyoacan. Hewn from coarse black lava, the roofless basilican church and brooding *convento* convey the same timeless monumentality as the ruined Aztec buildings scattered throughout the valley.

In the late 1550s, the Franciscan mission was ceded to the Augustinians, who wasted little time in starting construction of a substantial monastery. With a vast Indian labor force at their disposal, as well as an inexhaustable supply of building stone taken from demolished temples nearby, the friars erected a basilican church as well as a *convento* large enough to house a seminary.

The porous volcanic stone, known as *recinto*—exceedingly hard and difficult to carve—was perfectly suited to the monumental architecture, but ill-suited for indulging the Augustinian's taste for ornamental sculpture. There was no sacrifice of scale however. The massive church is accompanied by a seemingly endless sequence of conventual rooms and corridors.

After a severe earthquake in the 18th century, the roof of the basilica collapsed and was never rebuilt. In the 1900s, a new, smaller church was added awkwardly onto the southeast corner of the *convento*.

The Convento

The bleak *convento* is brightened by numerous 16th century frescoes in a mixture of styles. Executed in *fresco secco*—paint applied to dry instead of wet plaster—they picture a wide range of subjects dear to the Augustinian Order.

The vestibule beyond the L-shaped *portería* is decorated with a faded Ship of Friars mural depicting the arrival of the Augustinians in the New World, under the protection of St. Augustine. This was a popular theme for entryways; another famous example appears in the Augustinian monastery of Actopan (Chapter Two).

In one corner of the cloister, a pair of colorful, primitive frescoes explores another Augustinian motif, the Earthly Paradise. Against an idyllic landscape of rocks, caves and native vegetation, rendered in glowing colors against an azure sky, tiny friars pursue their tasks in a

Culhuacan, the basilica doorway

peaceable kingdom of naively drawn lions, rabbits and deer.

Around the upper cloister, large Renaissance murals of the Life and Passion of Christ are interposed with medieval-style portraits of Augustinian saints and martyrs. Located at the top of the stairs is a fragmentary Entry into Jerusalem, with the figures of the Twelve Apostles and a crowd throwing flowers. In the southwest corner is an elegant Adoration of the Magi, the most complete of the compositions.

Rows of martyrs line the south walk. First, a partial St. Stephen, then St. Nicholas of Tolentino, a prominent Augustinian preacher and healer, wearing an expression of beatific calm despite the loss of his severed right foot and left hand.

In the middle of the same corridor is a splendid panel of the Company of Augustinian Martyrs in an elaborate painted Plateresque frame. Clutching their books and palms, the martyrs crowd into the foreground, their rows of tonsured heads shining like peas in a pod.

The prior's room, on the western corridor next to the church, is identified by its paneled wooden door emblazoned with the Augustinian pierced heart and other symbols associated with the Order and the Passion of Christ.

The Basilica

From the dim north walk of the lower cloister, a dark passageway leads into the roofless church. Originally, its broad nave and side aisles were spanned by beamed roofs resting on two rows of stout pillars. The carved bases of the missing arcades still rest in the grass along the nave, marking off the side aisles.

Stepping through the gaping west doorway, the visitor can descend to the foot of the stone stairs and look up at the forbidding facade, cut from monolithic basalt blocks. To the right of the facade, behind an unobtrusive Tuscan portico, hides the arched sanctuary of the former open chapel.

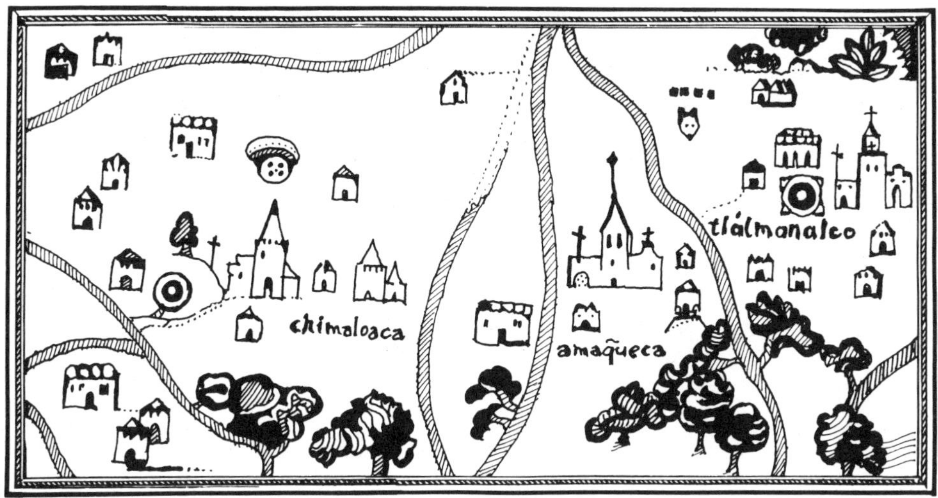

Colonial Tlalmanalco

TLALMANALCO

Place of Flattened Ground

In the winter of 1534, a line of cowled friars bore the body of their beloved Fray Martín de Valencia to its final resting place beneath the earthen floor of the primitive mission church at Tlalmanalco.

So ended Father Martín's ten eventful years as the moving force behind the Spiritual Conquest of Mexico. In 1524, as leader of the Franciscan Twelve, he undertook the awesome task of baptizing and converting the native masses to Christianity.

Formerly the Provincial, or head, of the Observant province of San Gabriel de Extremadura in Spain, he was personally committed to the apostolic path. He inspired the other friars by making long missionary journeys, often barefoot, across the plains and mountains to even the most distant villages.

After his death, as pilgrims flocked to the mission, popular demand mounted to erect a memorial to this venerated Franciscan pioneer. The magnificent open chapel at Tlalmanalco is that memorial.

Located at the foot of snow-capped Ixtaccihuatl, scenic Tlalmanalco was one of the chief towns of Chalco, a lakeside province that flourished before the warlike Aztecs arrived in the Valley of Mexico.

Like other valley lineages, by 1450 the proud Lords of Chalco found themselves under the yoke of Tenochtitlan. Bitter memories of this humiliation still festered when the Spaniards arrived in 1519, and the Chalcan nobles were quick to ally themselves with the newcomers against Montezuma.

Following the overthrow of the Aztec empire, Cortés remembered beautiful Tlalmanalco, where he had stopped on his first descent into the Valley of Mexico, and returned to claim its fertile lands and pine-clad slopes for his personal *encomienda*. The Franciscans came with him and fanned out through the Chalcan towns, baptizing, preaching and toppling the shrines of the native gods.

Tlalmanalco had been an important pre-Conquest religious center. In front of the main temple, elevated upon a platform that extended from the sloping hillside, stood the famous ceremonial dance floor which had given the town its name. The surface was paved with burnished red stucco, traces of which can still be detected on the floor of the open chapel.

The pagan shrine was torn down and in 1525, the mission of San Luis Obispo was erected in its place with stones from the demolished temple. By 1534, the year of Father Martín's death, a primitive church and friars' quarters had been added.

The Open Chapel

The ascetic Martín de Valencia might not have wished for such a splendid monument. Set against the majestic backdrop of the volcano, the open chapel at Tlalmanalco is a noble sight, one of the masterworks of 16th century sculpture in Mexico.

The design is elegantly simple. From the sanctuary, framed by a triumphal arch and Moorish *alfiz,* the walls of the chapel flare forward to embrace the broad arcade of the portico.

Sensuously carved from chocolate-colored stone by native artisans, the sculptural forms are a stylistic potpourri. "Half Indian, half European and all Mexican," John McAndrew, the art historian, has called them. Although the underlying forms are those of Renaissance grotesque decoration, medieval imagery and symbolism give the chapel an exotic and archaic appearance, like some long-forgotten Hindu temple.

But the unique significance of the chapel lies in its complex iconography, newly interpreted by the Mexican scholar, Gustavo Curiel. It is nothing less than a pictorial manifesto of late 16th century Franciscan beliefs on life, death and salvation—a sermon in stone designed to impress and instruct the native converts.

By the 1560s, when the chapel was being built, the friars' view of their mission in the New World had become increasingly pessimistic. The epidemics then decimating the Indian population were interpreted by the friars as divine punishment for the alarming resurgence of idolatry among their flock.

They saw these events as portents of the Final Days, when an apocalyptic struggle between the forces of good and evil would culminate in Christ's Second Coming. His triumph would precipitate the Last Judgment and establish the New Jerusalem—the Celestial City where, the friars believed, the righteous would dwell in joy forever. But if the Christian aspired to salvation, he must choose the path of faith and virtue. The temptations of sin and vice—works of the Devil—must be resisted and overcome. The alternative was damnation, a fate terrible to contemplate. Although some of the symbolism remains obscure, this is the message graphically conveyed by the sculpture of the open chapel.

The five arches of the portico picture sin and vice in all their guises, symbolized by wild animals, like horses, lions and monkeys, entwined in the rank foliage of untamed nature. People too, are caught in this jungle. Some resist heroically but others succumb to temptation with agonized expressions. Skulls and crossbones below the center arch symbolize the triumph of death, but the serene crowned head at the apex, flanked by the dragons of the underworld, represents the hope of salvation for man's eternal soul.

The elaborately carved sanctuary behind the arcade is the focal point of the chapel, containing the richest symbolism. Trees of Evil climb the flanking pilasters, headed by grim-visaged Angels of the Apocalypse on the capitals. Friezes of grimacing masks, animals and skulls continue around the *alfiz* and along the cornice, where a demonic zoo of fantastic animals—gryphons, birds of prey and hybrid creatures, half animal, half plant—emerge from the serpentine foliage.

A Pyramid of Demons ascends the jambs of the archway. Trapped by a welter of spiny tendrils, the contorted faces of sinners and fallen angels alternate with grinning goats' heads in a medieval bestiary of simians, hippogriffs, three-headed eagles and scaly locusts.

The archway itself represents the narrow road to salvation. From the chalices at the base—powerful symbols of redemption—a harmonious foliated design ascends to the radiant face of the New Adam at the apex. The knotted cord frames the arch, to emphasize the guiding role of the Franciscan Order along the perilous path to salvation.

In the spandrels, escutcheons display the Five Wounds, and crowned angels hold up the Instruments of Christ's Passion, by which Satan's power is vanquished.

Above the archway—the symbolic entrance to the Celestial City—stands Christ as Savior, with orb and scepter. The sun's rays, radiating

Tlalmanalco, the open chapel (detail)

behind his head, echo in stone the theophany repeated every morning as the sun rises above the chapel from the mists surrounding Ixtaccihuatl.

The Church

The square west front, anchored by the burly bastion of the north tower and topped with giant merlons, epitomizes the fortress style of the 16th century monastery.

Only the urbane north and west doorways challenge this initial impression. Both were rebuilt in 1591, after a series of destructive earthquakes, in the fashionable Mannerist style then being introduced from Europe into the cathedrals of Mexico City, Puebla and Mérida.

The Ionic west portal has a dentilled archway and cornice, with an ornamental relief of the Five Wounds and a dated plaque set in the spandrels. A diminutive statue of Louis of Anjou (San Luis Obispo), the titular saint of the monastery, is mounted in the scrolled niche above the doorway. St. Louis was an ascetic 13th century Franciscan of royal French blood, who eventually became an influential bishop.

The north doorway is more austere. Its *purista* frame of paneled jambs and fluted pilasters is inscribed with a Roman-style frieze.

At one time, the entire church interior was covered with a complex series of murals, executed in a subdued palette of red, green, mauve and earth colors. The remaining fragments appear to date from the early 1600s and are currently undergoing restoration. On my most recent visit, an epic Last Supper was materializing on the east wall.

The Altarpieces

In addition to the murals, the church is endowed with several exceptional colonial *retablos*. Originally designed as a side *retablo*, the altarpiece of the Virgin now stands behind the main altar. Its luxuriantly carved and gilded framework is typical of the ornate Solomonic style of the 17th century. Spiral columns, wreathed with the tendrils of curling vines, frame the two broad tiers of sculpture niches. Every surface is alive with scrollwork and spiraling foliage.

The niches house a set of fine-featured saints, attired in flowing *estofado* draperies, similar to those of the Xochimilco altarpiece. The central statue of the Virgin and Child projects an expressive melancholy. The intimate relief of the Visitation, above, shows Mary and Elizabeth—both with child—greeting each other against an angular architectural background. The pilgrim's hat dangling from Mary's hand is a nice anecdotal touch.

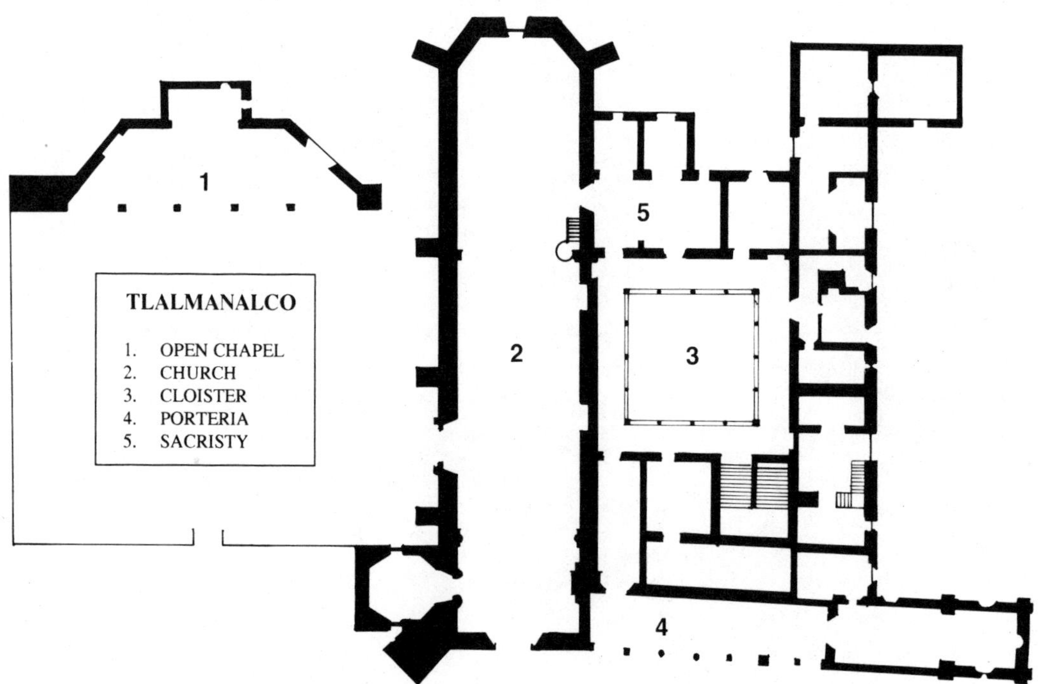

Tlalmanalco, Martín de Valencia

Several side altars have been removed or dismantled during the restoration. They run the gamut of Spanish colonial styles, from late Renaissance to neo-classical, and include paintings by recognized Mexican artists like Juan Correa, Luís Juarez and Juan Sanchez Salmerón.

The altarpiece of Jesus the Nazarene catches the eye with its bent figure of Christ bearing the cross to Calvary—a work by the 17th century sculptor Tomás Juarez.

Two large paintings hang beside the sanctuary, an Adoration of the Magi and a charming Nativity, possibly survivors from the original main *retablo*. Painted at the end of the 16th century, they are attributed to the Spanish master Baltazar de Echave Orío, whose canvases also adorn the great Xochimilco altarpiece. Both are dramatic Mannerist compositions that display the refined gestures and the warm palette of the Andalusian School, in whose canons the artist was trained.

Isolated specimens of 16th century stonework survive in the church: a pair of painted, gilded stone lecterns and the old wall pulpit. But my favorite relic is the monolithic baptismal font emblazoned with Franciscan insignia and the monograms of Jesus and Mary. Inscribed on the rim are Christ's uncompromising words to St. Mark: "He who believes and is baptized shall be saved. The unbeliever shall be damned."

The Convento

A wide pilgrim's portico of seven bays stands in front of the *convento*. It is entirely plain, conspicuously lacking the rich carving of the open chapel. However, vestiges of 16th century frescoes have been uncovered on the inner walls, the most interesting of which is the Arrival of the Twelve Franciscans, on the east wall. The friars file forward escorted by rows of Indians, Spaniards and musicians, all in authentic period dress. The mural is bordered by charming friezes of fruit, flowers and symbolic creatures such as hares, cranes and dolphins.

The cloister echoes the severe style of the *portería* with simple, molded arches and ringed Tuscan columns. Ghostly traces of ancient frescoes adhere to the scarred walls of the walks—here the faded outlines of a saint, and there a fantastical figure, half man and half beast. Pigeons, rabbits, even an anteater, peer out at the visitor from friezes along the walls and around the door frames.

Finally, the most complete mural, in the northwest corner of the cloister, pays tribute to Martín de Valencia. Portrayed in a panel next to St. Clare (a place traditionally reserved for St. Francis), the revered prelate emerges with a beatific expression from a decorous tangle of "roses without thorns"—a reference to his exemplary life.

A string of early colonial monasteries stretches south from Tlalmanalco along the foothills of the volcanoes. These include the primitive Dominican cloister at **Amecameca** and a little further south, the former Franciscan monastery of **Ozumba**, famous for its murals of Cortés greeting the Twelve, and the Niños Martires. For the story of the Niños, see **Atlihuetzía** (Chapter Three). But the pearl in the string is the little Dominican monastery of **Chimalhuacan**, located on the wooded lower slopes of Popocatépetl.

Chimal, the Royal arms

CHIMALHUACAN

Place of the Shieldbearer

Hidden away just outside the village, known locally as "Chimal", the tiny monastery of San Vicente Ferrer is hard to find, facing as it does away from the road. Its imposing tower, visible above the trees, is the only landmark.

It was at Chimal, according to tradition, that the illustrious Mexican poet, Sor Juana Inéz de la Cruz, was baptized in the monolithic carved font that still reposes in the church.

Erected in the 1540s by the Dominican friar-architect Fray Miguel de Zamora, a noted builder of aqueducts, Chimal's principal attraction is its exquisite Isabelline doorway—one of the most intricate 16th century portals in Mexico. The baskethandle archway is carved with entwined floral reliefs and a complex monogram of Christ.

The *alfiz* above the arch is pierced in the center by a niche enclosing a primitive statue of St. Vincent Ferrer, the patron saint of the monastery. This fiery 15th century Dominican preacher was famous for his efforts in converting the Jews and Moors of southern Spain. His elaborately staged didactic plays, often performed in the open air, were models for the evangelical dramas of the Spiritual Conquest in Mexico.

The *alfiz* frames what can only be described as a tapestry in stone. Four bold heraldic reliefs are set into an intricate *mudéjar* design of stars and braided strapwork. The upper escutcheons are emblazoned with the Spanish Royal arms on the right, and on the left, the arms of the Ferrer family—palms and coronets quartered with hearts and enclosed by a crown of thorns. Dominican *fleur-de-lis* crosses are skillfully carved on the lower *escudos.*

A recent facelift has given the little cloister a new lease on life. Isabelline pearl moldings add a decorative touch to stark arcades fashioned from pitted volcanic stone. Fragments of once brilliantly hued murals fleck the darkened corridors and, at the center of the sunlit patio, a rugged basalt cross stands like a mute sentinel atop its pedestal.

Chimal, the Dominican cross

Acolman, place glyph

ACOLMAN

Arm and Shoulder

According to an ancient Indian legend, when the gods created the First Man, they plucked him by the arm from the waters of Lake Texcoco and placed him, alone and dripping, on the heights overlooking the pristine Valley of Mexico.

On the site of this mythical Eden of the Americas, near the pyramids of Teotihuacan, now stands the imposing monastery of San Agustín Acolman. High on its facade is emblazoned the Aztec glyph for Acolman—the arm of the First Man, ringed by a halo of stone droplets.

Acolman is still an idyllic spot, located just beyond the smog and snarled traffic of Mexico City. The monastery is a solitary gray bastion in a sea of green cornfields, framed by cool blue hills. Here, in a grassy dell beside a spring, Fray Andrés de Olmos, the renowned Franciscan preacher and scholar, established a rude mission in the late 1520s. Its rough-hewn cloister and elevated chapel still remain, embedded in the fabric of the present monastery.

In 1539, the mission was ceded to the Augustinian Order, which rapidly developed plans for a grand new priory. Work began around 1540 on the church and a second, larger cloister. The entire Indian population was drafted for the massive project, using as a quarry the nearby temple of Quetzalcoatl, the "Feathered Serpent." By 1560, the monastery was essentially complete and by 1580, it was the most important Augustinian house outside the capital, serving at least ten outlying villages

The Atrium Cross

Mounted on a pedestal across the road from the western gateway is the primitive stone cross of Acolman. The melancholy, mask-like face of Christ appears in the center, crowned with thorns and surrounded by the Instruments of the Passion.

At the foot of the cross huddles the crude figure of the Virgin of Sorrows—unmistakeably the work of an untutored Indian stonecutter. A weathered skull and serpent rest at her feet, and the disk on her chest recalls the Aztec practice of insetting jades over the hearts of their idols.

The Church Facade

Descending through the terraced churchyard, we come face to face with the towering

Acolman, the atrium cross

churchfront. Braced by formidable buttresses and capped by a plain belfry, the crenelated facade frames a sculpted porch of unexpected sophistication.

This superb porch has been called the "The Queen of the Plateresque". It is probably the earliest and certainly the most ambitious example in Mexico of the elegant late Plateresque style of 16th century Spain. Startlingly innovative at the time, it exerted a powerful influence on many later churches, notably Metztitlán in Hidalgo (Chapter Two).

It was the viceroy himself, Don Luís de Velasco, who commissioned the work in the year 1560, according to the dedicatory plaque. Although the designer of this magnificent doorway is not known, it was surely an experienced Spanish architect or skilled master mason.

Crisply carved from gray-gold limestone, the lush Renaissance composition was once ablaze with color, as traces of pigment in the recesses reveal. Unfortunately, the sculpture is blurred in the lower section of the doorway, up to head height. Time after time during the colonial period, flood waters surged through the low-lying monastery, washing away the carved and painted details.

Ornate garlanded candelabra columns flank the triumphal arch of the doorway, although the twin cherubs on their lower sections have been melted like hot candlewax by the repeated flooding. Luckily, the patrician figures of St. Peter and St. Paul, looking down from the Gothic niches between the columns, stood safely just above the high water mark.

The richly carved archway is the centerpiece of the porch. Worn statues and goat's heads adorn the sculpted jambs, and the paneled arch is a banquet of fruits, ceremonial breads and other offerings, including the Augustinian pierced heart.

The spandrels above the arch tell the story of the Annunciation. The Archangel Gabriel, on the left, unfurls a banner of praise towards a startled Virgin Mary on the right.

Fanciful hippocamps or seahorses frolic along the frieze, between classical urns and grinning lions' heads. In the ornamental niche above the doorway, a headless young Christ strikes a magisterial pose, flanked by chubby cherubs playing the flute and viol.

A frieze of winged cherubs' heads frames the choir window above, supported by swagged Plateresque columns. At its apex, playful cupids tug on the beribboned insignia of St. Augustine. A plaque between the saint's miter and the pierced heart of Christ is engraved with lines from the *Confessions of Saint Augustine.*

Heraldic escutcheons project from the bare wall on either side of the window. On the left are the castles and lions of Spain, and on the right, the "dripping arm" emblem of Acolman.

The Church Murals

Inside the vast cool church, the eye is drawn towards the east end. Beneath an intricate webbed vault, the five-sided apse blazes with striking black, white and orange murals. A hierarchy of gigantic figures, seated in rows, scales the walls and reaches into the vault itself. Above a rank of lowly friars, stern-visaged prelates line the two middle tiers.

In the lunettes at the top, venerable apostles and Old Testament prophets sit uneasily among mythological figures borrowed from classical antiquity—naked youths, grotesque beasts and sibyls. The prophetic sibyls suggest the Second Coming, a theme that preoccupied the friars of the 16th century.

The Solomonic main altarpiece displays somber baroque paintings of the Passion of Christ. In front, a mitered St. Augustine leans on his staff, holding up a miniature church that may represent the Catholic Church or his City of God.

The Open Chapel

Between the church and adjacent *convento,* a broad archway opens on the upper level. This is the original open chapel of the monastery, which dates from the Franciscan years at Acolman. From its high balcony, the friars would preach to the Indians gathered on the terraces below. Recent restoration of this chapel has revealed a dramatic mural of St. Catherine of Alexandria, the patroness of preachers, shown in the act of beheading the King of Egypt. The mural is bordered by unusual tapestry-like decoration

The Convento

The Augustinian coat-of-arms—an intricate design of a heart pierced by arrows and enlaced

Acolman, St. Paul

with the tassels of a cardinal's hat—is carved above the doorway to the *convento* at the south end of the *portería.*

The two cloisters of the monastery are strikingly different from each other. The front cloister, built by the Franciscans in the 1530s, is the older and smaller of the two. Heavy beveled buttresses divide its austere arcades of black volcanic stone. In the patio, a rude pumice cross is carved with the Latin monogram of Christ.

A cycle of water-damaged murals illustrating the Life of the Virgin adorns the walls of the lower cloister. The Annunciation and the Adoration of the Magi are the most distinct, painted in a linear style that reflects the Flemish prints from which they were derived.

Wraith-like figures of apostles, prelates and the Fathers of the Church, as well as several gaunt Franciscan saints, gaze at us from the piers of the arcade. Behind St. Mark, the head of an Aztec Eagle warrior peers out, and jaguars slink along the decorative frieze—clearly the work of a native artist.

In its heyday during the 1580s, at least two dozen friars toiled at Acolman, teaching, preaching and ministering to the Indians. At the end of the day, the weary brothers sat down in the vast refectory beside the monastery garden. As they ate in silence beneath the painted vault, they listened to inspiring scriptures read from the wall pulpit.

It is an memorable experience to emerge from the dim refectory into the brilliantly lit rear cloister. The arcades of warm, reddish-gray limestone have been fashioned into a bold architecture that skillfully exploits the contrast between bright sunlight and dark shade. Smoothly rounded arches spring from powerful, cylindrical columns ringed by Isabelline pearls and headed by "feather" capitals of indigenous appearance. Double columns at the center of each arcade and triple shafts in the corners set in motion a compelling rhythm that reverberates around the cloister.

Twelve striking reliefs project above the arcades. They explore variations on the Augustinian pierced heart and the crucifix—one starkly set above a skull and crossbones. Another shows an Indian's head with an Aztec speech glyph issuing from the mouth—one more reminder of the Indian sensibility always lurking behind the European iconography.

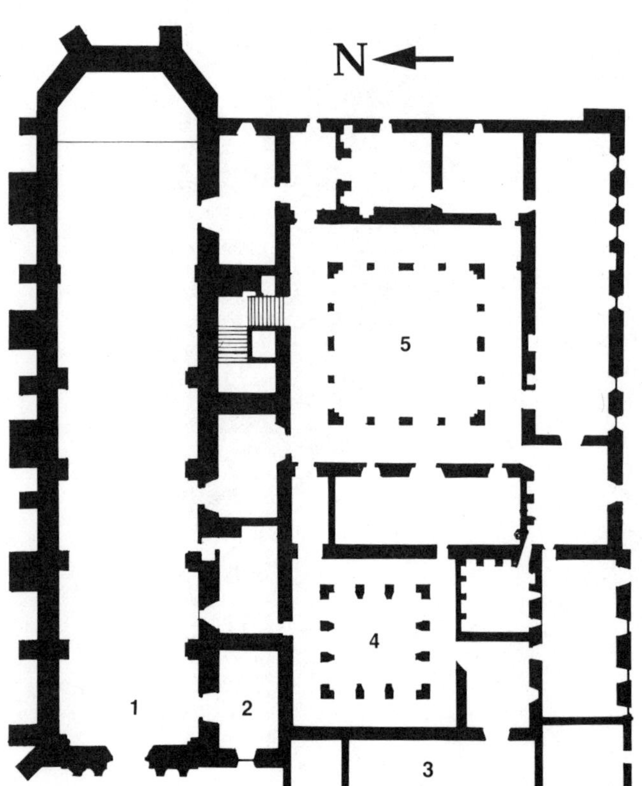

ACOLMAN

1. CHURCH
2. OPEN CHAPEL
3. PORTERIA
4. OLD CLOISTER
5. NEW CLOISTER

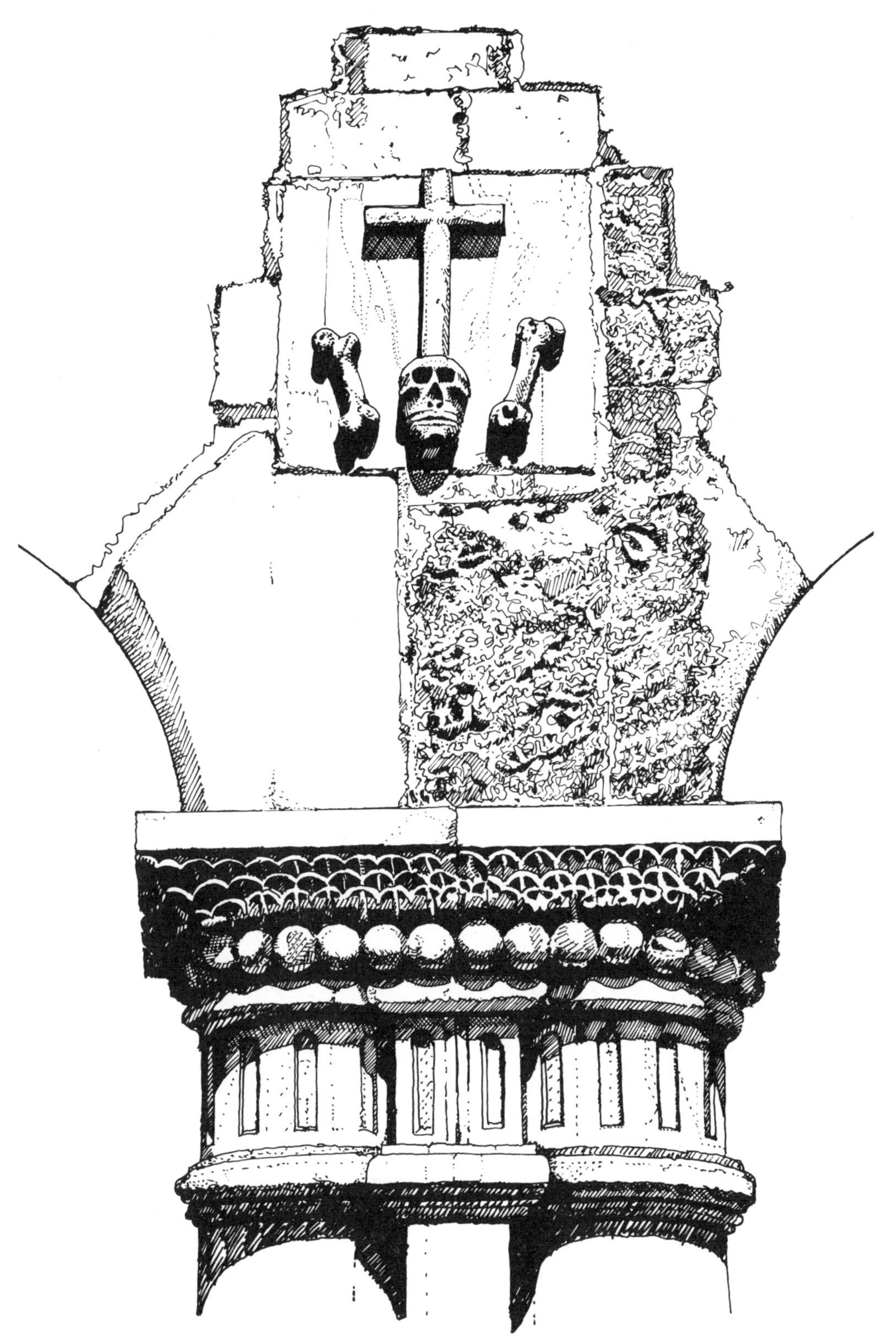

Acolman, cloister detail

The chapter room on the west side of the cloister is now a small gallery, displaying artifacts from the monastery as well as special exhibits. This was the *sala de profundis* of the monastery, so called because of the first words of Psalm 130, recited in Latin at the end of meetings: "Out of the depths (*de profundis*) have I cried unto thee, O Lord."

The Frescoes

Only a few mural fragments have survived the periodic inundations of the lower cloister. Proud eagles perch above painted colonnades, and words from the Psalms, entwined with delicate friezes of rosettes, link the decorative doorways along the corridors.

A handsome stone staircase on the north side leads to the treasures of the upper story: prehispanic artifacts, colonial canvases, religious sculptures in wood, stone and plaster, even a library of old leather-bound books.

But the most remarkable legacy is another cycle of late 16th century murals that unfolds around the upper cloister. Adapted from Northern European engravings and painted in charcoal tones with blue and tan accents, these faded frescoes narrate the central drama of Christianity— the Passion of Christ.

The sequence begins in the southeast corner, with the Scourging of Christ—a flogging administered by two robust Roman soldiers—and beside it, Christ Wearing the Crown of Thorns. Fragmentary scenes of the Road to Calvary follow along the south wall. But the finest and best preserved frescoes are in the northwest corner.

First, a Renaissance-style Crucifixion, in an Italianate landscape of steeples, trees and grottoes. The anguished figure of Mary Magdalene kneels at the foot of the cross, her long hair tumbling down like an ocher mane.

The Last Judgment, on the other hand, is a tumultuous medieval drama. In the upper part, Christ sits in majesty with sword and scepter among the massed ranks of the Blessed. A Latin banner proclaims the damnation of sinners to eternal fire while the dead struggle from their coffins.

Underneath, against a black background, the naked white bodies of the Damned suffer unspeakable torments: demons with grasping claws and gaping jaws tie their victims to trees, break them on the wheel and toss them into a steaming cauldron. Confronted with this nightmarish vision, who would not strive for salvation?

The corridors behind the cloister walks give access to rows of friars' cells. Sacred monograms and Augustinian emblems are painted above the doorways and faded fragments of devotional murals brighten the drab walls.

Like generations of friars in centuries past, today's visitors can look out from the window seats at the bucolic scenery and still imagine themselves in the Eden of the Americas.

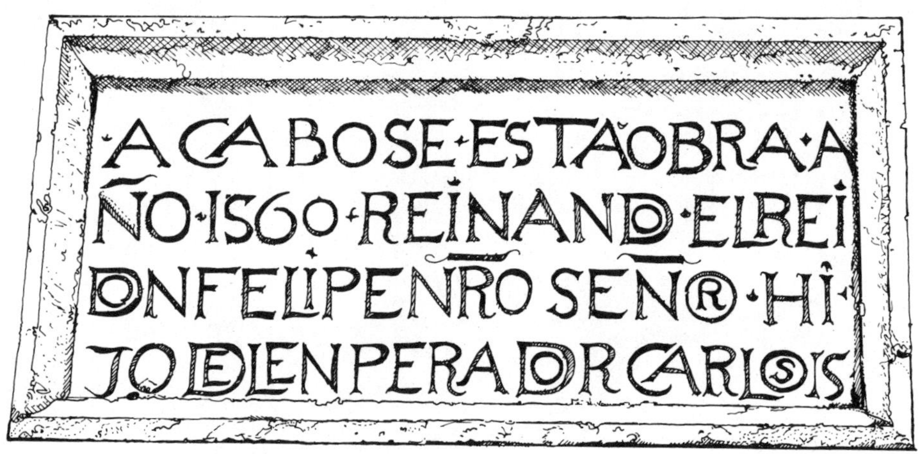

Acolman, the date plaque

Otumba, the choir window

OTUMBA

Place of the Otomí

On the 14th of July, 1520, in full retreat from Tenochtitlan after the disastrous Noche Triste, Cortés reached Otumba, where he faced a huge Aztec force. In one of the most decisive engagements of the Conquest, the weary Spanish troops and their Tlaxcalan allies, although vastly outnumbered, routed the flower of the Aztec military in a desperate and bloody battle.

High on the cold, arid northeastern rim of the Valley of Mexico, Otumba has the only regional place name to commemorate the Otomí, the aboriginal settlers of the valley. By 1520, the Otomí had long been a marginal people, dispersed by a succession of Nahua-speaking conquerors like the Aztecs.

The Monastery

In 1527, the Franciscans built a primitive mission of rude adobe atop the earthen mound of a former temple. With the completion after 1550 of the Arcos de Zempoala, a famous aqueduct which brought water over 45 kilometers from Zempoala (Chapter Two), Otumba prospered as an agricultural and trading center.

The present stone monastery replaced the early mission sometime after 1550, and may also be the work of Fray Francisco de Tembleque, the builder of the aqueduct. Although the fabric of the monastery has suffered over the centuries from neglect and thoughtless alteration, happily much of the original stonecarving has survived.

In contrast to the elegant Renaissance facade of Acolman, the stonecarving at Otumba is a prime example of the *tequitqui* style—a combination of Isabelline Gothic, Hispano-Moorish *mudéjar* and Romanesque motifs, unified in appearance by the traditional sculptural techniques of the Indian artisans.

Isolated in the middle of a blandly resurfaced west front, the porch is densely textured with relief carving. Slender colonettes, carved with tiny "baskets" and rings of pearls, divide the broad jambs of the doorway. The outermost column has been transformed into a knotted cord that extends upwards to form an *alfiz* over the doorway. Narrow relief panels of rosettes, flowers and vines snake between the columns and run along the imposts and over the flattened arch of the door. The same motifs are repeated around the choir window.

Inside the church, bands of star-like flowers between cord moldings border the underchoir, and Isabelline beading outlines the huge sanctuary arch. Carved stone basins in all shapes and sizes are dotted about the nave, several embellished with cords and eight-pointed flowers. The grand baptismal font, housed in a shell niche on the north side, sports huge ball pendants and an outlandish trumpet-shaped hood.

The Convento

Although the cloister and *convento* are now in ruins, the imposing double arcade of the *portería* has been restored. As with several other Valley monasteries, the *portería* also housed the open chapel. The carved sanctuary arch can be seen recessed into the rear wall behind the arcades.

The monastery entrance, at the north end of the *portería,* is similar in style to the church doorway, its triple jambs carved with narrow colonnettes and rich foliar decoration. Medallions of the Five Wounds and passages of *mudéjar* strapwork alternate with thistle-bearing vines around the arch.

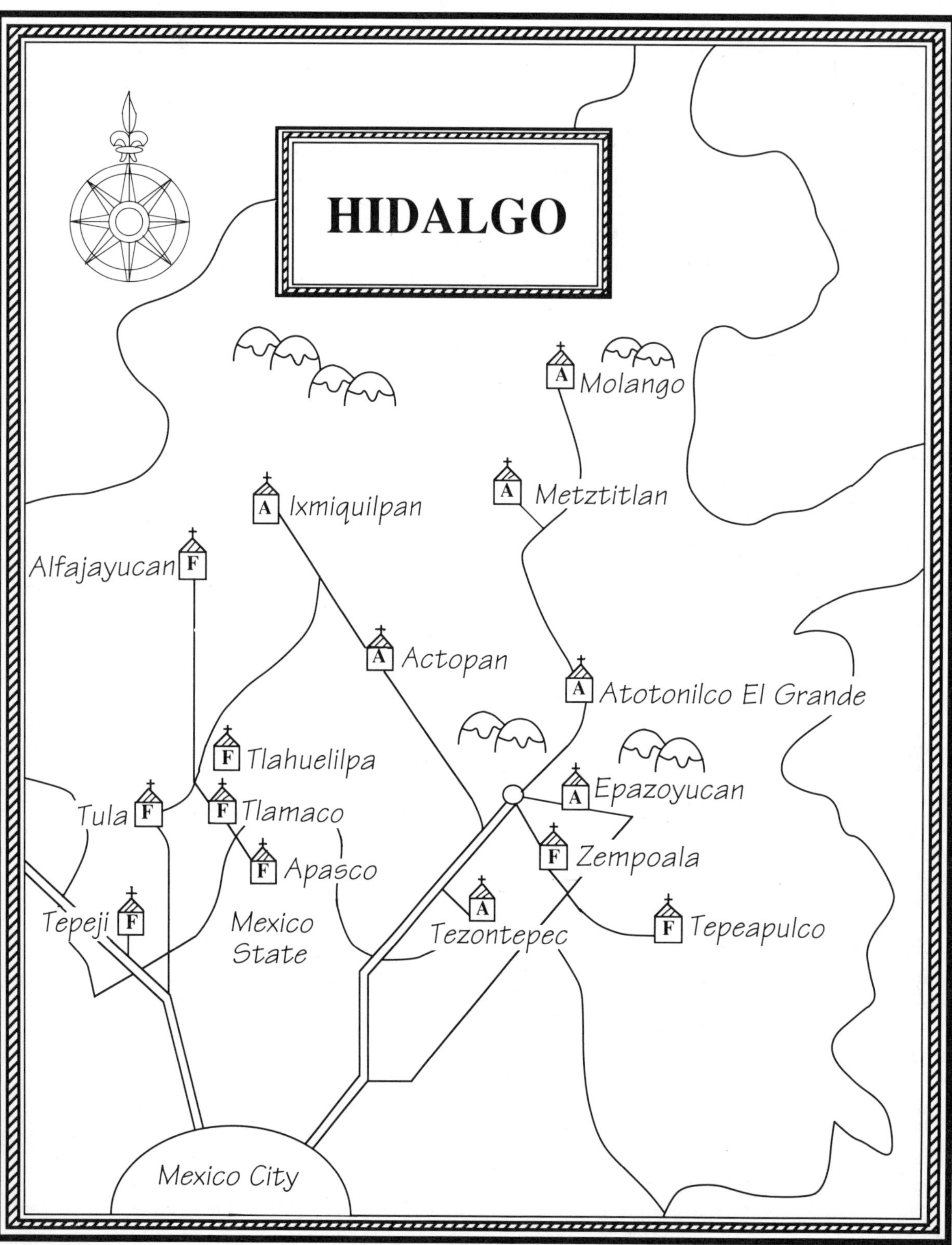

HIDALGO
Molango
Metztitlan
Ixmiquilpan
Alfajayucan
Actopan
Atotonilco El Grande
Tlahuelilpa
Tula
Tlamaco
Epazoyucan
Zempoala
Apasco
Tepeji
Mexico State
Tezontepec
Tepeapulco
Mexico City

Chapter Two

Celestial Citadels

The Monasteries of Hidalgo

The state of Hidalgo stretches northward from the Valley of Mexico across arid plains dotted with cactus and agave, a land of hot springs and volcanic cones. To the east, the land rises towards the high sierras, a scenic region of pine forests, misty mountains and deep canyons.

Following the Spanish Conquest, pioneering Franciscans and Augustinian friars ventured forth from the Valley of Mexico into this inhospitable region—at that time peopled by huge numbers of Nahua and Otomí speaking Indians.

Hidalgo is home to a surprisingly large number of 16th century monasteries. The fortress style of construction predominates, often achieving a monumentality unmatched elsewhere in Mexico. Architectural decoration shows great variety and is of high artistic quality. Severe Renaissance doorways often stand side by side with Plateresque, Gothic and *mudéjar* ornament. The region is especially rich in *tequitqui* stonecarving.

Although there are almost no surviving colonial altarpieces—the splendid baroque *retablo* at Metztitlán being the notable exception—the Hidalgo monasteries are celebrated for their ambitous, often brilliantly colored 16th century frescoes, which even today are being rediscovered, restored and reinterpreted.

This chapter is divided into two parts. The first part describes the Augustinian monasteries, counted among the grandest and most lavishly decorated in all Mexico. The second part deals with the more modest Franciscan houses of the region.

The Augustinian Monasteries

Here in Hidalgo, the Augustinians created their greatest artistic legacy. Two groups of monasteries are concentrated in the eastern half of Hidalgo. The first group is located in the dry central plain, known as the Mesquital, and includes **Epazoyucan, Actopan** and **Ixmiquilpan,** all of them outstanding for their monumental architecture and lavish murals.

The second group is a trio of fortress monasteries that extends into the rugged Sierra Alta to the northeast—from bustling **Atotonilco El Grande**, in the mining country north of Pachuca, to rustic **Molango,** high in the fog-shrouded sierras. Between the two, in the lush Tulancingo River canyon, lies the spectacular hillside monastery of **Metztitlán**, one of the most beautiful 16th century buildings in Mexico.

The Franciscan Monasteries

The Seraphic Order of St. Francis also established two clusters of monasteries, both close to the present boundary between Hidalgo and the state of Mexico. The sacred city of **Tepeapulco** in the plains of eastern Hidalgo, together with nearby **Zempoala**, form the first cluster and are noted for their extraordinary murals.

A second, larger group is centered around the formidable monastery near the ancient Toltec capital at **Tula**, and includes the smaller houses at **Tepeji del Rio**, **Alfajayucan** and **Tlahuelilpa**.

Tlahuelilpa is the jewel in a chain of early Franciscan churches and chapels that reaches eighty kilometers northwestwards from **Apasco** in Mexico State. Because of their extraordinary *tequitqui* carving, I have described these buildings in a section entitled **Valley of the Angels**.

The state capital of **Pachuca** is the most suitable base for visiting the Hidalgo monasteries. Outside Pachuca, tourist accomodations are sparse, with limited facilities. While the roads in Hidalgo are generally adequate, they often pass through congested market towns, so the going can be slow, especially on the heavily used commercial arteries.

The Augustinians in Hidalgo

The Augustinians got off to a slow start in Hidalgo. It was not until 1536 that the new custodian of the order, Fray Jerónimo de San Estéban, decided to mount an aggressive campaign of conversion among the Otomí Indians of the Mesquital and the Sierra Alta to the north.

Late in the same year, Fray Alonso de Borja, a veteran of missionary work in Morelos, Puebla and Guerrero, set out with two companions into the mountains, establishing a primitive mission at **Atotonilco El Grande** (1537). Two other missionaries, Juan de Sevilla and Antonio de Roa, whose names became legendary in the Sierra Alta, were chosen to evangelize this rugged high country. In spite of adversity, these stalwart friars succeeded in founding the monasteries of **Molango** (1538) and **Metztitlán** (1539).

When the Order replaced the Franciscans at Acolman in 1539, the stage was set for an Augustinian missionary presence in the Mesquital. In 1540, Fray Jorge de Avila began construction of a new monastery at **Epazoyucan**, a former Franciscan *visita*. By the late 1540s, large Augustinian houses were rising, first at **Actopan** and then at **Ixmiquilpan**, under the supervision of the friar/architect Fray Andrés de Mata. Once construction had begun, no effort or expense was spared to bring these monasteries to completion, a grand enterprise which was not finally concluded until 1570.

Epazoyucan, the atrium cross

EPAZOYUCAN

Place of Epazote

On a hill called Tlaloc, in 1540, Fray Jorge de Avila dedicated a new monastery to St. Andrew (San Andrés), by tradition the apostle of remote pagan peoples.

Twelve years earlier, Franciscans from Zempoala had evangelized Epazoyucan and built a primitive mission on the same site, which had sacred to Tlaloc, the ancient Mexican deity of rain and lightning.

However, it is to the Augustinian Order that we owe the present magnificent building. Father Grijalva, the 17th century Augustinian chronicler, records that their monastery at Epazoyucan was completed in seven months and seven days, an incredibly brief period that, although apocryphal, reflects the enthusiasm of the Augustinians in establishing their first mission among the Otomí.

The monastery is silhouetted against a panorama of volcanic hills sparsely covered with cactus and *maguey*. The sloping atrium has a few scattered tombstones, a carved cross and three of the original *posa* chapels. Instead of being incorporated into the atrium walls, as was customary, these *posas* are isolated, box-like pavilions with carved archways and decorative *fleur-de-lis* parapets.

The Open Chapel

Carved parapets also form a crest above the open chapel, which projects from the churchfront at the foot of the tower. This modest chapel may in fact be the structure described by Grijalva and thus the oldest part of the monastery.

Standing at the head of a broad flight of stone steps, the chapel looks like another, larger *posa*, with intricate filigree carving on the arch, jambs and quoining. Behind the altar was a large Crucifixion mural, now mostly effaced except for the figure of St. Nicholas of Tolentino, still resplendent in his star-spangled robe.

The Church

Epazoyucan is a fortress church, with great stepped buttresses and an unadorned square facade. A simple outline of moldings and cornices unites and articulates the doorway and choir window. Alternating sections of vertical and spiral fluting on the columns flanking the doorway provide minimal ornament. IHS and

Epazoyucan, west front

XPS, the Greek and Latin monograms of Christ, are incised in the upper facade—a decorative motif repeated inside the church.

Today, the vast interior is almost bare. A rough wooden floor overlays the recesses of the ancient pyramid below. The long nave was originally roofed by an exceptionally wide wood beamed ceiling, replaced circa 1700 by a stone vault, now badly cracked. The surviving *artesonado* choir balcony gives us an idea of the majesty of the lost ceiling. Its decking is inlaid with eight-pointed Moorish stars and supported by stout hand-hewn beams, blackened by the patina of time and with smoke from incense and candles.

The baptistery beneath the choir contains the only mural inside the church—a 16th century Baptism of Christ, featuring an angel recently rediscovered during restoration. The baptismal font is most unusual, its basin crisscrossed with pineapple-like Isabelline latticework.

The Convento

Excavations in front of the *portería,* on the south side of the church, have revealed the ancient stairway of the temple of Tlaloc. Long in a state of ruin, the *portería* has been partly restored, although it remains open to the sky. Two plain arcades bridge the deep, narrow entry, some of whose columns are headed with unusual foliated capitals—prototypes for the cloister arcades.

The plain molded arches and simple banded columns of the cloister arcades are transformed by the fantastic capitals, whose feathered scrolls swell like bulbs and curl up to embrace the rising curves of the arches. This striking effect is compounded in the multiple capitals of the corner piers.

Mullioned Venetian windows in the long corridors of the upper cloister offer uniquely framed vistas of the bare purple hills around the monastery.

The Murals

Every surface in the *convento* at Epazoyucan—walls, vaults, niches and door frames—was covered with frescoes. Among the richest and most complete program of 16th century mural decoration to survive in Mexico, the frescoes have been carefully restored by INAH, the government agency responsible for historic sites.

The lower cloister is painted with decorative

bands and borders, displaying complex patterns of ribbons, vines and grotesque figures as well as the ornamental lettered friezes favored by the Augustinians.

But the real focus of interest is the exceptional sequence of Passion scenes that decorates the niches at the end of each walk. Originally monochromatic, the murals were later accented with blues, reds and ochers that do not detract from the compositions. The native artist skillfully transposed these scenes from assorted print sources—Flemish, French and Italian engravings—to the larger scale of the monastery walls, enhancing their graphic strength and emotional power.

As we enter the cloister from the west, we first confront the Via Dolorosa, or Way of the Cross. In this dynamic composition, the head of Christ is awkwardly wrenched to one side of the cross, dramatically focusing the scene on his suffering. The painting is crowded with incident and anecdotal detail; note the little dog trotting by in the foreground.

The Crucifixion in the southwest corner is quite different. The Two Marys, elegantly robed and elongated in the Mannerist style, seem almost emotionless as they look upon the figure of Christ. Serene describes the bearded face of Christ looking out at us beneath the crown of thorns in the Ecce Homo at the east end of the south walk. In the Descent from the Cross opposite, by contrast, the emaciated body of Christ and the drawn, anxious faces of his family and friends convey an agonized immediacy.

An unusual tableau above the doorway in the southeast corner, entitled El Tránsito de la Virgen, portrays the death and coronation of the Virgin in a frankly medieval composition. The Apostles, individuals to a man, gather by the bier above a flock of mournful angels at prayer.

Inside the doorway, a ghostly head of Christ, etched in faded blue and ocher at the foot of the stairway, gazes enigmatically at us like the Cheshire Cat.

Sala de Profundis

A dim passageway to the left of the stairwell takes us into the lavishly frescoed *sala de profundis*.

Murals cover all four walls to the ceiling. Here, the later coloring has been removed to expose the well-preserved *grisaille* work underneath.

Epazoyucan, cloister capital

Once again, the murals illustrate the Passion of Christ, framed here by lettered borders and painted Plateresque niches. In panel after panel, the measured structure and sensuous lines of the composition complement the profound themes. The artist has used the triptych form—in which the central subject is flanked by supporting figures—to unify and dramatize the subject matter. The early episodes in the Passion unfold in a linked movement along the west wall, starting with the Agony in the Garden, continuing with the Kiss of Judas and the Flagellation, and ending with the Way of the Cross.

The Crucifixion is the focus of the south wall, flanked here by an expressive Pietá. Below the Crucifixion is a detailed frieze of the Last Supper, with an echo of Leonardo da Vinci. Scenes of Pentecost, the Descent into Hell and a moving *Noli me Tangere* grace the east wall, watched over by the august figure of St. Augustine. The powerful Renaissance influence on this unknown muralist is seen most clearly in the Resurrection on the north wall, in which the triumphant figure of the Risen Christ soars above the forests of an Umbrian landscape.

Take a moment to peer into the abandoned refectory on the south side of the cloister. Full length portraits of Augustinian saints and martyrs fill the dark walls. In another triptych at the east end, St. Augustine and St. Nicholas of Tolentino stand on each side of Christ Crucified.

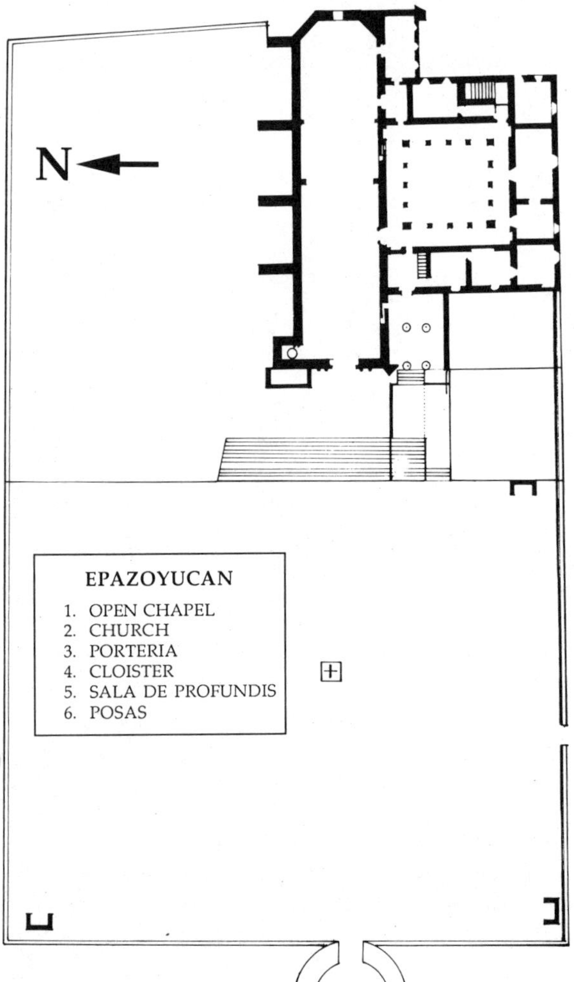

Note: *Epazote* is a medicinal herb used by the indigenous peoples of Mexico, with a bitter flavor and a strong smell reminiscent of skunk. A skunk (*zorrillo*) appears in the ancient place-glyph for Epazoyucan.

TEZONTEPEC

Basalt Mountain

Another cycle of frescoes—one of the most complete to be found in any Mexican monastery—can be seen at San Pedro Tezontepec, a hilltop Otomí village 25 kms southwest of Epazoyucan and readily accessible from the main Mexico-Pachuca Highway (Mex 85).

Beyond the unprepossessing exterior and overgrown atrium of the monastery, the plain cloister surprises the visitor with its wealth of 16th century murals, colored in a bright palette of blue, green and earth colors. Beneath painted ceilings of meandering ribs with floral bosses, the cloister walks are a gallery of large narrative murals and portraits of Augustinian luminaries, framed by extravagant Plateresque borders.

But the main attraction is the sequence of murals illustrating the Life and Passion of Christ. The figures are confidently drawn in sweeping strokes, whose vigor more than compensates for the occasional lack of subtlety in gesture and facial expression.

Starting with the Nativity in the northwest corner, scenes from the early life of Jesus unfold around the lower cloister, including a rarely depicted Flight into Egypt. Note the doll-like Christ and the tropical vegetation in the background.

The sequence continues around the upper level with episodes from the Passion, beginning with the Agony in the Garden at the top of the stairs, and ending with the Crucifixion in the northeast corner. Again, unfamiliar episodes are shown, such as Jesus in the House of Ananias and Christ before Caiaphas.

Actopan, place glyph

ACTOPAN

Fertile Land

Everything is on a grand scale at St. Nicholas Actopan, a palatial priory that was the foremost Augustinian house in Hidalgo. Its monumental architecture and visionary frescoes earn it a place among the greatest buildings of Mexico.

The eastern valleys of the Mesquital that lie beyond the picturesque eroded escarpment still known as Los Frailes (The Friars), were not evangelized until 1546. At a chapter meeting of the new Augustinian Province of the Holy Name of Jesus, held in Mexico City in 1548, Actopan was designated as the site for a major new priory, to be the focus for all missionary efforts in the region.

Several existing native communities were congregated into the new mission town, including the large villages of Atocpa and Ixcuincuitlapilco ("Dogtail" in Nahuatl).

By 1550, construction of the new monastery was going forward under the supervision of Fray Andrés de Mata. A friar of considerable learning, who had studied architecture and design in Italy, he was responsible for the overall planning and design of the monastery. The work was completed in the 1560s by his successor, Fray Martín de Acevedo, to whom Actopan's marvelous murals have been attributed.

The monastery stands squarely in the center of the bustling market town, set back from the main plaza behind a row of storefronts, its western gateway framing the visitor's first view of the vast paved atrium and the awe-inspiring facade. The portico of the *convento* extends to the right of the church and to the left, at the far end of the atrium, yawns the cavernous archway of the open chapel.

The Vault of Actopan

This local name for the open chapel succinctly captures its most striking feature, the soaring barrel vault painted with a handsome coffered pattern of crosses and octagons, based on the designs of the Renaissance architect Sebastiano Serlio.

But the true glory of the Actopan chapel is its spectacular frescoes, only recently discovered beneath layers of whitewash. Executed on a huge scale in vivid reds, blues, browns and ochers, they display the most vivid apocalyptic imagery of any Mexican murals of the 16th century.

Taken from medieval book illustrations, the images have undergone a metamorphosis in their translation to the chapel walls, acquiring overwhelming expressive power with the addition of color and the expansion of scale. The Christian iconography is liberally spiced with references to indigenous customs, including ritual cannibalism.

The complex sequence of paintings depicts episodes from Genesis and the Book of Revelation, as well as a lurid vision of Hell and its torments that explicitly details the fate awaiting sinners and backsliders. Even after 400 years and despite their fragmented condition, these cautionary paintings still have the power to shock the viewer. We can only imagine their riveting effect upon the impressionable Indian neophytes for whose eyes they were intended.

The main focus of the cycle is a panoramic Last Judgment spread across the end wall. Angels blow trumpets to awaken the dead, while the fires of Hell rage below. Serene above it all, the Company of the Elect floats atop a multi-hued rainbow.

Composite murals on either side below the Last Judgment juxtapose scenes from the Old Testament with images from the Apocalypse of St. John. The upper tier begins with the Creation of Eve on the left, followed by devils and angels emerging from the jaws of Hell. The sequence continues on the right with the Temptation of Adam and Eve, showing the serpent wrapped around the Tree of Knowledge, followed by the Expulsion from Paradise.

The lower panels portray Adam and Eve dressed in animal skins, digging and spinning. Beside them, War and Plague are personified by two of the Horsemen of the Apocalypse, riding out of the mouth of Hell. This is followed by the Flood, with Noah's Ark.

On the right is a chaotic Destruction of Babylon, with falling stars, tumbling buildings and gesticulating turbanned figures—possibly a reference to the razing of Tenochtitlan, which was viewed by the friars as a citadel of the Devil. The end panel is a terrifying scene of souls in Purgatory.

The imagery of the side walls projects a dark vision of human frailty and suffering. Full length panels immediately adjacent to the east wall display the enormous Jaws of Leviathan, vomiting the Damned into eternal fire.

Two tiers of murals on each side unambiguously picture the Torments of the Damned in graphic codex style. Grisly tortures, that include burning, flaying, dismemberment and cannibalism, are visited upon the hapless sinners by a brigade of nightmarish red demons with horns, bat-like wings and spiked tails. Inset in small corner panels are the Seven Deadly Sins, showing the vices to which the Indians seemed especially prone—temptations of the

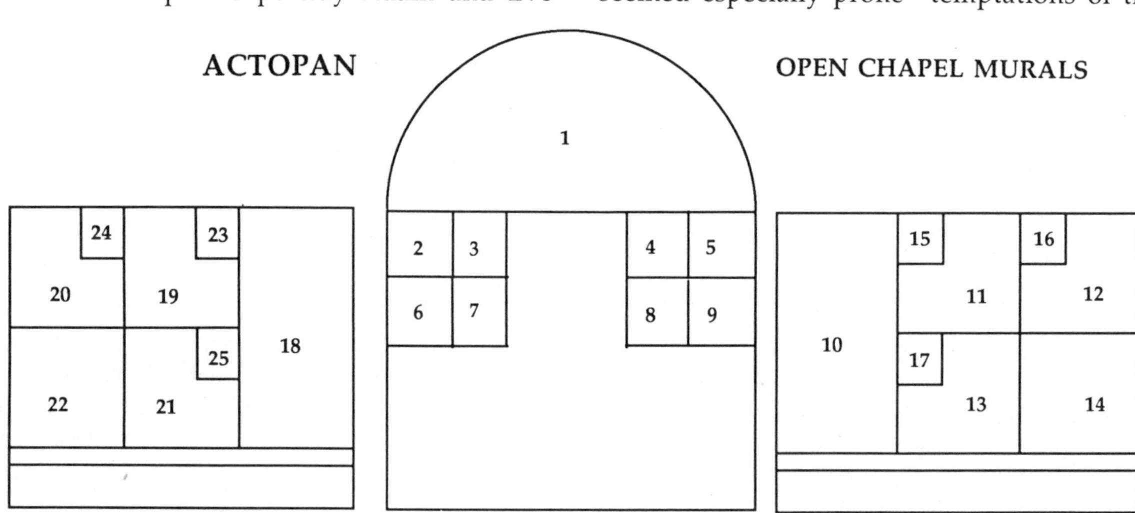

NORTH WALL

18 Jaws of Hell
19 Torments
20 Torments
21 Torments with cannibalism
22 Torments with cannibalism
23 Triumphant Demons
24 Drunkenness
25 Triumphant Demons

EAST WALL

1 Last Judgment
2 Creation of Eve
3 Hell with Devils & Angels
4 Tree of Evil
5 Expulsion from Paradise
6 Adam & Eve; War & Plague
7 The Flood
8 Destruction of Babylon
9 Souls in Purgatory

SOUTH WALL

10 Jaws of Hell
11 Torments
12 Torments
13 Torments
14 Torments
15 Idolatry
16 ?
17 Adultery

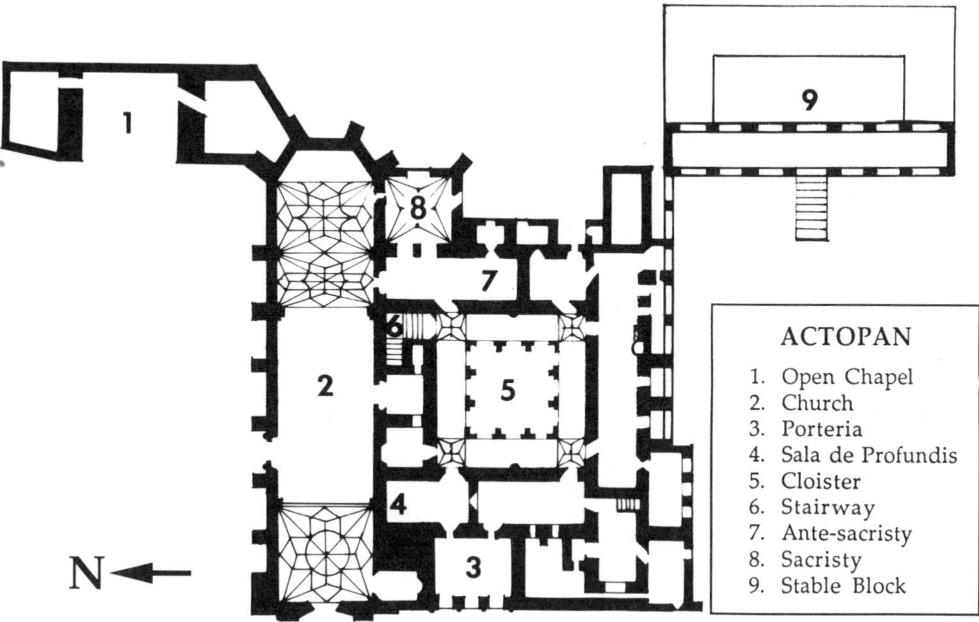

Devil in the friars' view: Adultery and Drunkenness on the north wall, and on the south side, Lust and Idolatry. In the last scene, an Indian and a Spaniard turn their backs on a pagan temple to adore a medallion of the Holy Name of Jesus.

Some have interpreted the horrific tone of these frescoes, probably painted in the 1570s, as a reflection of troubled times. For friars and Indians alike, it was a period of crisis. The Indians' continued adherence to the old gods beneath a superficial veneer of Christianity had called into question the enduring value of the missionary enterprise. The alarmed friars interpreted the fearful epidemics, then decimating the native population, as divine retribution for apostasy.

Within a decade, however, the strictures of the Council of Trent against nudity, profanity and apocalyptic themes in sacred art came into force in Mexico, and the chapel walls were covered with whitewash.

The Church

The vast fortress church is the centerpiece of the monastery. Outsize *garitas*, or mock sentry boxes, crown the nave buttresses while toothlike merlons march along the parapets. A massive battlemented Moorish tower magnifies the military effect.

The focal point of the facade is its gigantic west porch, fashioned from salmon-colored andesite brought from the nearby Cerro La Cantera quarry. Although derived from the porch at Acolman, the west doorway at Actopan has a quite different character. Renouncing the sculptural finesse of Acolman, the architect has opted instead for a formal complexity and Roman *gravitas* that deliberately manipulates the chiaroscuro effects of deep shadow and strong sunlight. Every element in the composition is intended to augment its imposing dimensions and visual drama.

The classical triumphal arch design incorporates a door-within-a-door motif. Paired Corinthian columns stand on each side of the inner doorway, set on high pedestals and placed at an angle for emphasis. Narrow Gothic niches with ornamental colonettes and crests are sandwiched between the columns. The recesses of the coffered arch are carved with angels' heads—each one varying slightly in form or expression—and winged cherubs crowd the frieze. Reliefs of St. Nicholas of Tolentino and St. Augustine, with his miter and crozier, occupy the spandrels.

Giant flanking columns, paired, fluted and set high on paneled two-tiered bases, frame the outer doorway. Its crowning cornice is also decorated with swags, rosettes and angel heads.

An elaborate coffered fan, inset with angels, fruit and flowers, artfully echoes and amplifies the archway below. Heraldic escutcheons of the Augustinian insignia correspond to the cameo reliefs of the inner doorway. The choir window overhead repeats the design but on a more intimate scale, with the addition of ornate swagged baluster columns.

In another parallel to Acolman, the local place glyph is emblazoned on the facade. Enclosed in a carved wreath to the right of the porch, a flowering corn plant sprouts from a clod of the rich soil which gave Actopan its name.

Despite the intrusion of vapid neoclassic altarpieces in the last century, the early colonial character of the church interior still resonates, especially in its refined stonework. The elegant wheel vault under the choir is one example: each intersection of the tracery is capped by a carved boss or pendant and the entire vault is supported by swagged, fluted columns. Majestic Gothic star vaults cover the two easterly bays of the church, and giant cushioned columns with lion's head capitals outline the sanctuary arch.

Yet another star vault roofs the spacious sacristy, adjacent to the east end of the church. A monolithic baptismal font occupies the center of the room, topped by a theatrically posed statue of John the Baptist.

Although the colonial *retablos* have gone, some of the old images survive in the *convento* museum. The statues of St. Peter and St. Paul, however, still preside over the church from their baroque niches in the apse.

The Convento

In a design that would not have seemed out of place in imperial Rome, the arcaded *portería* exemplifies the architecture of Actopan at its most monumental. Paneled Corinthian pilasters, set on high pedestals like those of the west doorway, bisect the massive fluted piers, separating the plain coffered arches of the portico. A Calvary cross is mounted in the attic above, flanked by Augustinian emblems and candelabra pinnacles.

The Portería Murals

Inside the dimly lit *portería*, details of the surviving frescoes slowly take shape. On the ceiling, portraits of Augustinian saints in black habits, including Santa Mónica, the mother of St. Augustine, are enmeshed in brown and yellow arabesques against the blue-gray vault.

Part of a rare 16th century Ship of Friars mural survives at the south end. Reclining uncomfortably on the ship's masthead, St. Augustine gestures towards the New World and the missionaries at work upon its shores. At the north end, in an idealized landscape dotted with friars, the saint appears as Protector of the Order, sheltering a host of followers beneath his ample cloak.

The Sala de Profundis

The dark vestibule, located between the *portería* and the cloister, was probably the former *sala de profundis*. Here, the theme of the New World as an idyllic but treacherous Paradise is explored in the next mural, the Allegory of the Eremitic Life, which takes up the entire north wall.

This complex composition celebrates the origins of the Augustinian Order in the caves and hermitages of the Egyptian desert. This mythic vision has been transferred to the unspoiled landscape of the New World, where the Augustinians hoped to create their City of God. The rocky outcroppings of Los Frailes in the upper left of the mural clearly link this utopia to Actopan itself.

From the top of the painting, God the Father looks down upon a red-robed St. Augustine, preaching to the assembled friars in front of a church. On each side, a motley of hermits, penitants, prophets, pilgrims and friars—some with speech-scrolls issuing from their mouths—are pictured in a wooded setting of caves and grottoes crisscrossed by winding paths and streams, drawn codex-style with native trees and animals.

Actopan, devil on the road (mural)

Stealing up the pathway in the lower part of the mural is the Devil, identified by his horns, large claws, forked tongue and serpentine tail. He is disguised as a *pochteca*—one of the Aztec merchants who often acted as imperial spies. Carrying his feathered badge of office and water jar, the Devil strains forward, the tumpline across his forehead securing a heavy burden of temptations. For just as the New World was seen as a New Eden—it was also the domain of the Devil, where evil still lurked.

The legend below the mural reads: "Hermits... Cenobites... Anchorites... Augustine radiates glory upon Saint Anthony." Cenobites were monks of the early church and St. Anthony, one of the Desert Fathers, was a famous hermit and pioneer of the monastic life.

Actopan, cloister & tower

The Cloister

Heavy paneled piers, similar to those of the entry portico, buttress the cloister arcades. But here, the arches are pointed and rib vaults cover the walks, becoming complex star vaults in the corners.

Although the larger murals have been effaced, numerous colorful friezes remain along the walks—beautifully drawn grotesque panels in red, mustard and aquamarine. Youths astride fantastic griffons emerge from thickets of spiraling foliage beside cartouches of saints and Augustinian emblems. There is a charming cameo of the Niño Jesús, and a pair of quails—the attributes of St. Nicholas of Tolentino, a popular Augustinian saint and the patron of Actopan.

The only narrative murals to survive in the lower cloister are found on the end walls of the ante-sacristy. At one end is an impressionistic Agony in the Garden, in which the figures of Christ and the sleeping Apostles are sketched in broad strokes. At the opposite end is another Last Judgment. Christ presides in terrible majesty over the company of the Blessed, while below, apprehensive kings and bishops rise from their tombs, summoned forth by the trumpets of doom.

The Stairway Murals

The most striking murals at Actopan surround the grand stairway to the upper cloister. In a configuration strongly reminiscent of the painted apse of Acolman, row after row of eminent Augustinians, identified by banderoles, fill the four sides of the stairwell. The top tier is reserved for the brightest luminaries: St. Augustine, St. Jerome and St. Nicholas of Tolentino in his starry habit. A stern, black-robed William of Aquitaine dominates the north wall, purposefully clutching his penitential scourge.

While humble friars occupy the lower rows, patriarchs, bishops and cardinals of the Order, all richly attired and seated on sumptuous thrones, fill the middle tiers. The ecclesiastics are framed by ornamental Plateresque arcades and elaborate friezes alive with fantastic birds and beasts. A vicious spitting demon over the stairway arch introduces the only jarring note in the decorous symmetry of the scheme.

A naive painted panel at the foot of the staircase shows Fray Martín de Acevedo, the second prior of Actopan, kneeling before the crucifix. The two native lords kneel behind him and the pinnacles of Los Frailes loom up in the background. History records that these lords supported the construction and decoration of the monastery during Fray Martín's tenure. This mural may commemorate their patronage.

The Upper Cloister

The upper cloister is more conventional, with colonnades of rounded arches set on plain shafts with slab capitals. The walks are roofed by newly renovated wooden ceilings.

Charming Renaissance friezes fringe the cloister and continue around the corridors behind, enlivened by *escudos* of miniature friars, quails and stars, decorative crosses and pierced hearts in red and black. Painted tracery weaves along the tunnel vaults, and the tympani at the ends of each corridor show scenes from the Passion of Christ, as well as another Last Judgment.

Several of the cells opening off the corridors contain fragmentary friezes and little painted Calvaries, but the most elaborate decoration is reserved for the prior's apartment, a suite of sunny rooms in the northwest corner of the cloister. Lifesize portraits of St. Peter and St. Paul flank the doorway of the spacious main room, which is located below the tower. In the four corners of the ceiling, angels with fluttering draperies tug on the ribbons of a wreathed crown that encloses a Latin monogram of Christ.

Emblazoned over the doorway is a florid escutcheon of the Mystical Arms of Christ with the Instruments of the Passion, surrounded by Augustinian emblems—most notably a tasseled pilgrim's hat surmounted by a heraldic plumed helmet. The lunette above the window shows St. Augustine and St. Nicholas kneeling in adoration before the Crucifix, in the dismal surroundings of Golgotha.

Nicholas of Tolentino

The Museum

A miscellany of colonial paintings, reliefs and statuary is haphazardly installed in a series of dimly lit rooms along the north side of the upper cloister. A scarred and bleeding figure of Christ is particularly memorable, as is the eccentric statue of St. Nicholas, kneeling half-naked in an act of self-mortification.

It seems almost a relief to leave the tortured *santos* and gloom of the monastery, and return to the sunlit atrium, filled in the late afternoon with the clamor of high-spirited schoolchildren.

Ixmiquilpan, west front

IXMIQUILPAN

Where the Quelite Grows

More than in any other Mexican monastery, the painted walls of Ixmiquilpan allow us to glimpse the visual imagination and skill of indigenous artists, at a rare moment when their expression was least restricted by Christian doctrine and European artistic canons.

The late 1500s were uncertain times for the residents of Ixmiquilpan. Expansion of Spanish settlement and the development of the silver mines north of Mexico City brought the colonists and Otomí villagers of the region into sharp conflict with the nomadic Chichimec tribes of the northern mountains.

In the Chichimeca Wars, the colonial authorities made a concerted effort to eradicate these last pockets of resistance to Spanish rule. During the hostilities, mission towns were frequently targets of guerrilla raids and the fortress monasteries truly served a defensive purpose.

Even fifty years after Cortés' defeat of the Aztecs, the problems of conflict with marauding native warriors were still immediate concerns rather than a distant memory. Ixmiquilpan itself was attacked by fierce mounted tribesmen as late as 1569—an assault successfully repulsed by the Otomí in a celebrated local victory. These events, compounded by the acute problems of evangelization of the Indians, preoccupied the Augustinian friars.

Some years earlier, in 1548, the *encomendero* Rodríguez de Escobar, one of Cortés' captains, had invited Augustinian missionaries to the populous Otomí town.

Fray Andrés de Mata arrived from Actopan, where he was supervising the construction of the great priory, to lay out the new monastery of San Miguel beside the main plaza. Construction proceeded apace under his energetic supervision and the monastery was completed by 1560—a remarkably short time for such a monumental building.

Although Ixmiquilpan is a simplified, scaled-down version of Actopan, it is still a substantial monastery, its severe military lines now obscured by the large shade trees of the park-like atrium.

The Church

The battlemented church is constructed of coarse-grained *tezontle* and braced by formidable exterior buttresses that radiate like spokes around the nave and polygonal apse. The massive south tower is also modeled on Actopan, although its paired bell openings and raised cupola have a more pronounced Moorish flavor.

Subtly-hued rose and lavender stonework distinguishes the imposing doorway—a triumphal arch design closely related to the porches of Acolman and Actopan. Flanked by Corinthian columns and Gothic shell niches, the coffered double arch of the doorway is carved with urns, cherubs, fruit and flowers. Winged horses prance along the frieze, and the Augustinian tasseled hat is emblazoned in the spandrels.

The Nave Murals

Polychrome murals beneath the choir expand on the themes of the facade. Two facing paintings create dramatic tableaux of sweeping strokes in bright colors—red, blue, black, orange and yellow.

The partially erased mural on the north wall echoes the left hand *escudo* of the facade. An eagle warrior perches, wings outstretched, on a spreading cactus, with a battle banner and feathered crest. Several speech scrolls issue from his beak, and fragmentary jaguars with plumed headdresses stand on either side.

The south mural is more complete, amplifying the themes of the right hand escutcheon. Here an eagle engages in a dialogue with two jaguars, one of which may actually be a coyote dressed in a jaguar pelt. The codex-style footpath reappears below, against a conventionalized mountain—possibly the Cerro de Nariz (Nose Hill), a local topographical landmark.

Ixmiquilpan, facade "escudos"

The Facade Escutcheons

As at Acolman, heraldic shields project on each side of the choir window. Although not easily decipherable from the ground, these *escudos* are highly significant. Their prehispanic imagery excludes any reference to Spanish or Christian symbols, foreshadowing the extraordinary murals inside the church.

The relief to the left of the choir window shows an eagle perched on a cactus sprouting from a rock above a lake. This motif was adopted by the Aztecs as their imperial symbol and is now the emblem of modern Mexico. Beside the cactus, the eagle is costumed as a warrior with a *tlauhquechol*, or plumed headdress, unfurling his war banner. A pair of eroded jaguar figures crouch carrying *chimalli*, native war shields.

The relief on the right portrays an eagle and jaguar on either side of a stylized footpath, again with water below. Comma-like speech scrolls curl from the mouths of the two animals, indicating a dialogue between them.

Ixmiquilpan, Jaguar warrior

Between the ribs of the choir vault overhead, another black eagle spreads his wings beside an Otomí warrior emerging from the tendrils of an acanthus vine.

For the native peoples of Mexico, the eagle and the jaguar symbolized opposing forces in a multi-faceted cosmic conflict: between the celestial and the terrestrial, light and darkness, life and death, good and evil.

This ancient drama, originally played out by the Aztec military orders of the Eagle and the Jaguar, was integral to the old religion and had been appropriated by the friars to dramatize related themes in Christian doctrine. Usually confined to colorful theatrical presentations staged outdoors on festive occasions, such religious dramas rarely found their way into the church.

The battle scenes along the nave at Ixmiquilpan are unique, the only pictorial record of such a drama in a Christian church, all the more remarkable for their frankly indigenous flavor. Hidden for centuries beneath layers of yellow paint, these spectacular murals only came to light in the 1960s. Starting from the underchoir, large-scale friezes continue eastward towards the sanctuary along both sides of the nave. Their underlying pattern is that of an antique grotesque, with urns, medallions and fantastic beings set amid undulating acanthus foliage, although in their imagery, color and pictorial style the murals bear an uncanny resemblance to prehispanic temple decorations and codices.

Clearly they are the work of a talented group of *tlacuilos*, or native artists, who were allowed unprecedented freedom. The figures are accented with red, brown and ocher touches, and the foliage is blue-green against a rich apricot background. The vivid graphic style and use of flat color washes have a modern look, reminding some observers of the work of Picasso!

The friezes graphically portray intense hand-to-hand combat between native warriors and various mythological and fantastic supernaturals. The combatants are two-dimensional, presented in outline with no modeling. Except for the eyes, anatomical details are shown in profile, and there are numerous authentic items of indigenous dress and gesture—speech scrolls, spotted jaguar robes and *huaraches* (native sandals) worn by centaurs.

On the south wall, eagle, jaguar and coyote warriors outfitted with *copilli* (quetzal-plumed warbonnets), shields and *macanas* (obsidian-edged native swords) do furious battle with centaurs and dragon-like hippogriffs that emerge like obscene growths from giant tendrils. This phytomorphic motif extends to the warriors themselves, who wear foliated skirts and whose *copilli* and speech scrolls also terminate in leaves.

Along the north frieze, plumed warriors subdue apparently pregnant women, who also emerge from giant acanthus buds. These bizarre figures are thought to represent the *cihuateteo*—souls of women who died in childbirth—sent by the Aztec earth goddess, Cihuacoatl, to harass mortals and tempt them into sin.

The giant foliage in these friezes works both pictorially, as a device to integrate the forms and figures of the design, and thematically, as a sinister intrusion of the netherworld into the land of the living.

Nevertheless, it is difficult to interpret these puzzling murals satisfactorily. The prehispanic imagery indicates that the murals were intended for a native audience. While superficially they may simply celebrate the triumph of the Otomís over the invading Chichimecs, on a deeper level they reflect the perennial Christian struggle between vice and virtue, between damnation and salvation—an obsession of the Augustinians during the turbulent 1570s, when these murals were probably painted.

The imminent danger to the Indians' souls, as perceived by the friars, may have inspired them to portray the spiritual struggle as a physical battle in traditional indigenous style—an effective visual sermon despite their general distrust of prehispanic imagery.

High above the apse, where the friezes end, an eagle warrior spreads his wings in triumph on the vault. He may symbolize the Archangel Michael, the patron saint of the monastery, who led the heavenly host in their victory over Satan's forces, and whose image, inexplicably, appears nowhere else in the church.

Another frieze runs around the nave at the roofline, using the same basic design and color-

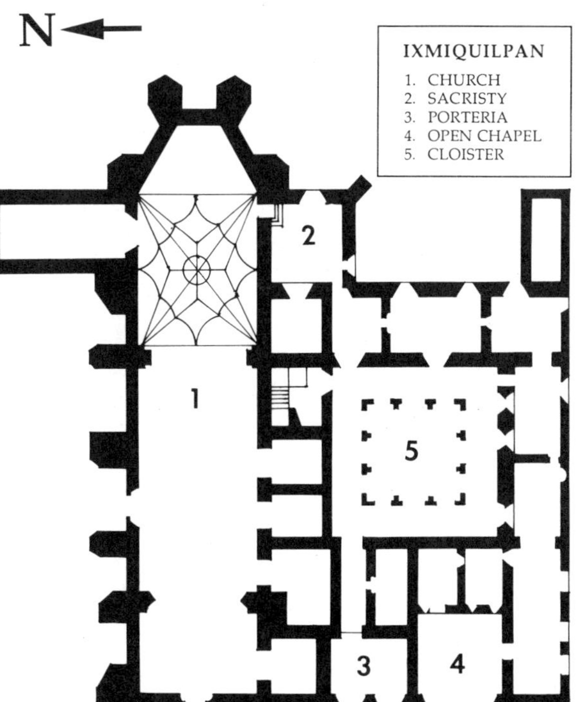

ation as well as some of the same imagery as the battle friezes—centaurs and other mythical beasts, medallions and acanthus foliage. But without the narrative drama and anecdotal detail of the lower frieze, its effect is dulled. Interestingly enough, unlike the battle friezes, this upper frieze was never painted over.

The Sacristy Frescoes

The sacristy murals are more conventional in iconography and style. Earlier in date than the colorful nave friezes, these black-and-white murals are firmly based on Renaissance engravings. Their compositions are static and the figures, with wide-eyed faces, are heavily outlined.

The devotional cycle depicts the Passion of Christ and begins with the Entry into Jerusalem, just inside the doorway on the right. Flanked by bearded Apostles, Christ sits astride a black donkey and blesses the crowd kneeling outside the city gate.

Proceeding clockwise around the room, on the east wall we come to the Apostles slumbering in the Garden of Gethsemane, while Christ converses with an archangel. Scenes of the Betrayal and the Flagellation follow, and on the south wall, large medallions of the Road to Calvary, an Ecce Homo and a Crucifixion are painted against a lattice of woven strapwork.

An eye-catching Resurrection dominates the west wall. In a landscape of cultivated fields and *maguey* plants, Jesus appears to the astonished Mary Magdalene in the guise of a gardener, with a scythe slung across his shoulder. Jerusalem and the Mount of Olives appear in the background. Note the design of the frieze above this scene, which may have been the prototype for the later nave murals.

In the corner panel, the Risen Christ appears to the Apostles, showing his spear wound to the sceptical Thomas. The cycle concludes on the north wall, with the Pentecost and the Ascension. Mary and the Apostles watch serenely as Christ rises into Heaven, leaving his footprints etched on the mountainside.

The Convento

The pointed arches of the *portería* and the recently unblocked archway of the adjacent open chapel are surprisingly plain, unadorned by architectural ornament apart from the paneled pilasters.

The lower arcade of the cloister also features pointed arches, similar to those at Actopan. Gothic vaulting covers the walks, terminating in star patterns above the corner bays. Painted Plateresque arcades cling to the walls, although the narrative murals they once framed have disappeared. A few decorative friezes remain, including one animated grotesque of youths mounted on griffons. Arabesques continue around the upper cloister, framing roundels of the Augustinian insignia, the Virgin Mary and a youthful Christ. Curiously, these medallions are painted on *amate*, a native paper made from maguey fiber, and then affixed to the wall—an unusual technique used to spectacular effect in the Franciscan church at Tecamachalco (Chapter Three).

Note: The ancient place glyph for Ixmiquilpan shows the *quelite* plant, or Mexican purslane, an edible succulent with blade-shaped leaves. The glyph depicts a bloodstained sacrificial knife set between sprouting leaves, symbolizing the link that prehispanic peoples saw between sacrifice and fertility.

Ixmiquilpan, winged lions

Atotonilco El Grande, St. Peter (facade medallion)

ATOTONILCO EL GRANDE

Thermal Waters

Sometimes called "The Gateway to the Sierra Alta," Atotonilco is split in two by the Mexico–Tampico highway, a heavily traveled artery that snakes across the Sierra Madre mountains to the Gulf coast. As a result, the congested market town is often choked with dust and traffic fumes.

Neglect and pollution have impacted the monastery of St. Augustine, located just a few paces from the main street opposite the Alameda, the former atrium. Despite its stained and crumbling stonework, the majestic scale of the church is still apparent—its long nave ringed by tall buttresses like a medieval walled city.

The 16th century Augustinian scholar and humanist, Fray Alonso de Veracruz, who resided here, was a connoisseur of architecture and design. He justified the much criticized lavishness of Augustinian monasteries in Mexico, "so that the Indians might forget their past labors and gentile tradition in the splendor of building, the richness of churches, the solemnity of festivals and in the divine cult."

The Church and Open Chapel

Bridging two buttresses on the north side of the church is an unusual exterior archway. This may have been the former open chapel of the monastery, although the blocked arch to the left of the facade, now barely discernible, seems a more likely candidate.

Set in the center of the rectangular west front is the porch, whose elegant Plateresque lines and finely carved details are difficult to appreciate in its present ruinous state.

Echoes of Acolman and Actopan reverberate throughout the design, although the forms are more severe and the sculpture less exuberant. Fluted double columns flank the clean-cut arched doorway, and relief medallions of St. Peter and St. Paul remain intact in the spandrels above.

The stonecarving inside the church has a more archaic flavor. Isabelline pearls, rosettes and thorn-and-ribbon moldings outline the triumphal arch of the sanctuary, which is roofed by a soaring Gothic vault. The archways of several side chapels are bordered with angels, flowers, vines and spiral moldings.

A sea of dingy yellow paint coats the walls, although underneath, a gallery of 16th century frescoes may still await discovery.

The Convento and its Murals

The sunken *convento* is older than the church. The *portería* remains blocked by an ugly modern facade and the sturdy south wing is closed off, now serving as the local penitentiary.

The cloister arcades are patterned after the rear cloister at Acolman. Smooth torus arches rest on slender shafts ringed by cannonball moldings. As at Acolman, the arcades are reinforced in the center and at the corners by piers with attached columns, setting up a complex rhythm unfortunately broken by unsightly buttresses in the middle of the arcades.

Virtually every surface along the lower walks is covered with black-and-white 16th century murals—a dazzling display of arabesque borders, spiral moldings, lettered friezes and painted Plateresque niches.

The corner frescoes illustrate Christ's Passion, and include a fairly complete Descent from the Cross and a Christ at the Column. The masterwork of the group is the Crucifixion in the northeast corner. Based on a Northern European Renaissance engraving, this vigorous composition is crowded with robed and bearded figures.

The stairway murals—one of the strangest sequences in Mexico—celebrate the cult of St. Augustine. Scenes from the saint's early life, including his birth and baptism, unfold along the top of the west wall. Below, he kneels in front of a hermitage set in a rocky landscape.

An enigmatic reclining figure, surrounded by spiny native succulents, sprawls above the stairway—perhaps a portrait of the saint as a hermit. Below the stairway, an angel pours a jar of water over another reclining figure, a pilgrim clutching a rosary—possibly depicting a dream. Augustine's Death and Apotheosis are recorded on the east wall.

Despite its poor condition, the large mural on the south wall, of St. Augustine sheltering members of the Order beneath his spreading cloak, is still impressive. His noble mitered head is surmounted by a Latin inscription proclaiming:

This Master teaches the secrets of Heaven. This Holy Doctor is the Prince of Theologians. If we believe his Word, we confess the Truth. He stands above all others in Sanctity.

On the side panels are busts of famous Greek philosophers and Roman statesmen—Socrates, Plato and Aristotle on the left, and Seneca, Cicero and Pythagoras on the right. Portrayal of this august company from classical antiquity was evidently intended to enhance the intellectual and moral stature of St. Augustine, and is unique in Mexican monastic art.

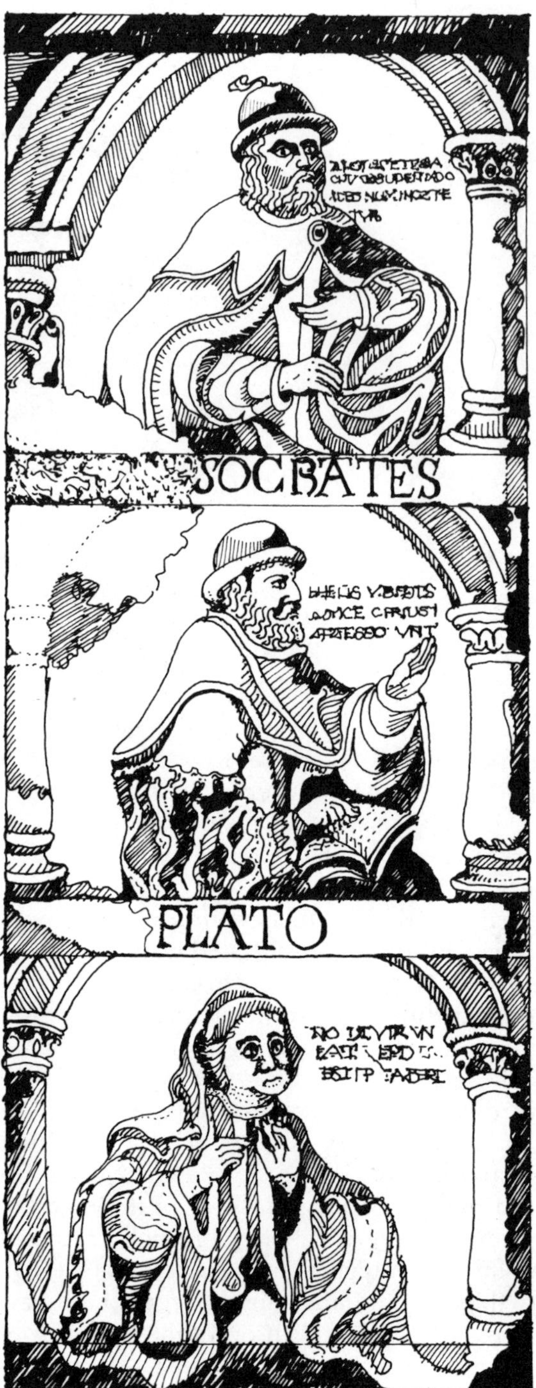

Atotonilco El Grande, ancient philosophers

Metztitlan, moon symbol

METZTITLAN

Moon in the Middle

Because of its location and authentic colonial flavor, Santos Reyes Metztitlán is one of the most rewarding of Mexico's 16th century monasteries to visit.

Just before the highway from Atotonilco climbs into the sierras, it crosses the Tulancingo River valley. At that point, a side road turns off to the north, following the canyon upriver. The narrow road winds through fertile bottomlands and groves of subtropical vegetation, passing several villages that cling to the sheer canyon walls. Finally, we arrive at the town of Metztitlán, whose steep cobbled streets and arcaded houses have scarcely changed since colonial times.

The Monastery

Soon after his arrival here in 1538, Fray Juan de Sevilla founded the first mission on low ground close to Lake Metztitlán, then much larger than it is today. Part of this early mission still stands—an arcaded building known as La Comunidad.

Frequent flooding, however, forced a change of location, and in the 1540s, construction of the new monastery of Santos Reyes began on its present site above the town. Although the *convento* was occupied by 1550, the huge church rose more slowly and was not finished until the 1560s. The only firm date is 1577, inscribed on one of the *portería* murals.

The monastery is built on a leveled ridge—part of the rugged canyon wall. Its vast terraced atrium, reputedly the site of a prehispanic Temple of the Moon, is now planted with rose gardens maintained by the town *barrios.*

A steep ramp climbs up from the town to the atrium, whose entrance is through a narrow opening cut into the crenelated west wall. Immediately opposite is a curious double open chapel, beside the church at the far end. Although originally linked by an *alfiz*, the two chambers of the chapel are separate, each with its own carved archway. The larger, slightly raised room on the left was the sanctuary, while the one on the right served as a choir or perhaps a baptistery. The colorful interior murals have been all but effaced by time, weather and graffiti.

One *posa* chapel crumbles away in the northwest corner of the atrium, a second faces the church and the remains of a third are embedded in the southeast corner of the atrium wall. A stately stone crucifix, carved with a crown of thorns, stylized wounds and globe finials, is mounted on a high pedestal in front of the church.

The Church

An imposing fortress church with tall flanking buttresses, rugged black and tan stonework, and battlemented parapets, Metztitlán is oriented north-south with a raised terrace in front. Its magnificent *espadaña*, or gable belfry, with seven bell openings, crowns the facade and soars high above the nave.

The entry porch owes much to the west doorway at Acolman. Although less ornate, the basic design is identical. Only the details vary, and their relative simplicity seems to enhance the

Metztitlan, facade

harmony of the forms. Simple swagged columns, headed by Corinthian lion's head capitals, enclose dignified statues of St. Peter and St. Paul. As at Acolman, plates of bread, fish and fruit are carved into the paneled doorjambs. Angels' heads and rosettes alternate around the archway.

Angels playing the lute and clarinet accompany the Child Jesus above the doorway, who, unlike his counterpart at Acolman, has managed to keep his head. The candelabra finials on each side are echoed in the slender baluster columns of the choir window—its only decorative touch.

Inside the church, a low ribbed ceiling, densely patterned with red, yellow and blue foliage, spreads across the underchoir. A large painted dado, similiar in size and coloration to the friezes at Ixmiquilpan, encircles the nave at eye level. Heraldic youths, grasping giant acanthus fronds, flank the Augustinian insignia. Fantastic bird and animal heads peer from the thickets, and long-tailed birds strut fastidiously along the foliated borders.

The lofty barrel vault draws the eye towards the sanctuary with its elegant Gothic wheel vault. The sanctuary arch, like the porch, is embellished with lion's head capitals.

The Altarpieces

By good fortune, or perhaps because of its provincial conservatism, Metztitlán, alone among the monasteries of Hidalgo, retains six of its colonial *retablos*. Their intricate gilded frames and painted saints create a thousand glinting lights in the darkened nave.

Perfectly framed by the flared walls and the coffered arch of the sanctuary, the main altarpiece is the only major *retablo* to survive in the region. It is a masterpiece of the Solomonic style, completed in the year 1700 by the celebrated native sculptor Salvador Ocampo, for the staggering sum of 6800 gold pesos.

Close to disintegration, the altarpiece was rescued by SEDUE, the Mexican agency for urban and ecological development, and is currently being restored. When completed, it will assume its rightful place among the finest examples of the style in Mexico.

The *retablo* is over fifty feet high with lateral sections sweeping forward like wings. The five tiers—a *predella* or base, three main stages, and a gabled top tier—are divided into five vertical sections, or *calles*. The wide center *calle* features large wooden reliefs, and is flanked by narrow sections containing figure sculptures. The wings frame a sequence of large paintings.

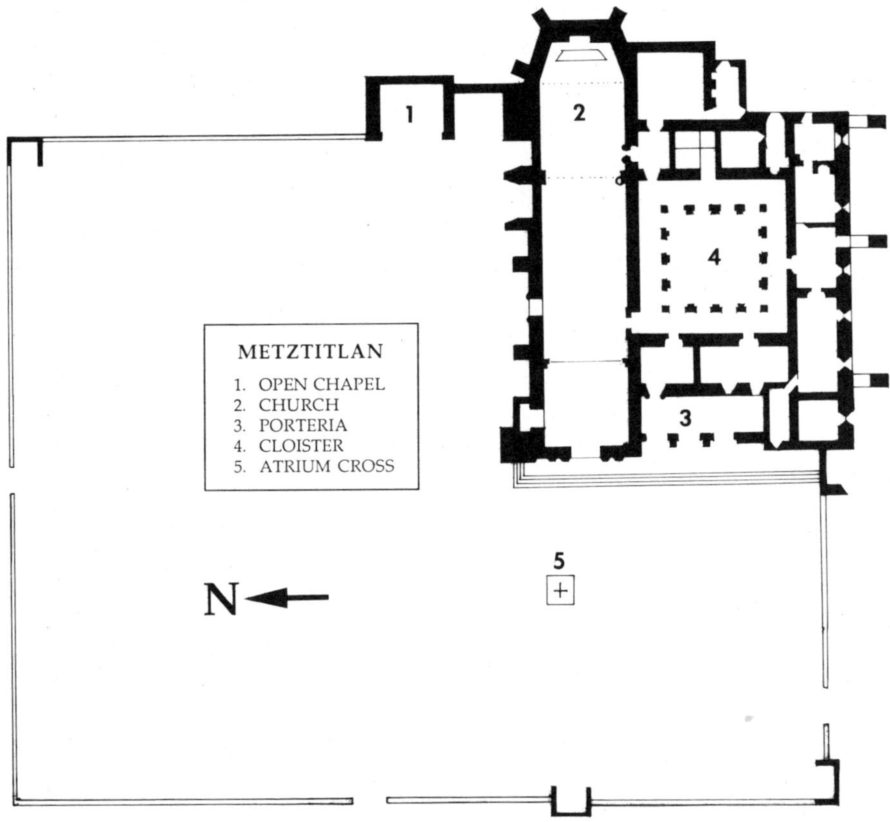

Spiral columns define the ornamental framework. Encrusted with twisting red and green vines and headed by ornate Corinthian capitals, they sound the dominant note in a voluptuous symphony of shells, scrolls, swags, dripping pendants and winged cherubs, against a rich counterpoint of strapwork and gilded foliage.

The central relief of the Three Kings, as well as the Crucifixion and a youthful Padre Eterno above, are believed to be from the accomplished hand of Ocampo himself, who is best known for the sumptuous choir stalls that he carved for the church of St. Augustine in Mexico City. The luxuriantly bearded kings in their opulent *estofado* robes gather around the infant Jesus and his mother. Considering its late date, the panel has an anachronistic Renaissance harmony, the idealized poses and serene expressions of the figures giving no sign of baroque restlessness.

Elaborately framed niches on each side of the center section house elongated statues of revered Augustinian saints. These include Nicholas of Tolentino and William of Aquitaine, on either side of the Three Kings, and Thomas of Villanova and John of Sahagún below. St. Clare and Augustine's mother, St. Monica, occupy the upper niches, while the monastic founders, St. Bernard and St. Benedict, appear on the predella, flanked by the Four Evangelists.

The six lateral paintings illustrate scenes from the lives of Christ and the Virgin, and are attributed to the painter Nicolás Rodríguez Juarez, a member of an illustrious family of Mexican artists. One of the leading painters of the Mexican Baroque, he was noted for his luminous but muted colors and the elegant Mannerist dignity of his figures.

Because of their soiled condition, the paintings are difficult to evaluate, and I look forward to the time when they are cleaned and installed in the restored frame. Only then will it be possible to appreciate how magnificently the religious intent of this altarpiece—the exaltation of Christ and his Mother and the glorification of the Augustinian Order—was realized, and fully comprehend its mesmerizing effect upon the congregations of 300 years ago.

The Convento and its Murals

The varied and unusual subject matter of the Metztitlán murals and their placement in the

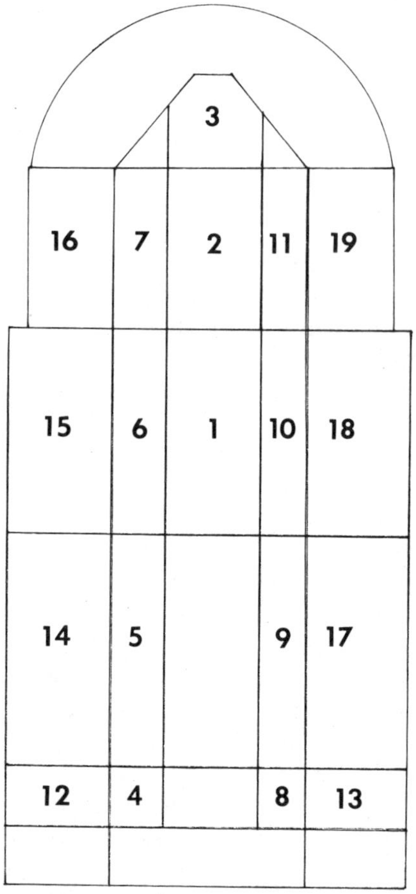

3

16 7 2 11 19

15 6 1 10 18

14 5 9 17

12 4 8 13

THE METZTITLAN RETABLO

Sculptures & Reliefs

1. Three Kings
2. Crucifixion
3. God the Father
4. St. Bernard
5. Thomas of Villaova
6. William of Aquitaine
7. St. Monica
8. St. Benedict
9. John of Sahagun
10. Nicholas of Tolentino
11. St. Clare
12. Sts. Matthew & Mark
13. Sts. Luke & John

Paintings

14. Adoration of the Shepherds
15. Circumcision
16. Ascension of Christ
17. Nativity of the Virgin
18. Presentation at the Temple
19. Assumption of the Virgin

monastery tell us much about the function of 16th century religious art.

Location was important. The murals in the *portería* and lower cloister were directed primarily at lay viewers—mostly Indian neophytes—and emphasized the principal pillars of the Church and the Augustinian Order. The frescoes of the stairwell and upper cloister were generally accessible only to the friars. Here, the murals stressed the triumph of faith through sacrifice and virtue, no doubt to bolster the friars' morale and underscore the value of their arduous mission in this beautiful but isolated corner of the New World.

The Portería

Although plainer and smaller, the Metztitlán *portería* recalls the grand portico of Actopan. Supported on robust paneled piers and set atop a flight of steps, the arcade frames a broad vista of the surrounding canyon with moon-shaped Lake Metztitlán beyond. The round lake, or perhaps the reflection of the full moon upon its calm waters, gave Metztitlán its aboriginal name. The man-in-the-moon motif that appears throughout the monastery is a visible reminder of this poetic origin.

Ornamental lettered friezes and arabesque borders outline the *portería* walls, beneath a painted vault of ribbons and rosettes. Two narrative frescoes of great interest adorn the east end. The smaller of the two, framed in an ornate Mannerist niche on the north wall, depicts the Virgin of the Immaculate Conception—a subject rare in 16th century mural art. The only other known example is in the cloister at Huejotzingo (Chapter Three).

The elongated figure of the Virgin stands on a crescent moon, elegantly robed and surrounded by several objects mentioned in her litany, including the Tower of David, the Gate of Heaven, the Morning Star and the Mirror of Justice, each identified by a lettered banner. A demon writhes defiantly beneath her feet. The artist deployed an unusually broad palette of colors: blue, green, purple and a range of reds, browns and ochers, many of them faded despite, or possibly because of, recent cleaning.

Filling the entire east wall is a complex fresco of the Tree of Redemption. Although the upper part, which included the head of Christ, has been erased, the central image of the Crucifixion is intact. Branches spread out from the foot of the cross, linked to medallions picturing the Seven Sacraments. The blood of the Redeemer flows into the Fountain of Life below, where a baptism is witnessed by an assembly of well-dressed worshippers. Known to be based on an engraving by the Italian Mannerist, Bartolomeo de Olmo, this allegorical mural is dated November 6, 1577, and almost certainly commemorates the baptism of a particular individual.

The Cloister

The cloister is a model of Roman sobriety. Paneled piers support plain molded arches and cornices of austere refinement.

Although the cloister is small, the walks are broad, roofed by high barrel vaults painted with *artesonado* designs and fringed by grotesque friezes. Ribbed vaults cover the corner compartments, colorfully decorated with angels and foliage. A painted balustrade of convoluted Mannerist design, a riot of wild bearded heads, waterfowl and swagged strapwork, runs along the cloister walks.

Huge beribboned Augustinian emblems have been added at eye level around the lower cloister, possibly obscuring more 16th century wall paintings. The only visible narrative murals are the portraits of the Four Evangelists and the Doctors of the Church in the lunettes of the

Metztitlan, Tower of David

corner bays. The richly appareled Doctors—Gregory, Jerome, Ambrose and naturally, Augustine—sit in splendor on elaborate thrones against a classical backdrop. The Evangelists are painted in a more impressionistic style and are shown with the Tetramorph—the four creatures who traditionally symbolize the Evangelists. St. Luke, mounted on his muscular ox among celestial clouds, is especially virile.

On the south wall of the stairwell, another beautifully drawn bull, festooned with garlands, represents the Triumph of Chastity. Derived from engravings by the 16th century Flemish artist Martin de Heemskerck, this is the best preserved of a unique cycle of allegorical frescoes illustrating the Triumph of the Christian Virtues. The other virtues are difficult to identify precisely, although Patience is on the opposite wall at the top of the staircase.

Bull and garland motifs are also worked into the multi-colored dado surrounding the upper cloister, where, as on the lower level, the only surviving narrative murals are in the lunettes of the corner bays. Stylistically, they are similar to the portrayals of the Evangelists in the lower cloister, and are probably by the same artist. Figures and landscapes alike are boldly sketched in impressionistic strokes, with scant attention to detail. This unique sequence of murals links scenes of the Passion story with episodes from the Old Testament, to illustrate the triumph of faith through sacrifice.

Only two of the six identifiable murals are complete: the Sacrifice of Isaac and the Road to Calvary—both in the southwest corner. In the first, a rarely shown biblical scene that prefigures the sacrifice of Christ, Abraham raises his sword while a blindfolded Isaac kneels, awaiting the fatal blow. The Road to Calvary reminds us of the Via Dolorosa at Epazoyucan. Christ stumbles under the weight of the cross amid a crowd of Apostles, onlookers and helmeted Roman soldiers with pikes and halberds.

A fragmentary scene of Moses and the Bronze Serpent is found in the southeast corner, another unusual Old Testament episode considered to be prophetic of the Crucifixion. Vestiges of the Crucifixion itself, the outline of a Resurrection, an Agony in the Garden, and the Betrayal of Christ (only the heads of Judas and Christ remain) occupy the other lunettes.

A splendid star pine grows in the cloister patio, its symmetrical form reflecting the harmony of the cloister.

Metztitlan, Abraham & Isaac

Molango, angel with cross

MOLANGO

Place of Mola

Molango is a quintessential Sierra town, high, cool, and frequently blanketed with fog. Its multistoried houses cascade down a steep ridge overlooking a green valley and ranges of blue hills.

The monastery occupies a sensational site, high on a raised platform that seems suspended between the sky and the valley below. This was at one time the location of the great Temple of Mola, a local god whose oracular cult was widespread in the Sierra region.

Molango is forever linked with Fray Antonio de Roa, the first Augustinian missionary to arrive here. Legend has it that he hurled the stone idol of Mola down the hill where it smashed into a thousand pieces—an iconoclastic feat that evidently impressed the Indians.

Although Fray Antonio was a man of great physical size and strength, the spirit of this mercurial "Apostle of the Sierra" was in constant turmoil. In 1537, alone except for one Indian companion, he set off into the inhospitable Sierra Alta, an unknown land peopled by hostile tribesmen. Filled with self doubt and discouraged by the privations and apparent futility of his mission, he abandoned it within the year and resolved to return to Spain. His superiors, however, persuaded him to try again. Despite severe hardships, made worse by his penchant for self-mortification and traveling barefoot, he persevered and the next year founded a primitive mission in Molango.

By the precipitous western entrance to the atrium, reached by a steep ramp and a tortuous stairway, stands a freestanding *espadaña*. Originally mounted on the wall, this belfry may be the only surviving remnant of Fray Antonio's first mission.

The Church

Massive arched buttresses brace the rough-hewn walls of this isolated fortress church. Built in the 1540s, its most remarkable feature is the ornamental stonecarving.

The west porch is unlike that of any other Augustinian building in Hidalgo. Carved in *tequitqui* style, it is closer in feeling to the Franciscan doorways of the region—at Tepeapulco, or in the Valley of the Angels.

Its most innovative feature is the welcoming frieze of angels around the soffit of the archway. They stand full-length with wings spread, holding large crosses against a background of cactus-like clouds. One or two of the faces are still inset with their original obsidian eyes. The broad jambs of the doorway are densely carved with stylized foliage—a profusion of leaves, vines, buds and flowers, which extends onto the capitals and around the arch, creating an enveloping tapestry in stone. An *alfiz* of ornamental candelabra crowns the porch.

The upper facade is pierced by a rose window—one of only a handful in Mexico. Gothic *flamboyant* tracery outlines the eight petals of the rose, and a triple frame of winged cherubs, rosettes and vines encircles the window. Rosettes and vines also decorate the north door, a simplified version of the west doorway, recently brought to light by the removal of the Guadalupe Chapel.

The teardrop lights of the choir window obliquely illuminate the dark church interior, where we find more rustic stonecarving. Rosettes, crosses and sacred monograms frame the sanctuary arch and ring the baptismal font.

Although the wooden roof of the nave has been replaced by a new concrete vault, carved wood beams still support the narrow choir loft. Another uncommon feature in the church is a tribune gallery above the sanctuary, still linked by an arcade to the adjacent cloister.

The Convento

Completed in the 1560s, the cloister is currently in a dismal state of repair. The upper arcades have gone and only three of the lower walks are still standing. With its blackened, crumbling stonework, the cloister retains little of its original harmony of design.

Stylistically, the cloister is closely related to those of Atotonilco El Grande and Acolman. The plain columns, ringed by pearl moldings, are paired in the middle of each arcade and banded together to form the corner piers. Archaic reliefs of Augustinian insignia and angels displaying the Instruments of the Passion are emblazoned above the archways.

After laboring for long years as a missionary at Molango and other Augustinian missions that he had founded in the fastnesses of the Sierra Alta, Fray Antonio de Roa finally retreated to the life of a hermit. The "Monster of Piety," as the Indians affectionately called him, lived out his last days in a local cave that still bears his name.

Molango, angels on door jamb

The Franciscans in Hidalgo

The Franciscans were the first to evangelize the region. Friars from Texcoco crossed the southern plains of Hidalgo, founding monasteries at **Tepeapulco** and **Zempoala**.

To the west, missionaries from Mexico City pushed north along the Tula River Valley, establishing a major house at **Tula**, with satellite monasteries at **Tepeji** and **Tlahuelilpa**.

Tepeapulco, winged lion

TEPEAPULCO

Beside the High Hill

When the Spaniards arrived in Mexico, the cult of Huitzilopochtli, the Aztec war god, held sway in Tepeapulco. His dominion was short-lived, for immediately after the Conquest, Cortés personally ordered the destruction of the deity's bloodstained shrine that towered above the town.

Franciscan missionaries arrived in Tepeapulco in 1527, led by Father Toribio Motolinía, one of the original Twelve, a dedicated missionary and chronicler of the Spiritual Conquest. The monastery was founded in the following year by the eminent preacher and scholar Fray Andrés de Olmos, also one of the Twelve.

The imposing new monastery of San Francisco was built atop the Aztec pyramid, using the stone of the demolished temple. But it was slow work. Construction was often interrupted by plagues among the Indians and a perennial shortage of friars. However, both church and cloister were complete when Fray Bernardino de Sahagún stayed here from 1558 to 1560, while working on the *Primeros Memoriales,* the first part of his epic account of native society and religion.

From the town plaza, a flight of stone steps climbs steeply to the western gateway of the atrium—a huge enclosed area of shady gardens crisscrossed by stone-flagged pathways. At the far end, another broad stairway of prehispanic origin leads to the monastery itself, set high on an upper terrace.

The Church

Although the church was substantially rebuilt in the 18th century, its plain facade is original. The tower, dated 1530 by a plaque on its north face, is very early—possibly the first ever built in Mexico. Officially prohibited by the constitutions of the Order, towers were especially rare in Franciscan churches of this period.

The west porch is exemplary. Its simplicity of design and richness of detail established a

Tepeapulco, west front

pattern for numerous other church and chapel doorways throughout the region. Derived from an even earlier doorway at Texcoco, it features broad jambs, a carved archway and surmounting *alfiz* framed by the Franciscan knotted cord. Most of the decorative carving—rosettes, garlands and dense foliage—is rendered in low relief. Angels on jaguars ride around the archway in a frieze with crosses, acanthus leaves and codex-style speech scrolls. All the details are intricately modeled in the round, in the same manner as on the great open chapel at Tlalmanalco (Chapter One).

In contrast, the relief of St. Francis Receiving the Stigmata above the door is primitive, the rudely formed figures set in a locally inspired landscape of cone-like hills and *maguey* plants. (*Maguey* sap is the source of *pulque,* the mildly alcoholic native beverage, for which Tepeapulco was famous in colonial times.)

Beside the church doorway, stands a stone cross prominently sculpted with the Instruments of the Passion. This is one of several 16th century crosses found throughout the monastery. Another, carved with the diminutive figures of Christ and two Roman soldiers in a primitive medieval style, is mounted on the wall of the church sanctuary—the only feature of interest in the interior, apart from a pair of primitive holy water stoups by the entrance.

The Convento and its Murals

Simplicity is the keynote in the long *portería* arcade that extends to the south of the church. Six bays of arches with exaggerated concave moldings rest on folk Doric columns with plain slab capitals. This generous *portería* doubled as an open chapel in the early years of the monastery. A third sculpted cross, set beside a niche in the rear wall, probably marks the location of the original altar.

The simple forms of the arcade are repeated in the small tree-shaded cloister, whose surrounding corridors and conventual rooms are a picture gallery of 16th century murals. Narrative scenes, friezes and coffered ceilings—all are remarkable for their range of color and inventive composition.

Although the larger murals of the lower cloister have been mostly effaced—only a faded crucifix remains on the north wall beside the entrance—the unusual upper frieze is still there, a complex arabesque border of fruit and foliage, replete with demonic heads and trumpet-blowing angels. The strange device of a heron pursuing a fish against a watery blue backdrop appears at intervals along the frieze.

Immediately below the frieze, a looped and knotted cord runs around the cloister. This motif, which appears throughout the monastery—often superimposed on earlier murals—may have symbolized the binding vows of the Franciscan Order.

The former *sala de profundis*, now used as a sacristy and parochial office, contains the most complete cycle of narrative murals in the *convento*. The entry doorway, opposite an enormous baptismal font, is marked by the Stigmata painted above it. At the far end of the room, the entire wall is covered by a handsome triptych framed by a painted arcade with delicate arabesque friezes.

The Nativity in the center panel is flanked on the left by a fine Adoration of the Magi, in which the robust Three Kings overshadow a meek Virgin and Child. On the right, a touchingly domestic Holy Family is shown against a background of draped crosses that prefigure the Crucifixion.

The elongated figures are based on Northern European Mannerist engravings. The draftsmanship is self-assured, with bold lines shaded in a blue-black *grisaille* and accented with ocher washes. The folding draperies, expressive hands and somber faces of the figures are all finely observed. The Italianate landscapes are alive with incident—stars and crosses, gesturing figures, hills, trees and turreted medieval castles.

More figural frescoes, in the same style, survive in the upper cloister. These portray incidents from the Life and Passion of Christ, in the corners, with large-scale portraits of renowned saints and martyrs along the walks. Tall, elegantly clad figures appear against backgrounds filled with anecdotal detail.

St. Sebastian suffers stoicly, pierced by the arrows of a muscular duo of helmeted Spanish archers, and an impassionate St. Lawrence holds his grill of martyrdom.

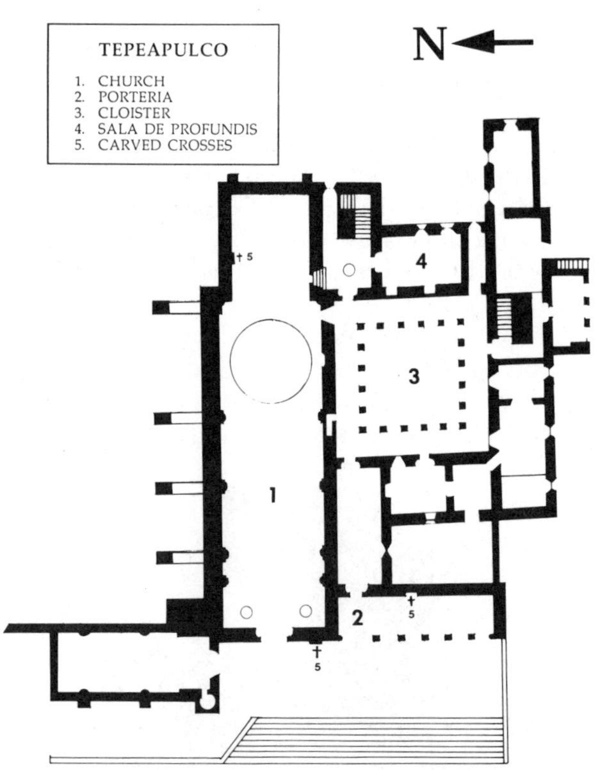

The fragmentary corner frescoes include the Crucifixion, at the top of the stairs, and a Nativity with two friars. But the most interesting mural of the group is a well-preserved Mass of St. Gregory in the northeast corner.

This rarely illustrated subject concerns an apocryphal story in which the saint, while celebrating mass, experienced a vision of the Risen Christ, surrounded with the Instruments of His Passion. Accompanied by two deacons, St. Gregory is seen elevating the host before a panoply of the Arms of Christ. Unfortunately, Christ's face has been obliterated by the overpainted looped cord.

Here, as elsewhere in the monastery, the painted friezes are always imaginative. The upper border, like that above the sacristy frescoes, artfully weaves cartouches of the Five Wounds and the young Christ into an lively arabesque of cherubs, birds, fish, leaves and fruits. Rattlesnakes entwine with doves in a frieze decorating one of the friars' cells.

End your tour of this outstanding monastery by visiting the attractive little museum, located in a suite of rooms just off the lower cloister, where ancient artifacts from archeological excavations at the monastery and the nearby prehispanic site of El Tecolote are on display.

You will also enjoy taking a stroll up the road behind the monastery to the famed Caja de Agua. This communal fountain and washhouse, built in 1545 to channel spring water from a 20 kilometer-long aqueduct, is one of the few early colonial examples left and is still in use after 450 years. The stumpy pinnacles atop the building are carved with reliefs of local flora including corn, cactus and, of course, *maguey*.

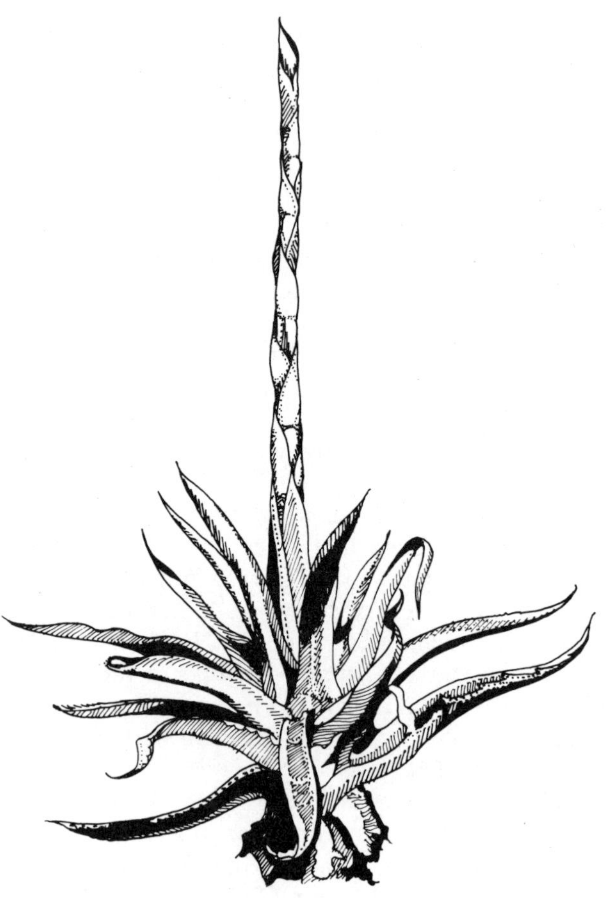

Zempoala, west front & gateway

ZEMPOALA

Place of the Twenty Count

Just a few years ago, the parish priest of Zempoala noticed that fragments of murals underlay the peeling white walls of the church. This exciting discovery of a hitherto unknown cycle of 16th century frescoes decorating the apse was a first among Franciscan churches in Mexico.

Zempoala started life as a modest *visita* of Tepeapulco, but with the completion, about 1570, of Father Tembleque's celebrated aqueduct from Zempoala to Otumba, a vast labor force of 5000 Indians was put to work building a new monastery.

Imposed against a stark landscape of dry plains and volcanic hills, the monastery of Todos Santos Zempoala has a palpable 16th century ambience. Ongoing restorations are slowly bringing the fabric of the monastery back to its original condition.

The Ionic arcade of the atrium gateway frames an unobstructed view of the monastery's austere west front. On the north side of the church stands the roofless open chapel, a structure that predates the rest of the monastery. From the hexagonal sanctuary, the side walls flare out to meet a wide transverse nave—reminiscent of the influential Franciscan open chapel at Cuernavaca (Chapter Four). The missing wooden roof beams rested on Tuscan Doric arcades, of great simplicity and elegance, that still stand. Much work will be needed to clear and rebuild this classic open chapel.

The Church

A lofty tower of Florentine dimensions adds interest to the plain, rectangular facade. The west porch follows the severe *purista* style of the late 1500s, with fluted Corinthian half columns and a coffered doorway—a design further elaborated at Tula and Tepeji. The rounded choir window has a Romanesque simplicity.

Inside the church, tall fluted pilasters and a running cornice, cut from local black basalt, articulate the nave. The dark ribs of the vaulting stand out dramatically against a celestial blue ceiling dotted with cherubs.

The Murals

With the assistance of SEDUE, the government environmental agency, the frescoes in the apse have been uncovered and restored.

An action-filled sequence of Old Testament scenes unfolds in four tiers on each side. The compositions are drawn in a lively graphic style with dramatic poses and closely observed details, subtly accented with blues, greens and earth colors, and framed by painted Plateresque arcades

Although a comprehensive study of these intriguing murals remains to be done, there are several familiar themes. On the south wall, for example, Moses examines the tablets presented to him by God. Below, in a medieval battlefield filled with tents and waving banners, David squares off against a heavily armored Goliath.

High on the north wall, Judith stands over the headless corpse of Holofernes, and on the lower tier, we can clearly identify Daniel and the fiery furnace. Kings, patriarchs and prophets crowd the frescoes amid scenes of sacrifice and martyrdom.

An impressionistic frieze along the nave, best preserved on the north side, restates the heron-and-fish motif we saw at Tepeapulco in an almost abstract swirl of color and line. A forceful grotesque dado of acanthus leaves and Roman military paraphernalia is outlined in black and white on the lower part of the wall.

The Convento

A single Doric column and a row of broken bases protruding from the weeds are all that remain of the *portería* arcade, but the charming cloister behind remains intact.

The heavy arcades, despite their flattened arches, stumpy ringed columns and overbearing slab capitals, are country cousins of the slender colonnades of the open chapel on the other side of the church.

Although tantalizing vestiges of colorful murals mottle the cloister walls, they are irretrievably damaged. Sadly, we shall never know how they compared to the magnificent frescoes in the church.

Note: Twenty was an important and sacred number for the Aztecs and other Mesoamerican peoples. Their month was 20 days long and they used the vigesimal system for counting.

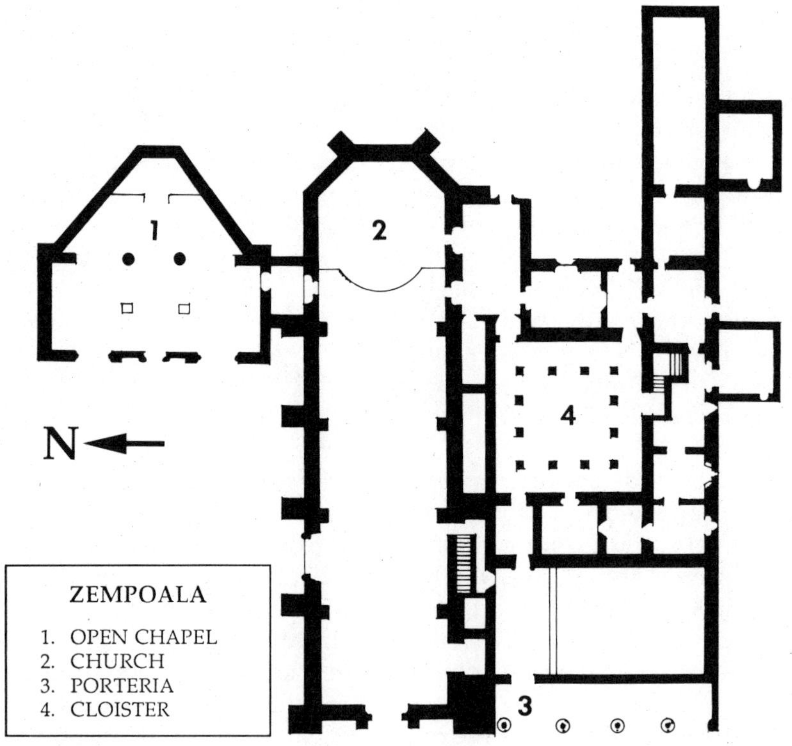

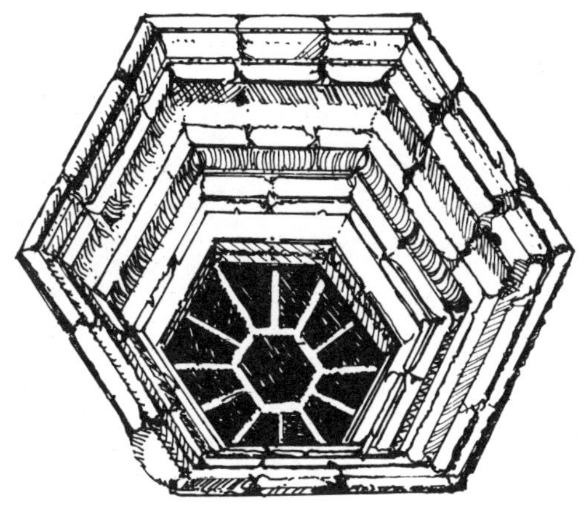

TULA

Place of the Reeds

When I last visited Tula it was the feast day of the Virgin of Guadalupe. Festive crowds in their Sunday best filled the vast monastery atrium. Little girls dressed like the Virgin, with dolls pinned into their shawls, and little boys as diminutive Juan Diegos, with ponchos and penciled mustaches, were being photographed against brightly painted backdrops, adding a touch of color to the gray monastery behind.

Now a shadow of its former self, San José de Tula was once the focus of the entire Franciscan missionary enterprise in the region. Much of its 16th century character has been compromised by later accretions, ill-considered renovations and sheer neglect. Nevertheless, its majestic scale and stylish architectural detailing make the monastery well worth a visit.

As early as 1529, evangelical friars from Mexico City, led by Fray Alonso de Rengel, ventured to the cactus-covered Llano de Tula, erecting their first rustic mission in the abandoned ruins of Tollan, the imperial Toltec capital.

Predecessors of the Aztecs, the Toltecs were nomadic warriors from the north, who descended on central Mexico around A.D. 900. Although Tollan was abandoned by the late 12th century, the Toltec heritage—especially its popular cult of Quetzalcoatl, the "Feathered Serpent"—shaped many of the later cultures throughout ancient Mexico.

In the late 1540s, the omnipresent Father Motolinía, by then the Franciscan Provincial, decided to build a great new monastery to replace the primitive mission. He sought the help of Fray Juan de Alameda, the distinguished friar/architect whose Pueblan monasteries are described in Chapter Three.

A new site for the mission town was selected at a distance from the main ruins and by 1550, the fortress monastery was rising atop a manmade platform ten feet high—the foundation of a temple formerly dedicated to Quetzalcoatl. The atrium extended over 200 feet to the west of the monastery and was enclosed by a battlemented wall 14 feet high, pierced by Moorish gateways.

Such ambitious siting was typical of Fray Juan, who may also have designed the church and supervised its construction, to judge by its classical architecture and beautifully executed stonecarving.

The Church

The exceptionally high walls of the church are veneered with cut stone and braced by cyclopean prow buttresses topped with turreted *garitas.* A crenelated parapet encircles the church at the roofline. The soaring rectangular facade retains its 16th century severity, even with the later addition of an ornamental *espadaña.*

Despite its eroded stonework, we can still appreciate the elegant Renaissance design of the west doorway—which was a model for the entries at Zempoala and Tepeji. Panels of

Tula, north side thru gateway

diamante coffering frame the archway, which is flanked by Corinthian half columns and surmounted by a rounded pediment. By good fortune, the matching north doorway has been enclosed since the 18th century by the Trinity Chapel. Protected from the elements, it is well preserved and, except for the triangular pediment, virtually identical to the west porch.

Although recently touched up with whitewash and gold paint, the interior is still awe-inspiring. The audacity of the rib vaulting shines through, most notably in the splendid star vault that covers the sanctuary.

The superior quality of the stonework is obvious in the molded nave windows and the ornate baroque entry to the elaborate Chapel of the Virgin, just beside the sanctuary. A particularly tormented and bloodied folk image of Christ, on a side altar, adds an earthier touch.

The Convento

The *convento* is modest, of ruder workmanship than the church. Now undergoing restoration, it was in ruins until recently.

The two-level arcaded *portería* has been completely rebuilt, with none of the original carving or decoration in place. But the cloister arcades are authentic—retaining a pleasing simplicity of design and finish. The deeply cut concave arches of the lower arcade sink directly into the columns, without capitals. Isabelline arches frame most of the niches and doorways around the walks. The gray limestone of the lower arcades makes an attractive contrast with the pinkish-brown masonry of the upper level.

Frescoes in varying stages of decay cling to the walls of the staircase and the upper walks, many of them weathered portraits of anonymous saints and friars. A Desert Father, possibly St. Jerome, reclines over the stairwell, and above the entry arch to the upper cloister, St. Francis holds up a crucifix to saints Anthony and Bonaventure, who kneel in adoration.

Facing a primitive St. Sebastian across the cloister, St. Peter manages to appear dignified inside his peeling niche.

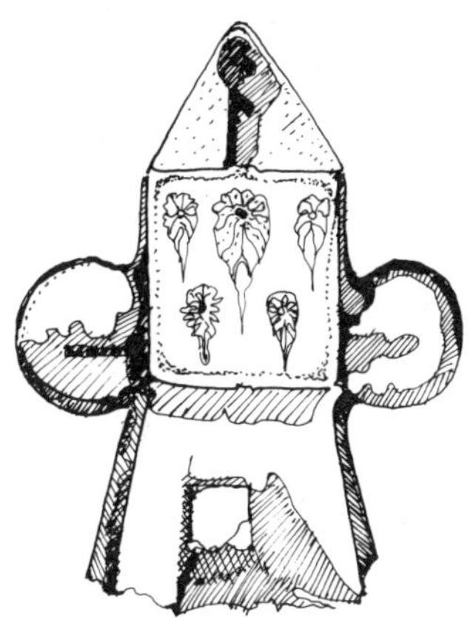

Tepeji, "eared" merlon

TEPEJI DEL RIO

On Broken Hill

Like Tlalnepantla in the Valley of Mexico (Chapter One), San Francisco Tepeji was a mission town deliberately located between two hostile villages—one Otomí, the other Nahua speaking.

The monastery was founded here in 1558 by Franciscans from Tula, on steeply sloping terrain above the town. The west end of the atrium was excavated from the hillside and the fill was used to build up the monastery foundation on the east. Atop this great earthwork, the narrow apse of the church looms above the town.

The sunken atrium is protected by high crenelated walls with unusual "eared" merlons. Although the four corner chapels have disappeared, one was still standing within living memory.

The Church

Built in the 1560s, the church still has an archaic, provincial look. The whitish-gray ashlar facade is flanked by flaring buttresses in the fortress style. Despite its coffered baskethandle arch, the doorway is unclassical, with broad two-stage pilasters on each side, headed by peculiar triple cornice capitals, a plain *alfiz* and a simple molded choir window. An ornamental escutcheon of the Stigmata sounds the only decorative note. By contrast, the north doorway is a model of classical correctness—closer to its counterpart at Tula. Diamond-point coffering again outlines the entire doorway, while fluted Corinthian half columns and a dentilled, triangular pediment complete the frame.

Inside the church, we can just trace in the dim light of the underchoir the worn outlines of winged lions and the Five Wounds around the primitive stone font—motifs repeated in fading grotesque friezes along the nave.

On the north wall hangs a large, somewhat insipid painting of Purgatory, signed by Juan Correa, the popular mulatto artist whose work achieved great acclaim in 18th century Mexico. Primitive *santos* line the nave. From one crucifix hangs a squat Christ, scarred and yellowed with age. Nearby, another red-robed *cristo* sits awkwardly astride a black donkey.

Tepeji, open chapel arch

The Open Chapel

The open chapel is embedded in the monastery wall to the right of the church. The flared opening attracts the eye to the intricate carving of the archway.

Studded with rosettes, the arch springs from rustic Ionic capitals—the most interesting feature of the chapel. Slotted scrolls curl outwards from the acanthus clusters at the base of each capital to cup "bleeding" rosettes from which issue catkin-shaped wounds. A low, spiraling thorn-and-ribbon *alfiz* surmounts the archway.

The *convento* is a warren of dark chapels and chambers, linked by narrow stone stairways. The cloister arcades, cut from coarse oolitic limestone, share the rustic style of the open chapel, with flattened arches and scrolled Ionic capitals—a motif seen again on the stairway by the monastery entrance.

Despite the best efforts of the National Institute of Fine Arts (INBA), whose restorers worked here in the mid-1970s, the surviving murals are confined toa few black and white friezes in the lower cloister—fragmentary arabesque panels, with scantily clad cherubs enmeshed in a swirl of foliage and strapwork.

ALFAJAYUCAN

Where the Waters Rise

Located in the chaparral-dotted badlands of the western Mesquital, about 50 kms north of Tula, San Martín Alfajayucan is a spartan monastery in the mold of Zempoala.

The churchfront is a cliff of ashlar stonework, whose muted hues of ocher, rose-red and hyacinth create a subtle patchwork on a monumental scale. Coffered *diamante* panels around the arches of the west door and the choir window are their only adornment.

The *convento* is located on the north side of the church—a rarity in this region. Four of the five bays that make up the long portico have been filled in, blocking our view of the *portería* chapel behind. From the single open bay a long, narrowing passage leads the visitor into the cloister, plain like the facade. Ringed columns with slab capitals and bases support unmolded arches, whose severity is somewhat softened by the pink and lavender tones of the stonework.

Although most of the multi-colored frescoes that once embellished the cloister walks have disappeared, enough fragments remain to demonstrate a pictorial sophistication unexpected in these austere precincts. Above the Isabelline arch of a doorway along the north walk appears a partial figure of St. Francis Receiving the Stigmata. The door frame itself is painted with Plateresque candelabra and dated 1576—the only firmly dated 16th century mural in Mexico. A vivid black-and-white frieze runs around the lower cloister. Angels, demonic masks and mythological beasts are picked out in white against the black background.

Mounted on a pedestal in the center of the patio is the magnificent atrium cross. Chiseled from dark red *tezontle*, it bears the symbols of the Passion densely carved in flat relief.

Alfajayucan, atrium cross

VALLEY OF THE ANGELS

East of Tepeji, the Tula River winds north from Mexico State into arid central Hidalgo. A picturesque chain of smaller 16th century Franciscan monasteries and *visitas* follows the river valley. I have dubbed this the Valley of the Angels, because of the angels that abound in the architectural sculpture.

Starting at **Apaxco**, actually located in an arm of Mexico state that juts up into Hidalgo, we travel north to **Atotonilco de Tula**—not to be confused with the Augustinian monastery of Atotonilco El Grande, described earlier in this chapter.

Stopping en route to view the primitive mission at **Tlamaco**, we eventually arrive at the exquisite little monastery of **Tlahuelilpa**, a treasure trove of *tequitqui* stonecarving.

Apaxco, angels displaying the Stigmata

APAXCO

In the Cooking Pot

The brownstone facades of this modest hillside church and its adjacent open chapel display some of the finest *tequitqui* carving in Mexico.

The raised open chapel is the older of the two structures, to the right of the church overlooking the verdant atrium. The arcaded front projects like a bay window, each of its three arches framed by an *alfiz* carved with vines, angels' heads and the Five Wounds.

But the most prominent sculptural features of the chapel are the paired angels above each archway. Similar in style to the *posa* reliefs at Huejotzingo (Chapter Three), they hover in midair, their robes flying out behind.

On the side arches they hold up the Stigmata, and above the center arch they flank an inscribed plaque surmounted by a freestanding carved crown. A monogram of Christ, encircled by a crown of thorns, is affixed to the keystone.

The more expansive churchfront boasts a Plateresque porch modeled on the Franciscan doorways at Otumba and Tepeapulco. The broad jambs of the doorway are divided by decorative spiral columns and capped by complex panels of winged cherubs, rosettes and slotted scrolls. Grotesque panels of birds, animals and demonic heads decorate the jambs and an unusual braided molding, carved with entwined foliage, follows the archway.

The double-framed niche above the doorway, carved with cherubs and giant tassels on the outer frame and featuring a zig-zagged inner arch, houses a primitive statue of St. Francis. A huge *alfiz*, in the same style as the open chapel, frames the entire porch.

Inside the church, more grotesque reliefs encrust the sanctuary arch, which frames an attractive 17th century gilded altarpiece illustrating scenes from the life of St. Francis.

ATOTONILCO DE TULA

Beautifully sculpted from soft golden limestone, the west porch of Atotonilco stands out sharply against the coarsely textured facade. Although more classical in outline than the Apaxco doorway, its sculpture remains archaic.

As the sun creeps across the facade, the enormous winged angels' heads seem to fly out from the archway. The door jambs are embellished with arabesques of coy cherubs, posing in a stylized garden of birds, fruit and flowers—all modeled in the round.

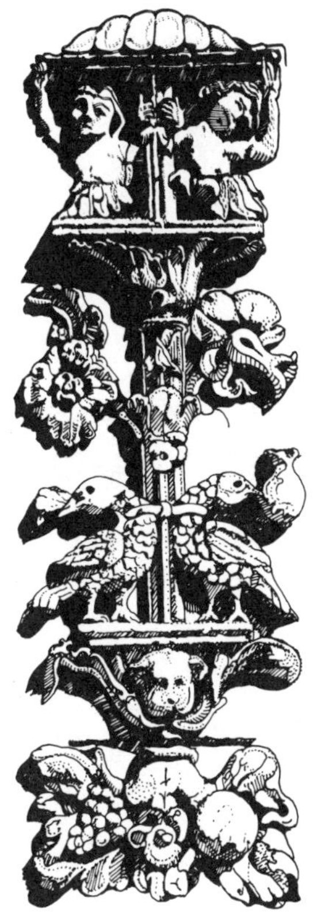

Atotonilco, door jamb

Atotonilco, St. Paul

The haloed figures of St. Peter and St. Paul on either side of the doorway have a stylized simplicity. The saints shelter beneath soaring Gothic canopies carved with crouched animals and winged cherubs—motifs repeated in the pinnacles crowning the cornice. The cruciform openings and intricate tracery of the rose window bring touches of refinement to the rough masonry of the upper facade.

A much whitewashed relief of the Five Wounds, flanked by fluttering angels with crosses on their heads, is set into the wall beside the church, marking the site of the demolished *convento*.

Tlamaco, west doorway

TLAMACO
Place of Sacrifice

This domed *visita* stands on a bluff within sight of the folk baroque facade of Atitlaquia, its mother church across the Tula River. Its intimate scale and open, elevated site, girt by the carefully trimmed hedges of the churchyard, make Tlamaco a delightful stop.

The diminutive church and its arcaded open chapel were built in the 1570s from apricot-colored *cantera*, a fine-grained local stone.

The west porch presents variations on the sculptural themes we saw at Apaxco and Atotonilco. Angels' and dogs' heads peer out through an intricate grapevine pattern around the archway. Bands of rosettes decorate the jambs and form an *alfiz* above.

The most original element in the porch is the ornamental triangular pediment. A carved thorn-and-ribbon molding capping the doorjambs curves sharply around the base of the pediment, rising steeply on each side. At the apex is a rosary enclosing the Marian insignia, and above it, an openwork *fleur-de-lis* cross. Unlike the carved church doorway, the handsome portico of the open chapel is entirely plain.

TLAHUELILPA
Well-watered Gardens

The diminutive monastery of San Francisco Tlahuelilpa is the "archangel" of the Valley of Angels. Its extraordinary stonecarving is the high point of what might be called the Franciscan Gothic—an exuberant fusion of medieval, Renaissance and *mudéjar* ornament, unified by the indigenous stonecarvers.

Tlahuelilpa was evangelized by friars from Tula late in the 1530s. They built the mission on a raised plaza—probably an old temple site—in the center of the settlement.

The elevated open chapel is the earliest part of the monastery. Its most striking feature is the broad scalloped archway, formed by nine medallions. Each giant oval is carved with decorative foliage and the occasional skull and bones, framed by vine leaves. A relief of the Stigmata is emblazoned on the center medallion, encircled with a crown of thorns and flanked by two hovering angels, whose long gowns ripple across into the adjacent medallions.

The candelabra of the *alfiz* frames several eroded reliefs above the archway. The headless image at center probably represents the praying figure of La Purísima, the Virgin of the Immaculate Conception, the first patroness of the monastery. She is flanked by angels displaying the Instruments of the Passion, and the crude figures of St. Francis Receiving the Stigmata, on the left, and his companion Fray Leon on the right.

The squared doorway of the little church is less adventurous. Rosettes outline the jambs, the arch of the doorway and the *alfiz*. Rosettes, with winged cherubs, also frame the sanctuary arch inside the church, which is carved with enormous sprouting plants and magnificent bas-reliefs of Peter and Paul, not unlike those at Atotonilco.

The wooden roof that covers the narrow nave is fringed by a multi-colored 16th century frieze

Tlahuelilpa, west front

of meandering red and blue foliage, inset with medallions of the Stations of the Cross. The stout wooden beams of the choir rest on *zapata* brackets carved with foliage and mythical birds—part eagle, part parrot and part dove. More exotic birds, with demonic heads entwined in foliage, enliven the jambs and arch of the baptistery doorway, whose ornamental capitals are carved with naive lions' heads.

The baptistery itself is a low-ceilinged room, located underneath the elevated chapel and filled with crosses and old stone fonts. Its rear door opens into the flower-filled cloister beyond—also a garden of sculptural delights. Arcades of luxuriant spiral columns, capped with curling folk Ionic capitals, blossom with angel heads, curling vines and acanthus leaves around each archway. Gothic doorframes along the cloister walks erupt in a cornucopia of crowns, cherubs and foliage, scarcely contained by the knotted cord moldings.

* * *

The exquisite stonecarving of the Franciscan monasteries and chapels of Hidalgo serves as an appetizer for the sculptural banquet that awaits us in the monasteries of Puebla (Chapter Three)—the *chef d'oeuvre* of the Franciscan artistic heritage in Mexico.

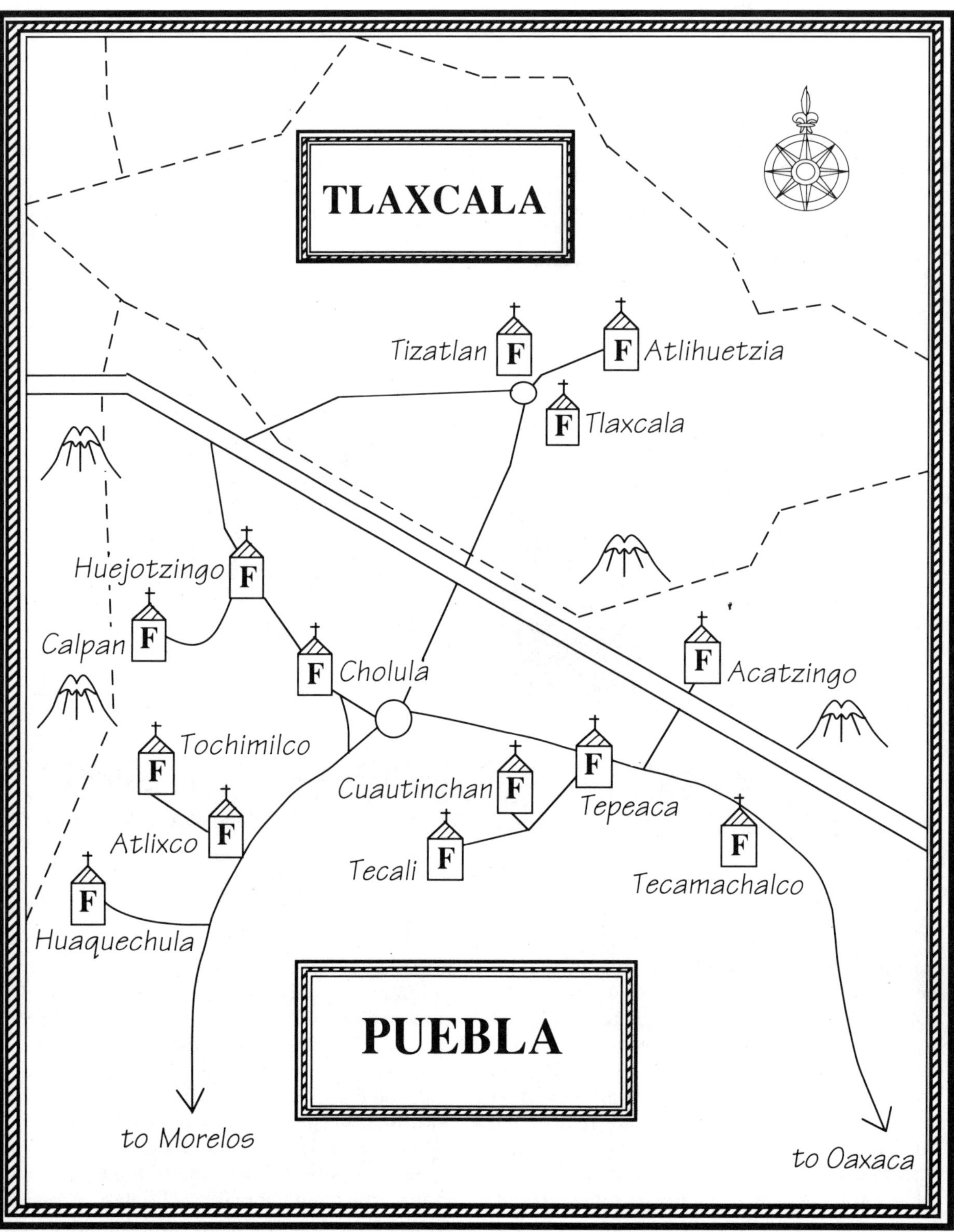
TLAXCALA
Tizatlan
Atlihuetzia
Tlaxcala
Huejotzingo
Calpan
Cholula
Acatzingo
Tochimilco
Cuautinchan
Tepeaca
Atlixco
Tecali
Tecamachalco
Huaquechula
PUEBLA
to Morelos
to Oaxaca

Chapter Three

Under the Volcanoes

Puebla and Tlaxcala

As he stepped ashore near Veracruz, Fray Juan de Alameda knelt and kissed the ground. Here, on Mexican soil, he and his fellow Franciscans hoped to build the Celestial City in the New World.

Fray Juan was one of a select group of friars who sailed from Spain in 1528 with Juan de Zumárraga, the Franciscan humanist and utopian reformer, newly appointed by the Emperor Charles V as Archbishop of Mexico.

With their arrival, the Spiritual Conquest began in earnest. One of Zumárraga's goals was to establish mission towns across the fledgling colony. He envisioned a network of Christian Indian communities, working and worshipping in peace and harmony under the benevolent guidance of the Seraphic Order of St. Francis.

To accomplish this task he brought with him a talented group of friars noted for their special skills: linguists, teachers, medical practitioners, preachers and one experienced architect—Fray Juan de Alameda.

Fray Juan de Alameda

Although we know little about Alameda's prior work in Spain, his contribution to monastic architecture in New Spain was enormous. An energetic worker and traveler, he designed and supervised the construction of several outstanding early monasteries. Although he is credited with planning the great monastery of Tula (Chapter Two), it is in the Puebla region that we can admire his best work.

He was closely associated with Huejotzingo, one of the earliest and most influential of Mexican monasteries, and may also have designed the neighboring mission at Calpan. He traveled throughout Tlaxcala advising on monastery construction and is said to have worked on the preliminary plans for Puebla Cathedral. His name is linked with the hill missions of Atlixco and Tochimilco, but his undisputed masterpiece is the delightful mountain monastery of Huaquechula, where he died in 1570.

Art and Architecture

All of the monasteries described in this chapter were Franciscan. These pioneering friars enjoyed a virtual monopoly in Puebla and Tlaxcala, which was their first missionary venture outside the Valley of Mexico.

The Pueblan monasteries inaugurated the fortress style—massive masonry structures with crenelated walls and carved doorways.

Their architectural sculpture is the richest and most imaginative of any in Mexico. Its forms are suffused with Gothic, *mudéjar* and Plateresque motifs, as well as complex iconography which mirrors the apocalyptic concerns of the early friars. The abundant murals, monochromatic for the most part, are among the earliest in colonial Mexico and also reflect the millenarian outlook of the Franciscans.

The Puebla/Tlaxcala region is also rich in colonial altarpieces, including several early examples—notably the magnificent *retablo* at Huejotzingo, one of the priceless treasures of Mexican art.

The Monasteries

Most of the Pueblan monasteries are located in the southwestern part of the state—in a narrow north-south corridor along the foothills of the volcanoes Popocatépetl and Ixtaccihuatl. All are within easy reach of the City of Puebla, the state capital.

Our first stop is at **San Miguel Huejotzingo**, the most famous of the Franciscan monasteries, located in a busy market town at the foot of Ixtaccihuatl. Close by, but higher up on the slopes of the volcano, stands the sculpted monastery of **Calpán**.

Further down the valley we come to the grand monastery of **San Gabriel**, located in the ancient city of **Cholula**. Continuing south, we enter the lush Atlixco Valley, home to several hill monasteries perched on the slopes of Popocatépetl: **Atlixco**, **Tochimilco,** and my personal favorite in Puebla, **San Martín Huaquechula**. Between the volcanoes of Orizaba and La Malinche in the southeastern part of the state lies a cluster of three major monasteries, **Tepeaca, Tecali** and **Tecamachalco,** each with its own artistic personality.

The last part of the chapter is devoted to adjacent **Tlaxcala**, a tiny state off the tourist track. The main attractions here are the historic monastery of **San Francisco** in the city of Tlaxcala, the exquisite painted chapel of **Tizatlán** nearby, and the picturesque ruined monastery at **Atlihuetzía**, in the hills to the north of the city.

Five Wounds

HUEJOTZINGO

Where the Willows Grow

Every morning on the stroke of ten, Brother José de Jesús climbs the fourteen steps leading to the great arcaded gateway. Fishing an ancient key from beneath his brown habit, he unlocks and swings open the iron gate. Passing through the carved archway, like thousands of his fellow Franciscans over the centuries before him, he crosses the shaded atrium and enters the hallowed halls of the monastery.

Huejotzingo was a strategic town in Aztec times, guarding the high passes between the Puebla Valley and the imperial capital of Tenochtitlán. Chafing under Montezuma's yoke, the proud citizens of Huejotzingo were quick to assist Cortés and his allies in their conquest of the Aztecs.

The Monastery of San Miguel

After the Conquest, the Franciscans picked friendly Huejotzingo as the site for their first monastery outside the Valley of Mexico.

At the time, much of the population, scattered by the turmoil of the Conquest, was living in inaccessible ravines on the upper slopes of the volcanoes, seriously thwarting the missionary task. In 1529, Fray Juan de Alameda boldly decided to move the people to a town site in the valley below. Shortly afterwards, a primitive church and *convento* were built, dedicated to the Archangel Michael (San Miguel), traditionally the messenger of Christ to far-flung pagan lands.

After further reorganization of the town in the late 1540s, work began on a much grander monastery, the "Queen of the Missions" as it became known—a project not finally completed until the 1570s.

As well as a man of vision, Juan de Alameda was also a gifted architect and engineer. San Miguel Huejotzingo was the first of his many projects in Mexico and contemporary witnesses were amazed at the scale of the monastery. Critics carped at the unseemly splendor of its ornament in what was, after all, "only an Indian town."

Viewed from the atrium, the scale and splendor of the monastery are still impressive after 450 years. The entire complex—church, *convento* and *posa* chapels—is remarkable for its rich, varied carving and the wealth of religious art displayed within its walls.

The Atrium and the Posa Chapels

Our exploration of the monastery begins in the vast plaza of Huejotzingo. Picking our way past the vendors of the excellent local apples, pears, walnuts, cider and honey, we come to a rugged basalt cross—the former atrium cross of the monastery. The gateway to the elevated atrium stands directly opposite, across the main street at the end of a stone-flagged walk.

However spacious the church may seem today, in the 16th century it was far too small to hold the vast congregation of newly converted Indians. By necessity, the friars preached outdoors, celebrating mass in the atrium. On feast days, friars and acolytes moved in procession around the perimeter, stopping briefly to pray at the four corner chapels, known as *posas*—from the Spanish *posar*, meaning "to pause."

Built by the principal Indian *barrios* of Huejotzingo to honor their local saints, the *posas* were maintained throughout the colonial era by *cofradías*, the religious brotherhoods of the community.

This quartet of chapels is one of the few complete sets of 16th century *posas* to survive intact in Mexico. Capped by a distinctive pyramidal roof, each one is elaborately carved on its two open sides. In addition to its remarkable decorative qualities, the complex sculptural program is designed to link the Christian story with the Franciscan Order.

The archway of each *posa* is framed by clustered Gothic colonettes and linked fetter moldings—possibly symbolizing the bonds of sin. The Franciscan knotted cord outlines the rectangular *alfiz* and then loops around the arch, ending in a prominent tassel.

At the center of each *alfiz*, an ornate monogram of either the Holy Name of Christ or the Virgin Mary is surmounted by a row of relief medallions displaying the Five Wounds of Christ. This central symbol of the Passion—intimately

Huejotzingo, west front

associated with the receiving of the Stigmata by St. Francis and thus doubly meaningful to the Franciscans—was universally emblazoned on their buildings in the New World.

Although all the facades have a common format, the iconography differs. Pairs of angels, frozen in flight, present the various Instruments of the Passion, in a sequence that runs counterclockwise around the atrium.

Northeast Posa

The south face of the first chapel, to the left of the church door, depicts the amphora and ewer of water used by Pontius Pilate and the lantern by whose light Christ was discovered and arrested. Displayed above the adjacent archway, we see the lance and sponge of vinegar, complete with a cup of honey. The date 1550 is carved on the roof, beside a skull and crossbones.

Northwest Posa

On the east side, angels with trumpets sound the Last Judgment, while on the south face, another angel brandishes the sword of Saint Peter. Note the belt-like representation of the thirty pieces of silver.

Southwest Posa

Here, the angels carry the cruel tools of the Crucifixion. On the north side, the scourge, the cane and the flagellation column with the cockerel crowing on top, and on the east face, the crown of thorns.

Southeast Posa

Unfortunately, the reliefs on the last posa have been defaced and are indecipherable.

The chapel interiors are all empty now. The altars and shrines that once adorned them have been removed and only a few patches of colored fresco remain. Tree crosses, also carved with the Instruments of the Passion, once stood atop each chapel roof. Only one such cross has been preserved. It now stands in a crown of thorns on a pedestal in front of the church.

The Church

San Miguel Huejotzingo looks like a medieval Italian citadel. Parapets of pierced merlons run along the sheer walls and swallow-tail battlements crown the stepped buttresses.

The West Porch

Set between angled buttresses against a rose-colored ashlar facade, the forceful porch design is a prime early example of the Mexican Plateresque style. Slender Gothic colonettes frame the porch, the door and the choir window. The beveled *mudéjar* arch casts an undulating shadow across the doorway.

Over the door, a row of relief medallions with the monograms of Jesus and Mary is surmounted by a looped and tasseled knotted cord, which also frames the choir window and the flanking emblems of the Stigmata.

The North Doorway

This extraordinary portal has long been blocked up and is now accessible only through an iron gateway, to which the guardian has a key. Ask him to open it for you.

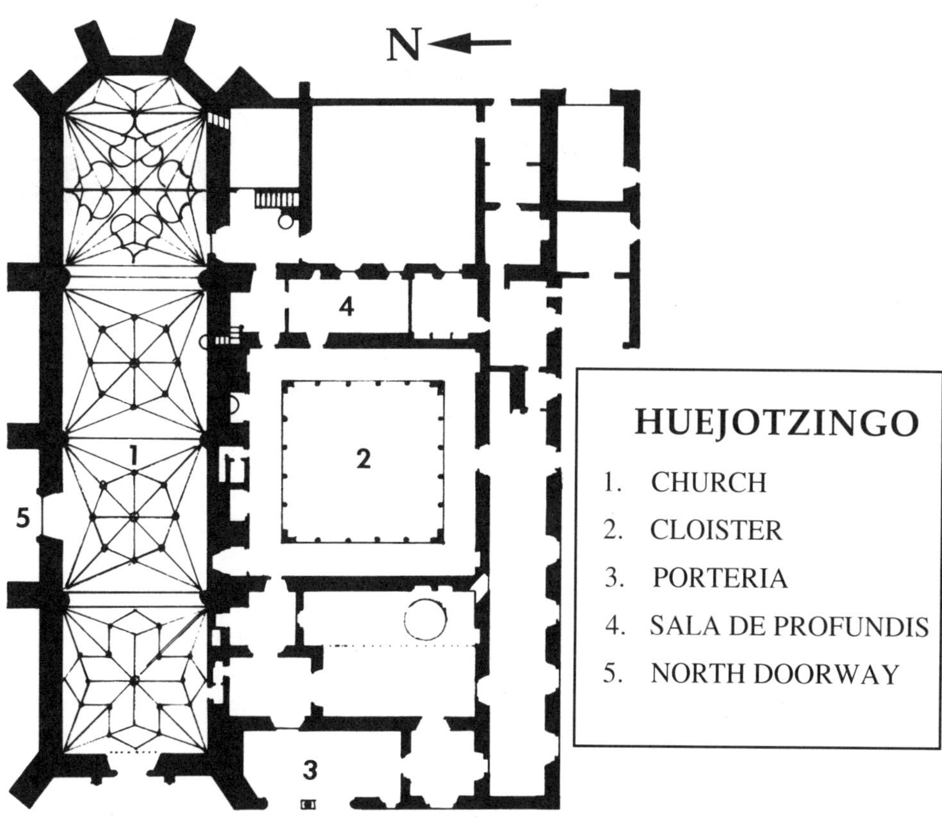

Huejotzingo, north doorway

More sensuously carved than the west doorway, the north entry was influenced by the Manueline style—an ornate amalgam of late Gothic, Moorish and oriental architecture that flourished in 15th century Portugal.

Like all the sculpture at Huejotzingo, the exotic detailing of the north porch reflects religious symbolism, in this case related to its historical function. From medieval times, the north doorway of the church had held special significance for the Franciscans. The *portiuncula,* as it was known, commemorated the rebuilding of the tiny ruined chapel of Santa Maria degli Angeli, just outside Assisi, by the young St. Francis. The preferred processional entry to a Franciscan church, it was opened only on special feast days, when plenary indulgences were granted to the faithful.

Known as the Door of Jubilee, it also symbolized for the friars the portal of Paradise, the entry to the New Jerusalem. Some believe that the Huejotzingo design was based on an Old

Testament description of Solomon's Temple—one of the biblical models for the Celestial City that would be established after the Second Coming of Christ.

The broad, foliated doorjambs are divided by unusual half columns, bracketed by bulbous "baskets" at the top and bottom. To the center of each column are affixed heraldic shields displaying the Keys of Heaven, superimposed upon crucifixes hung with crowns of thorns. The columns are headed by huge finials of curling acanthus leaves topped by bunches of grapes.

A distinctive chain molding, thought to represent the chain of the Golden Fleece, outlines the archway. This may allude to the aristocratic religious/military order of the Golden Fleece, headed by the Spanish Emperor Charles V—a monarch who sponsored the Franciscan mission in Mexico. This chain is quite distinct from the fetters that decorate the *posas* and the *portería*.

The floral motif above the archway is especially opulent. Leaf clusters and swelling buds sprout from the wall, vigorously modeled in the round, in contrast to the low relief sculpture elsewhere. The Stigmata appear above the doorway, framed by a generous *alfiz* studded with rosettes.

The Church Interior

The medieval ambience intensifies inside the church. Golden panes of *tecali*, a beautiful translucent alabaster mined in the Puebla region, glaze the high windows along the nave, casting an eerie amber glow into every corner of the church.

The Gothic vaults above are woven into complex star and wheel patterns from clusters of painted ribs. Other examples of early stonecarving include two fluted fonts embossed with sacred monograms. The archaic 16th century pulpit, accessible from the *convento* through a narrow stairway inside the north wall of the nave, is carved with acanthus leaves, Isabelline beading and, once again, the knotted cord. But the most accomplished interior work is the sacristy doorway, on the south side near the altar, clothed in a stone tapestry of rosettes and braided *mudéjar* strapwork.

A compelling sequence of murals, long obscured by overpainting and side altarpieces, recently came to light on the nave walls. The murals date from about 1600—a time when plagues and famine ravaged Mexico. On the south wall, rows of barefoot penitents and flagellants in white habits, including women and children, walk in grim procession. Between them, somber lines of hooded black figures wearing the badges of religious *cofradías* hold up banners and objects from the Passion story. Some carry saints on litters.

The procession continues along the north wall, culminating in scenes of the Crucifixion, the Descent from the Cross and the Entombment. Pallbearers carry the shrouded body of Christ, a reference to the powerful local *cofradía* of the Santo Entierro (Holy Sepulcher). These powerful murals mirror the penitential customs of the age—a unique document of those anxious times.

The Pereyns Altarpiece

Nine altarpieces, in styles from every colonial period, line the nave. The masterwork of the collection is the main altarpiece, one of two superlative 16th century altarpieces to survive in Mexico—the other being the *retablo* at Xochimilco (Chapter One).

Like the Xochimilco altarpiece, the Huejotzingo *retablo* reflects the religious concerns and evolving artistic tastes of the period. For unlike the architecture of the church, which draws on a medieval past, the Pereyns altarpiece looks to the future. It is considered the pivotal work in the stylistic transition from the Plateresque to the Renaissance in Mexican religious art.

Simón Pereyns was a Flemish court painter who came to Mexico in the 1560s. He established a workshop in the capital that attracted some of the best European artists and craftsmen of the time. Drawn by new opportunities in the Americas, these artisans introduced the innovations of the Renaissance.

Completed in 1586 and signed by Pereyns, the Huejotzingo altarpiece was a collaborative effort. Its design, production and cost are well documented. Pereyns himself supervised the overall design and executed most of the paintings, while the statuary was the work of the Andalusian sculptor Pedro de Requena. Skilled members of Pereyns' workshop, including native artisans, were responsible for the architectural carving, painting and gilding.

Four tiers high and divided into seven vertical *calles,* the altarpiece soars up to fill the polygonal apse. The sides flare out like a folding screen into the nave, enticing the spectator into its mysteries. The framework is highly structured. Doric and Ionic columns with carved and fluted shafts articulate the lower two tiers, changing in the upper tiers to ornate baluster columns—an ornamental tribute to this earlier Plateresque form. Renaissance cupids and garlands festoon the shell niches and the intervening panels. Even a few baroque touches—scrolled pediments and oval frames—make an appearance in the top tier of the altarpiece.

As with every work of art at Huejotzingo, the altarpiece has a message. Its iconography links the story of Christ with the founding and building of the Church, emphasizing the role of the Mendicant Orders—especially the Franciscans. Statues of luminaries of the primitive Christian Church and Franciscan saints alternate with large paintings that illustrate key episodes in Christ's life.

The Sculptures

Realistic, careworn portraits of Apostles, the founding fathers of early Christianity, are carved along the base panels. On the lower tiers we are shown the Doctors of the Church, the teachers and philosophers whose writings were the building blocks of the Church. Sober and bearded, these patriarchal figures are dignified by their opulently textured *estofado* draperies. St. Augustine and St. Gregory, at bottom left, epitomize ecclesiastical dignity.

The middle tiers are dedicated to the founders of the monastic orders and include prominent Franciscan saints. The sumptuously attired figures of St. Bernard and St. Dominic flank the central panel of St. Francis Receiving the Stigmata, a large relief carved by Pedro de Requena at a cost of only 150 pesos, according to the original contract!

Martyrs and prophets, the conscience of Christianity, occupy the outer compartments and the top tier. These include St. Lawrence and the Spanish ascetic, San Antonio Abad. An unclothed St. Sebastian and John the Baptist, conspicuous in his wolfskin, stand apart from their elegantly attired companions. Above a large relief of the Crucifixion, God the Father, in flowing cape and beard, gestures majestically from the crowning pediment.

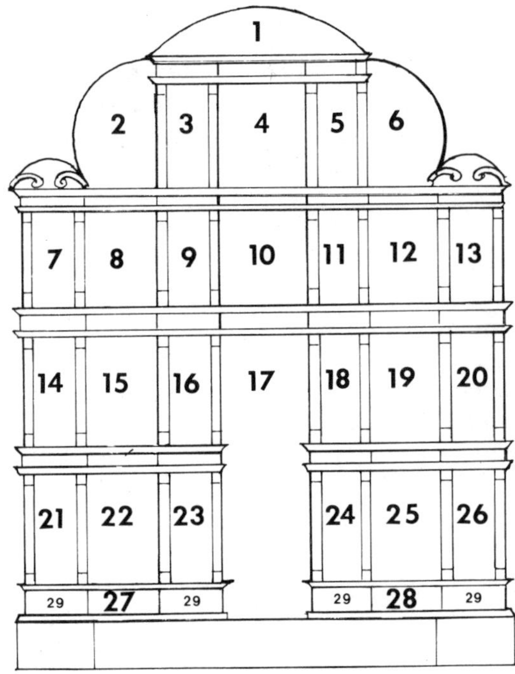

The Pereyns Altarpiece

1. God (*Padre Eterno*)
2. Christ at the Column
3. St. John the Baptist
4. The Crucifixion
5. *San Antonio Abad*
6. The Road to Calvary
7. St. Lawrence (*San Lorenzo*)
8. The Resurrection
9. St. Bernard
10. St. Francis receiving the Stigmata
11. St. Dominic
12. The Ascension
13. St. Sebastian
14. St. Anthony of Padua
15. Circumcision of Christ
16. St. Bonaventure
17. St. Michael
18. St. Jerome
19. The Presentation at the Temple
20. *San Bernardino de Siena*
21. St. Augustine (*San Agustín*)
22. Adoration of the Shepherds
23. St. Gregory
24. *San Pedro Damiano*
25. Adoration of the Magi
26. St. Ambrose
27. Mary Magdalene
28. Mary of Egypt
29. Twelve Apostles

The Paintings

Pereyns' paintings dramatize the significant episodes of Christ's life. Derived from Renaissance prints by the Flemish engraver Martin de Vos, the panels show a decided Mannerist influence, with a sharp eye for detail. Although the faces retain their classical serenity, the compositions display a vitality of gesture and movement that anticipates the baroque.

The most accomplished and accessible paintings are on the lower tier: a charming Adoration of the Shepherds (left) and the arrival of the Three Kings (right). The figure of St. Joseph is particularly well realized, as is the sensuous reclining figure of Mary Magdalene on the base panel—the only work signed by the artist.

The Convento

Large and well-built, complete with its upper and lower cloister, dormitories, cells and orchard.

This terse description, left to us by a visiting friar over 400 years ago, gives no indication of the intriguing architectural detail and abundant early murals that grace the precincts of this classic Franciscan *convento.*

The Portería

The double archway of the monastery entrance is divided by a massive baluster column—a primitive progenitor, perhaps, of the Plateresque shafts in the main altarpiece. Carved pleats, feathery fluting and a capital crowned with acanthus leaves animate its bulbous form.

Distinct decorative motifs frame each of the two broad arches. Intricate eight-pointed crosses cover the right hand arch in a coffered band and around the left hand arch, the fetter motif carved on the *posas* is repeated on a larger scale.

Beyond the monastery vestibule, we pass into an open courtyard, formerly the chapel of the Third Order of St. Francis. Note their emblem of crossed arms above the baroque doorway. The wall confessionals in the anterooms on the far side communicated with the nave of the church, enabling the friars to hear confessions without leaving the *convento.*

The Cloister

The fountain and orange trees in the patio create a refreshing oasis at the heart of the *convento,* framed by the symmetry of the cloister arcades.

Huejotzingo, Penitant (nave mural)

Along the north walks of both levels, adjacent to the church, niches studded with carved rosettes and monograms have been cut into the thick wall. Some are outlined by the Franciscan cord and painted friezes, and many contain altars and colonial *santos*—suggesting the involvement of Huejotzingo's influential *cofradías*. The gracious figure of St. Francis in the lower cloister is the best preserved of the images.

The Cloister Murals

Above the arch in the northwest corner of the cloister, a pair of angels like those on the *posas* holds up the Arms of Christ—the cross surrounded by the Instruments of the Passion.

An unusual and complex black-and-white mural, depicting the Virgin of the Immaculate Conception, appears above a narrow Gothic doorway in the northeast corner.

She is surrounded by her attributes as described in the Song of Solomon, each one carefully captioned, and is flanked by Saint Thomas Aquinas, the Dominican schoolman, and the Franciscan theologian Duns Scotus, wearing his ecclesiastical *biretta*.

These two medieval scholars were the principals in a dispute concerning her Immaculate Conception—a doctrine championed by the Franciscan Order.

Beyond the doorway lie the sacristy and *sala de profundis*. Emblazoned above the entry is a spirited representation of the Annunciation. The Archangel Gabriel appears on the left, opposite a militant St. Michael with fearsome spiked wings.

Sala de Profundis

A fascinating series of 16th century murals flows around the walls and over the doorways. Remarkably complete and still in excellent condition, they are justly famous. The most celebrated fresco stands above the main doorway and shows the first Franciscans, the apostolic Twelve, arriving in New Spain. They kneel humbly before the cross, their names inscribed above their heads. This unique mural is an important historical as well as artistic document.

Prominent Franciscan saints, with St. Francis at their head, are enshrined in scalloped Plateresque niches along the west wall: St. Bonaventure, St. Anthony, St. Clare and St.

Huejotzingo, the Twelve

Barbara, together with Peter and Paul. Christ washes the feet of the Apostles above a canopied water stoup on the east wall, carved with cherubs emerging from the tendrils of a vine.

The workaday south wing of the *convento* houses a long refectory and the monastery kitchen with its great open hearth. A huge tiled lavabo dominates the washroom at the far end.

A complex system of channels runs along the entire south side, at one time fed by an aqueduct built by the friars. Runoff from the slopes of the volcanoes flowed through conduits along the walls of the garden into the monastery, and from there down into the town. A few stunted fruit trees stand in the vast enclosed garden—a far cry from the lush *huerta* admired in the 1580s by the same visiting friar.

The "brothers' john"—an old latrine block formerly connected to the drainage system, remains isolated at the southeast corner of the monastery.

At the top of a broad stone staircase that winds up from the refectory, we find ourselves in a long corridor hung with colonial oil paintings. Off the corridor are the friars' cells, surprisingly light and spacious, with south-facing windows.

The south walk of the upper cloister provides an excellent vantage point for admiring the rugged fabric of the church. Recessed windows and stepped buttresses punctuate the massive sweep of the nave wall, painstakingly constructed from course after course of cut stonework. The former monastery library, situated above the *portería*, has been converted into a small exhibition gallery.

Returning to the atrium, it is pleasant to pause awhile beneath one of the towering cedar trees. Contemplating this peaceful monastery, we may once more glimpse Brother José going about his routine tasks as did the friars of 400 years ago—reassuring evidence of continuity in a world beset by wrenching changes.

An exciting but less peaceful time to visit Huejotzingo is during its famous Lenten Carnival. To the accompaniment of earsplitting gunfire, the townspeople boisterously reenact the Battle of Puebla, where in 1862, to its eternal glory, a ragtag Mexican army routed an invading force of Napoleon's elite troops.

Calpan, seraph with Stigmata

CALPAN

Place of Many Houses

The monastery of San Andrés Calpan is a gem of early Franciscan architecture, seldom visited by travelers. From Huejotzingo, an unpaved road meanders for about ten kilometers up to Calpan, a sleepy hill town set among cornfields and walnut groves on the slopes of Ixtaccihuatl.

These days, only the sigh of mountain breezes through the moss-covered pines of the walled atrium disturbs the silence of this monastery that time has passed by. Most of the religious life of the village is now centered on the baroque parish church nearby. Only on special occasions, such as the feast of St. Andrew (San Andrés), in late November, does a solitary priest journey from Huejotzingo to celebrate mass in the church.

The monastery was founded in 1548 by Fray Juan de Alameda, who also drew up the plans and may have supervised the early construction. The monastery is generously laid out on a leveled site, possibly the location of a former prehispanic temple.

The atrium is cut deep into the hillside at the west end, where a flight of stone steps descends steeply from the raised gateway. To the east, the apse of the church and the rear of the *convento* stand tall above the sloping hillside, commanding a panoramic view of the entire Puebla Valley.

The Posa Chapels

Calpan's atrium is a 16th century sculpture garden, its *posa* chapels justly famed as the most elaborate and best preserved in Mexico.

The four *posas* of Calpan are unique in their imaginative stonecarving and complex iconography, surpassing the *posa* chapels of the mother monastery at Huejotzingo. Their sculpted reliefs are a triumph of *tequitqui* ornament, exquisitely carved by native artisans in the service of their Franciscan patrons.

As at Huejotzingo, the imagery illustrates the redemptive power of Christ's Passion, as mediated by the Franciscan Order. But here, the theme takes on a more urgent tone, intens-

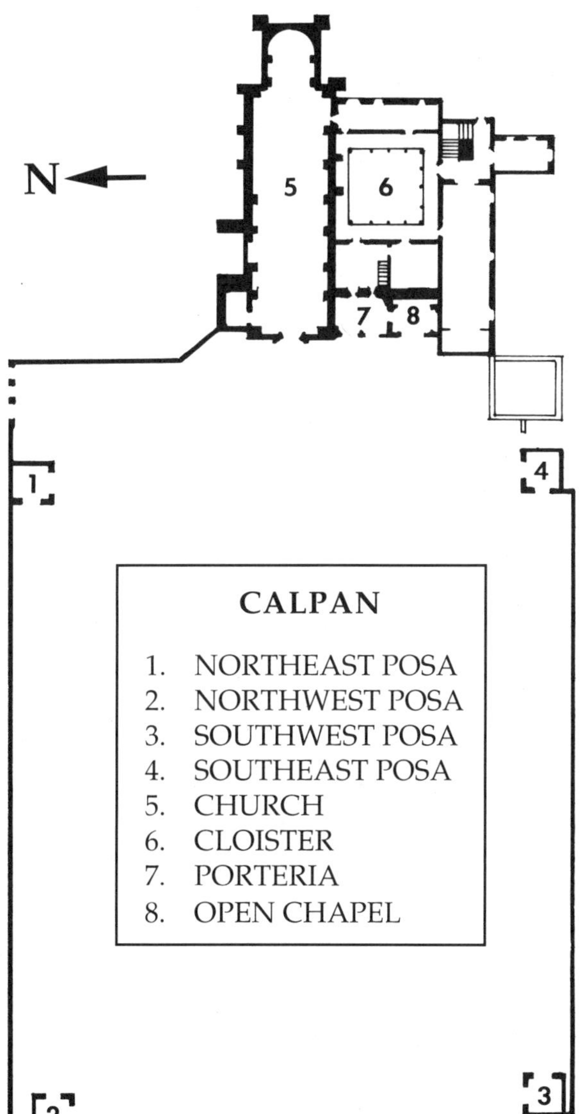

ified by apocalyptic visions of the Second Coming and divine judgment.

Northeast Posa

Dedicated to the Virgin Mary, this first *posa* stands just inside the arcaded gateway on the north side of the atrium. Sculpted reliefs, each framed by carved panels of rosettes and intricate foliage, enrich three of the sides.

A dramatic relief of the Virgin of Sorrows covers the eastern facade. Giant swords with engraved hilts and dagger-like points crisscross Mary's grieving figure—an image of suffering that prepares us for Christ's agony on the cross. The Coronation of the Virgin is carved over the south-facing archway, encased in a U-shaped frame. Here she is swathed in a voluminous robe amid a cloud of cherubs who display the crown above her head. Four angels hover with candles and swinging censers.

The Annunciation embellishes the third face of the *posa*. The Virgin Mary sits on the left, with the Archangel Gabriel on her right. A vase of lilies symbolizes the purity of the Mother of God, and the Holy Spirit in the form of a dove descends through exaggerated rays of heavenly light. Monograms of Christ and the Virgin are linked on the jambs, friezes and roof medallions. The steep pyramidal roof of the chapel is topped by a crown and a tree cross shaped like a cactus.

Northwest Posa

This chapel is dedicated to St. Francis, reinforcing the link between the Franciscan Order and the Passion of Christ. The roof dome is boldly outlined by the knotted cord. The statue of a praying friar—probably St. Francis himself—perches on the corner of the foliated parapet.

Large, intricate medallions of the Five Wounds of Christ are carved on both faces of the second *posa*. The stylized, gushing wounds are in high relief, flanked on the east side by a pair of fluttering angels bearing the Instruments of the Passion. On the south face, the wounds are surmounted by a seraph with six spreading wings. Note the chain moldings around the arch and *alfiz*.

Southwest Posa

The Archangel Michael, patron saint of this *posa*, is identified by name and occupies the

Calpan, Last Judgment

center spot over the north arch. He is flanked by two other archangels, symbolizing the triumph of the heavenly host. Above the east doorway is the acknowledged masterpiece of architectural sculpture at Calpan—a graphic depiction of the Last Judgment, derived from medieval book illustrations.

Christ sits in majesty beneath the sword and the lily. Angels descend from his throne bearing the cross and sounding the trumpets of doom. The Virgin, enfolded in a vast flowing robe, and St. John the Evangelist kneel on either side. Below, diminutive figures of the dead emerge from their gaping tombs. The facade is framed by carved bands of hearts, shells and foliage. Winged angels and scrolled Gothic crockets climb the steep sides of the roof, towards the crowning papal tiara of St. Peter, the keeper of the gate to Paradise.

Southeast Posa

This last *posa* is dedicated to St. John the Evangelist, author of the biblical Book of Revelation. The figure of the saint stands in the center niche over the west archway, surrounded by the Tetramorph—the symbols of the Four Evangelists—a sign believed to be revealed only to the righteous upon their arrival in Heaven. Finally, a partial relief on the east side depicts Christ reigning with the angels over the Celestial City.

The *posa* of St. John is the only one of the four to retain its 16th century altarpiece, now in poor condition, with eroded wooden reliefs and carved frame.

The Church

The church is modest and provincial, built in the fortress style from the same charcoal colored stone as the *posas* and the rest of the monastery. Its outstanding feature is the Plateresque porch, whose eclectic architecture embraces many of the sculptural motifs carved on the *posa*s.

The imposing paneled door frame is almost eclipsed by an ornate cartouche of the Five Wounds overhead, presented by two enormous winged angels with dynamic flying draperies. Tall columns rise on each side of the porch, interrupted at intervals by foliated capitals. Sacred monograms and *escudos* of the Stigmata appear on the columns, along the friezes and in the intervening wall space.

Wedged beneath the choir window is a primitive relief of St. Andrew, the patron saint of the monastery, embracing his distinctive X-shaped cross. A looped Franciscan cord with penitential knouts encases the twin lights of the medieval choir window, and the entire ensemble is incongruously but effectively capped by a classical shell pediment. Somehow, the sheer variety and zest of the *tequitqui* carving holds the design together.

The Convento

This section of the monastery has recently undergone much needed reconstruction. The *portería* arcade, in front, and the arch of the open chapel, to its right, have been attractively restored. (The upper arcade is a later addition.) The modest cloister is also being renovated.

Although Calpan enjoys a family resemblance to Huejotzingo and the other Pueblan monasteries associated with Father Alameda, it is set apart by its magnificent *posa* chapels—records in stone of 16th century Franciscan ideas as well as monuments to the art of the native stonecarver.

Calpan, west porch

Cholula in 1580

CHOLULA

Where Men Leap

When the Spaniards first glimpsed Cholula in 1519, they could scarcely believe their eyes. "Temples and shrines rise like lofty towers above the city," wrote an awed Bernal Díaz, the chronicler of the Conquest. "The main temple, an object of much veneration, is larger than any in Mexico."

This was the great Temple of Quetzalcoatl, the "Plumed Serpent," sacred to the Aztecs and famous throughout Mesoamerica. It was in this walled temple precinct that Cortés, fearing a trap, massacred the assembled Cholulan chieftains in a pre-emptive attack. This former killing field is now Cholula's main plaza, a tranquil expanse of gardens and fountains.

The Monastery

San Gabriel Cholula is the grandest monastery in the Puebla region after Huejotzingo, and is distinguished by its formidable fortress church and the unique colonnaded Capilla Real, orRoyal Chapel.

When the dust and disruption of the Conquest had subsided, the Franciscans hastily erected a wood and adobe mission on the site of the razed temple of Quetzalcoatl. By the late 1540s, this primitive structure had decayed beyond repair and work promptly began on a permanent monastery, under the supervision of Toribio de Alcaraz, one of the few professional architects to design monastic buildings.

The foundation stone was laid in 1549 and the monastery was dedicated in 1552. Construction continued for many long years, but by 1581 the finished monastery was described as "sumptuous, well-built throughout, with a church and a cloister of twenty friars and a large school."

The terraced double atrium lies to the east side of the main plaza, enclosed by high, castellated walls. The church and adjacent *convento* are located on the right, and the Capilla Real is set back on the left, linked to the church by the baroque Chapel of the Third Order.

The larger, lower terrace, in front of the Capilla Real, has two corner *posas* topped with impressive merlons, and in its center, a carved 17th century cross. The upper terrace, bordered by the churchfront and the L-shaped *portería* of the *convento*, has its own gateway. Virtually every surface is faced with newly painted white and yellow stucco.

La Capilla Real

Travelers who have seen the famous mosque in Córdoba, Spain, may experience a sense of *déja vu* on entering the Capilla Real. The broad Renaissance facade, surmounted by classical cupolas, hardly prepares the visitor for the surprising interior, aptly named the "Hall of a Hundred Columns."

This elaborate structure was the Indian chapel. It is the oldest part of the monastery and may occupy the former inner shrine of Quetzalcoatl's temple, explaining its special sanctity for the native community, which commissioned its construction and paid for its maintenance throughout the colonial era.

As designed by its Spanish architect, Luís de Arciniega, the chapel had no less than nine aisles side by side, each divided into seven bays by colonnades of octagonal and round shafts—creating a dense forest of columns. Originally, the bays were roofed with brick vaults and wooden *artesonado* ceilings similar to those at Córdoba. These were replaced in the 18th century by the tiled and lanterned domes we see today. During the same period, the long arcaded west front, formerly open to the atrium, was enclosed and fitted with classical portals. The spectacular flanking turrets have gone, and only a few candelabra finials still project above the facade to remind us of its original dramatic outline.

The interior furnishings include numerous colonial paintings and statues, but the most striking artifact is the huge baptismal font, carved with acanthus leaves and the knotted cord. Although it may lack the rich Moorish detailing of its Andalusian ancestor, the Capilla Real of Cholula is nevertheless one of the most ambitious examples of colonial architecture in the Americas.

The Church

Enclosed by tall flaring buttresses, the towering churchfront has an imperious severity. Roughly textured, buttressed walls of charcoal-colored basalt, capped with crenelated parapets, reinforce the look of impregnability.

The austere geometry of the Renaissance portal is accentuated by stout studded doors, stark crosses set on the surmounting pinnacles, and isolated medallions and monograms. The doorway frieze bluntly proclaims: "This door will be open to those sinners who repent." A *tequitqui* relief of urns and slotted scrolls ringing the

Cholula, Capilla Real

rose window above the porch provides the only concession to ornament in the facade.

More inviting than the west porch, the Plateresque north doorway is attractively carved in smooth white limestone—an island of finesse in the dark rubblework of the nave wall.

A spiraling ribbon molding, engraved with Latin verses from the Psalms, outlines the archway, while in the spandrels, seraphs hold up shields of the Five Wounds. The inscription from Revelation on the frieze is more encouraging: "I am the doorway of the Lord; whoever enters by me shall be saved."

Inside the church, the Gothic tracery of the windows and soaring vaults only seem to emphasize the barn-like scale of the nave and its uninspired, wedding-cake decor. The glowing painted *retablos* have been replaced by neoclassical altars and everything, including the vaulting, has been overpainted in monotonous white and gold.

The Convento

The arcades of the long L-shaped *portería* to the south of the church remain blocked up. Sole access is now through the sacristy. Vestiges of a 16th century mural on the theme of the Entry into Paradise have been found inside the *portería*.

The *convento* is not usually open to the public, although the priest or sacristan may give you permission to look around the cloister. In the 16th century, many prominent scholars were drawn to the Franciscan school here. While strolling in the colonnaded cloister, they meditated upon devotional murals, of which only fragments now remain.

Portraits of Franciscan saints and martyrs line the lower walks, alternating with naively painted episodes from the life of St. Francis. In one lively scene, the boyish saint disrobes before the scandalized Bishop of Assisi, seated upon a Renaissance throne. In another, St. Francis dons the habit in front of a youthful Pope Honorius, who gives his sanction to the new Order of Friars Minor.

In the upper cloister, a black and white fresco depicts the mystery of the Mass of St. Gregory, a uniquely Franciscan subject. Christ rises from the sepulcher in a composition crowded with the Instruments of the Passion. A virile St. Sebastian, the martyr and popular protector against the plague, is shown in an adjacent mural, but he is the only other recognizable figure.

During the first week of September, the vast atrium comes to life as masked folk dancers celebrate the Festival of the Virgin of Los Remedios.

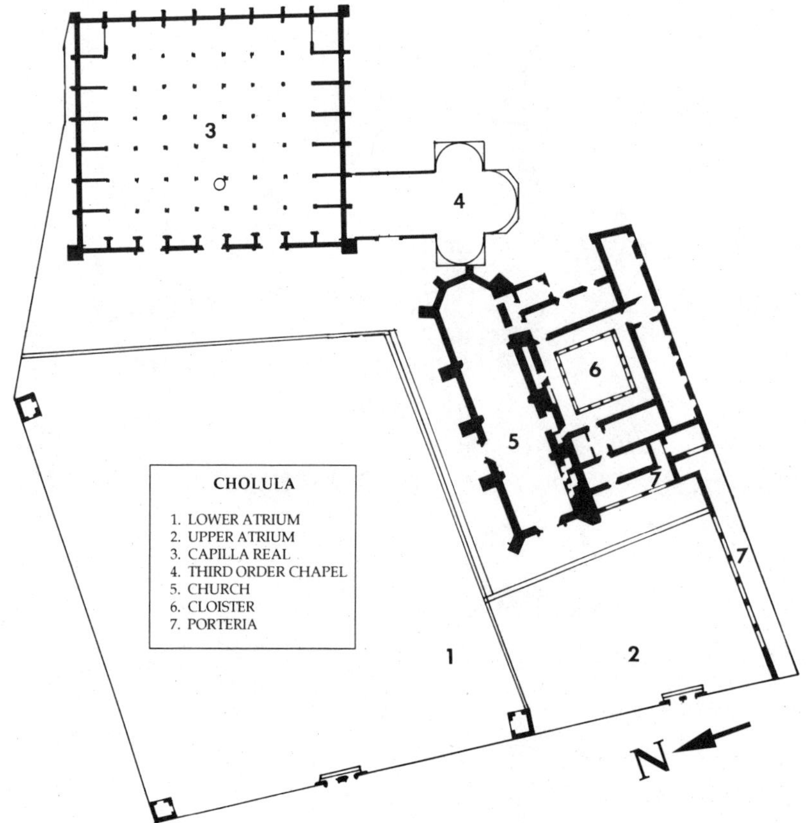

THE ATLIXCO VALLEY

Twenty kilometers southwest of Cholula, we descend into the benevolent Atlixco Valley. Warm and well-watered, it is the most fertile and scenic of the Pueblan valleys, famous for its spas and dairy farms. Both wheat and sugarcane flourish here, and in colonial times it was a center of the silk industry.

The monasteries of the Atlixco Valley are located in communities all along the foothills of Popocatépetl, especially in the attractive colonial town of **Atlixco** and its more isolated neighbor, **Tochimilco**.

To the south lies **Huaquechula**, the most delightful of the Pueblan monasteries, easily reached by a new paved road.

These valley monasteries are readily accessible from the city of Puebla via a new superhighway that joins the Oaxaca Highway (Mex 190) just outside Atlixco. A more leisurely route from Cholula skirts the west side of the congested state capital, passing en route several tiled and stuccoed churches in the picturesque Pueblan "folk baroque" style, notably at Acatepec and Santa Maria Tonantzintla.

ATLIXCO

On the Face of the Water

Atlixco is an attractive hill town with a marked Spanish flavor. It is well known for its 17th and 18th century churches with ornate stucco facades. Among these are the Guadalupe Chapel of San Agustín, La Merced, and the Third Order Chapel, noted for its opulent *retablo* and the quaint figures of Franciscan saints on its facade.

Narrow cobbled streets, lined with houses painted in a rainbow of pastel shades, wind up past little squares to the monastery of San Francisco, perched like a medieval citadel on the heights above the town. Although few visitors find their way as far as the monastery, it is well worth the journey, not least for the bird's-eye view of the Atlixco Valley stretched out below.

Toribio de Motolinía, the Franciscan chronicler and missionary, founded Atlixco about 1550 in what was then the native quarter above the Spanish town. During his long tenure as Guardian, he first built the *convento*, and then the church with the help of Fray Juan de Alameda, who advised on its design and construction.

The entire monastery is squeezed onto a narrow platform cut into a rocky crag, which falls away precipitously on three sides. Giant mimosa trees line the irregularly shaped atrium. Stepped terraces of red and black volcanic *tezontle* lead up to the church, snug against the hill on the left, and the *convento*, which projects towards the precipice on the south side.

Despite its present air of neglect, Atlixco remained an important Franciscan house until late colonial times. Funds were available for a costly refurbishing of the church in the 18th century and fourteen friars were still living here as late as 1755.

Braced by angled buttresses on each side, the monumental churchfront clearly belongs to the 16th century. Spiral Solomonic columns—a baroque addition—flank the Plateresque porch, whose flattened archway rests on banded Gothic colonnettes with thistle capitals. Twelve rosettes bespangle the area above the door, symbolizing the Twelve Apostles, and eleven *tequitqui* medallions, carved with the Five Wounds and emblematic Latin and Greek monograms of Christ and the Virgin Mary, frame the choir window.

A primitive statue of St. Francis set in the niche over the doorway and the use of the knotted cord throughout the porch remind us that this is a Franciscan house. The Moorish bull's-eye window in the upper facade was added in the 18th century, along with the tower. The crowning parapet is inlaid with Jerusalem crosses of black basalt.

Inside the church, early and late colonial works vie for our attention. Both nave and sanctuary are roofed by elegant 16th century Gothic vaults with patterned tracery. The windows are glazed with thin panes of *tecali*, which diffuse a golden

Atlixco, west front

glow throughout the church. A sumptuous Churrigueresque altarpiece, crowned by a great rounded pediment, fills the apse. Giant spiral columns, festooned with vines and headed by scrolled capitals, dominate the design. Ornate gilded and polychrome woodcarving encrusts the framework, replete with fruit, flowers and rococo flourishes, almost eclipsing the paintings. These seven canvases of the life of the Virgin were painted by the popular 18th century artist Francisco Martínez, who may have created the entire *retablo*.

Two early stone fonts, still in use, stand under the choir. One is a cracked monolith in the shape of a bulbous basket—a typical Isabelline motif. The other is a shell-shaped clay stoup, rimmed with angels, medallions and serpentine foliage.

The large first bay of the arcaded *portería*, anchored to the steps by a powerful stone bastion, probably functioned as the open chapel of the monastery. Open on three sides, it commands the entire atrium from its elevated position.

The cloister arcades are disarmingly simple—octagonal *mudéjar* shafts headed by plain molded capitals.

Faded traces of large murals linger along the cloister walks: fragments of a Christ at the Column and a melancholy Agony in the Garden around the lower cloister, and remnants of strange, surreal landscapes in upstairs corners. The ascetic countenances of a few Franciscan saints still stare out from the defaced walls of the refectory.

The recently revived folkloric festival of Huey Atlixcoyotl enlivens Atlixco each year on the last Sunday in September. Masked revelers from the neighboring towns converge on the Cerro San Miguel to dance until dawn.

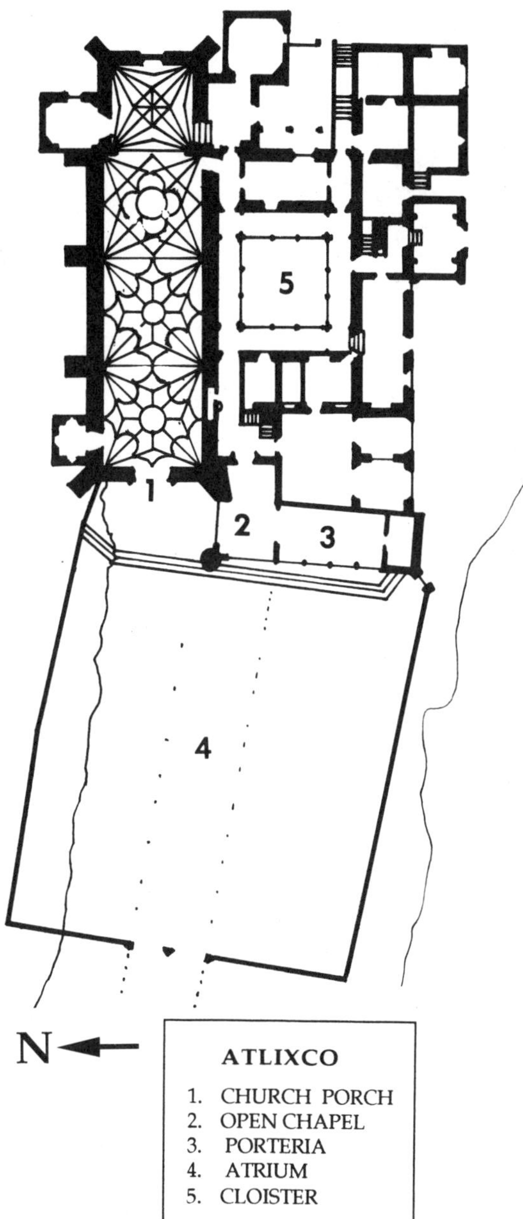

TOCHIMILCO

Field of Rabbits

The hill village of Tochimilco is located about 15 kms west of Atlixco, on a poorly marked, unpaved road. The fountain in the plaza, surmounted by a handsome crest carved with reliefs of rabbits, agave plants and dated 1558, is reputedly the oldest working specimen in Mexico.

The rugged monastery of San Francisco Tochimilco stands on high ground above the plaza, its walled atrium neatly planted with beds of cilantro. Its lofty churchfront is a checkerboard of dark *tezontle* blocks set in white mortar, an eye-catching backdrop for the handsome Plateresque porch. The pediment above the doorway frames a charming relief of the Virgin and Child, and relief rosettes outline the mullioned choir window overhead.

Inside the church, soaring Gothic vaults—as beautiful as any in Puebla—cover the nave and underchoir. Angular reliefs from a major 16th century altarpiece, including a panel of St. Francis Receiving the Stigmata, have been reused in several later *retablos* .

The most unusual feature of the monastery, however, is the open chapel. Its great archway, elevated above the squat *portería* arcade, was blocked up for centuries and only reopened in the 1960s. Unfortunately, the overzealous restorers destroyed several 16th century murals in the process, including a huge St. Christopher painted on the side of the tower.

Tochimilco, 16th century fountain

Huaquechula, St. Martin

HUAQUECHULA

Bird of Rich Plumage

Virtually forgotten for 300 years, this jewel of early monastic architecture was rediscovered in the 1940s by Manuel Toussaint, the dean of Mexican colonial art studies.

His voyage of discovery was an ordeal. The town and monastery were accessible only by "an abominable road, an ocean of ruts, ravines and rivers—some wet and some dry." For today's visitor, this tortuous journey is a thing of the past. A new paved road has just been completed from the main highway to the plaza of this idyllic village perched on the southern slopes of Popocatépetl.

Founded by Five Flower, the legendary Toltec king and mentor of Quetzalcoatl, Huaquechula guarded a strategic pass into the Valley of Mexico and was encircled by a stout wall. The lords of Huaquechula were proud of their ancient lineage and erected many fine temples, including one dedicated to Quetzalcoatl.

With the approach of the conquering Spaniards, the lords followed the lead of the Huejotzincans, offering their help to Cortés and swearing loyalty to the Spanish king. In response, the Aztec emperor sent 3,000 of his finest warriors to garrison the town. In October 1520, Cortés stormed the citadel and, with the help of the inhabitants, routed the Aztecs, killing them to the last man.

It was late in the 1530s before a tiny band of friars reached the walls of Huaquechula, weary from their trek up the mountainside from Huejotzingo. They were warmly received by the native chieftain, who took pity on the ragged friars and sent for a wagonload of homespun to clothe them.

The chief was the first to receive baptism and was appropriately christened Don Martín, after Martin of Tours, the 4th century knight who divided his cloak with a beggar and was immediately converted to Christianity by a vision of Jesus. Don Martín insisted that all his subjects be baptized too and before long, thousands of Indians from the surrounding area were pouring into town.

Once the initial conversion was accomplished, the Franciscans turned their attention to founding a monastery in Huaquechula, which they also dedicated to St. Martin.

Huaquechula is best known as the final resting place of Fray Juan de Alameda, its founder and architect. A modest plaque in the church records his burial there, but his chief memorial is the monastery itself. Like a single, giant work of sculpture, this is one of the most satisfying 16th century architectural ensembles in Mexico. All the buildings, including the magnificent open chapel, are fashioned from rich golden limestone streaked with sinuous red and orange veins.

The Open Chapel

Ministering to the host of new converts was a formidable task. The first priority was to erect an open chapel. Built in 1565, this was the focus of the outdoor church and provided a vantage point from which the friars could survey the Indian congregation assembled in the atrium below.

But as the era of evangelism passed and the Indian population declined, the chapel fell into disuse. In late colonial times, the archway and the *portería* arcade were enclosed to create a Lady Chapel.

The great chapel arch, raised above the *portería* arcade as at Tochimilco, was recently unblocked, exposing a spectacular rib vault with carved bosses over the sanctuary. During restoration, the elaborate capitals of the supporting pilasters were uncovered, still carved with cherubs and inscribed with the names of archangels.

The Church

The Huaquechula doorway is a classic example of the Mexican Plateresque. An intricate tapestry of relief foliage flows from the jambs over the archway and around the outer columns.

Winged cherubs in the spandrels hold up reliefs of the Stigmata, and a massive double cornice projects above the doorway, supported by scrolled *zapata* brackets and trimmed with the knotted cord. The coffered recesses between the brackets are also painted and carved with inscriptions and cherubs.

Above the doorway, protected by a broad *alfiz*, is a delightful relief, in spirited Gothic style, of the mounted St. Martin, turning in the saddle to cut his cloak with his sword. The sculpture still bears traces of the original red and blue paint.

Note the carved inscriptions embedded in the upper facade and on the powerful flared buttresses. One carries the date "Six Flint" in Nahuatl glyphs—1576 by our calendar.

The North Doorway

Tucked away on the shaded north side of the church is an even more remarkable doorway. Bas-reliefs of St. Peter and St. Paul, guardians of the entry to the Celestial City, adorn the niches on either side of the doorway. Despite their elaborate robes, the saints' feet are bare and their misshapen haloes resemble the caps worn by 16th century Flemish burghers—no doubt copied from Northern European woodcuts.

Crisply carved above the flattened archway is the Last Judgment. Christ of the Apocalypse sits in the center, his sword to hand, flanked by four fluttering angels sounding the trumpets of doom. Below the angels, saints kneel in awe wearing crowns of salvation.

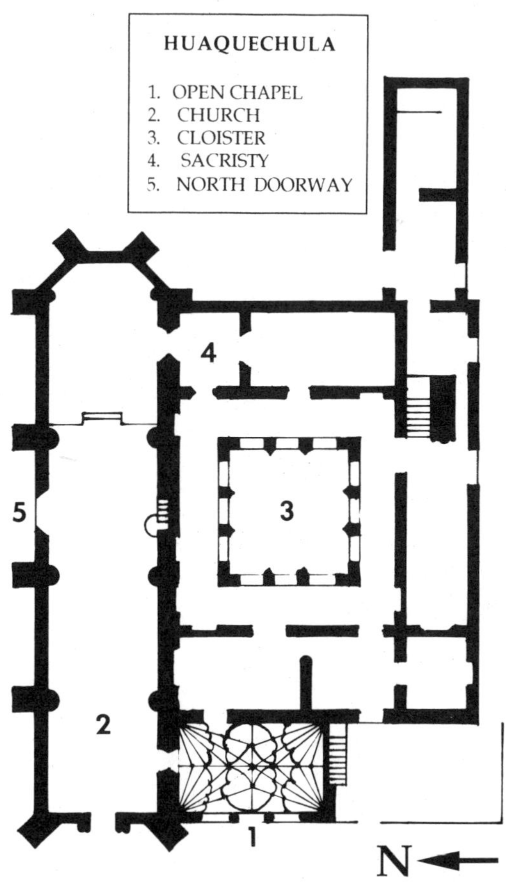

Huaquechula, west front through gateway

Look for the relief of an Aztec warrior embedded at the base of the north wall. Rising from the earth in his plumed helmet, he brandishes a spear and his decorated *chimalli*, or war shield.

The Church Interior

This is Father Alameda's church. His memorial plaque is mounted in the north wall under the choir, beneath a startling frieze of grotesque serpent masks with Aztec speech scrolls. The subdued interior, completed about 1570, is almost certainly Alameda's last work. Covered by a network of Gothic vaulting, the nave is a treasury of colonial religious art, containing ornamental altarpieces, baroque paintings, local *santos* and carved stonework.

The Main Altarpiece

Time has not been kind to the splendid 16th century altarpiece. Dirty, neglected and atrociously overpainted in the last century, it is a tarnished colonial masterpiece.

The Plateresque frame was probably fabricated around 1570. Slender baluster columns divide the four principal tiers, supporting classical entablatures decorously carved with Renaissance cherubs and swags. Many of the relief carvings also date from this time, notably God the Father at the apex, and the Apostles and Evangelists along the base, whose expressive bearded faces and strong sinewy hands embody the faith of these pioneers of the early Church. The image of St. Martin occupies the place of honor in an ornate shell niche at the center of the *retablo*.

Many of the original paintings and statuary were replaced 100 years later with a cycle of 17 canvases by the renowned Mexican artist Cristóbal de Villalpando. Signed and dated 1675, this sequence of paintings is the earliest, most complete, and probably the finest work of this influential baroque painter, predating his only other known complete cycle, the *retablo* of St. Rose of Lima at Azcapotzalco (Chapter One).

The most ambitious paintings are the large outer canvases of familiar scenes from the life of the Virgin. They are painted in an elegant Mannerist style using a subdued palette—very different from the richly colored, dramatic baroque compositions of the artist's later career. Many of the pictures have fascinating genre details. In the Adoration of the Shepherds, for example (bottom right), a peasant woman offers the Christ Child a fresh egg from her basket.

A second group of paintings, located at the top and difficult to see clearly, includes a graphic Crucifixion flanked by panels of the Ascension of Christ and the Assumption of the Virgin. Carelessly retouched and in a precarious state of preservation, these irreplaceable colonial paintings stand in urgent need of restoration. The group of narrow canvases flanking the central *calle* portray somber Franciscan saints, probably replacing earlier figure sculptures.

Huaquechula, flying angel on pulpit

Close by, the imposing bearded figure of St. Luke sits astride his bull, holding up the book of his gospel. This dramatic lifesize statue may be one of a set originally belonging to the main altarpiece.

Carved stone angels like those of the north doorway hover in flight on the paneled wall pulpit, toes peeping out below their robes. Every fold of the robes is painstakingly represented in flat relief by the native stonecarver, although some details, such as the faces and tassels, are more fully modeled.

The Convento

If the church is Father Alameda's, then the *convento* belongs to the present custodian, Don Cándido, who has taken care of the monastery for over twenty years. Obliging and friendly, he is a mine of information, especially about the buildings and their restoration by INAH in the 1960s, in which he played a part.

The original monastery entrance behind the *portería* remains blocked. Access to the *convento* is through an enclosed courtyard to the south, whose walls are emblazoned with another Nahuatl date, "Twelve House"—the equivalent of 1569 and the earliest date found in the monastery.

Passing through a dark room filled with dismantled church furnishings and dismembered *santos,* we emerge into the lower cloister. This is the oldest part of the monastery, built before 1540. Braced by thick prow buttresses and covered by misshapen tunnel vaults, the heavy arcades have a primeval strength. Faded friezes skirt the shaded walks and an escutcheon of the two-headed Hapsburg eagle appears over the sacristy door in the northeast corner.

Twelve canvases by an accomplished Pueblan painter, Luís Berrueco, are on view in the sacristy. Originally hung in the cloister, they relate the miracles of St. Francis in an allegorical but pleasingly anecdotal style. A follower of Villalpando and Juan Correa, this much married artist specialized in the portrayal of women. The sensuously delineated figures of the women and courtiers gleam with sparkling jewelry and exquisitely embroidered clothing. By contrast, the features of the friars are starkly realistic.

Fragments of architectural stonework and colonial altarpieces line the long refectory on the south side of the cloister. A charming lavabo, carved with angels and the Franciscan cord, is set in the wall at the end nearest the kitchen.

Unlike the lower cloister, the upper walks are filled with sunlight streaming through the open colonnades to illuminate the ornamental niches in the north wall. Although stripped of their saints and altars, these shrines are still bright with multi-colored murals of Franciscan saints in Italianate landscapes bristling with cactus and other local plants. A row of hooded flagellants in black and white penitential robes advance around the walls of one niche. Uncovered by Don Cándido himself, these painted figures are in the same style as those in the church at Huejotzingo.

Don Cándido keeps the *convento* immaculately clean. He has his quarters on the west side of the cloister and emerges to greet the occasional visitor. He does not spend the night here because, he says, the spirits of the past disturb his sleep.

Back in the atrium, we cross to the far end where a flight of steps leads up to the arcaded western gateway. There, in the golden glow of the late afternoon, the archway frames an unforgettable view of the monastery front.

On such an afternoon, it is pleasant to relax in the tree-shaded town plaza, enjoying a cold drink or a snack from the nearby refreshment stall. There too, we can admire the unusual cast-iron Victorian bandstand and examine the ancient monoliths and calendar stones arranged around the plaza.

Huaquechula, date stone

"Twelve House"

Tecamachalco, west front

Between the Volcanoes

Another string of imposing monasteries stretches across the southeastern neck of Puebla, between the two volcanoes of La Malinche and Orizaba. Starting in the south at **Tecamachalco**, celebrated for its painted choir ceiling, we travel northwest, pausing at the classic fortress monastery of **Tepeaca** and its sister mission of **Acatzingo**. Lastly, we visit the ruined Renaissance monastery of **Tecali** and its neighbor **Cuautinchan**, located in the hills just south of the city of Puebla, both noted for their fine colonial altarpieces.

TECAMACHALCO

Jaws of Stone

Native artists have left their imprint at Tecamachalco. In the sculpture and above all in the paintings, the art of the indigenous craftsman is seen at its finest.

Facing a vast, dusty atrium cut into the hillside, the formidable west front of the monastery is stepped like a giant's stairway. A massive 16th century tower rises above the church on the north. The glaring white facade, built up of great stuccoed blocks of *tezontle*, stands in the middle and below it to the south, lies the ruined *convento* block. The toothlike rank of merlons atop the facade seems to echo the serrated ridge above the town—the inspiration for Tecamachalco's toponym.

Emblazoned on the tower base is a heraldic relief of a helmeted eagle, who bristles with the Aztec symbols of war, fire and flood. This escutcheon is also carved with Spanish and Aztec dates that commemorate the founding and the completion of the church.

An unusual notched outer frame encloses the west porch. Broad paneled jambs flank the doorway, supporting an undulating mixtilinear archway—one of several Hispano-Moorish arches in the monastery. Beaded rosettes outline the arch and *alfiz*, as well as the handsome Isabelline choir window overhead. Around the corner is blocked north doorway of the church with its intricately carved, lobed frame.

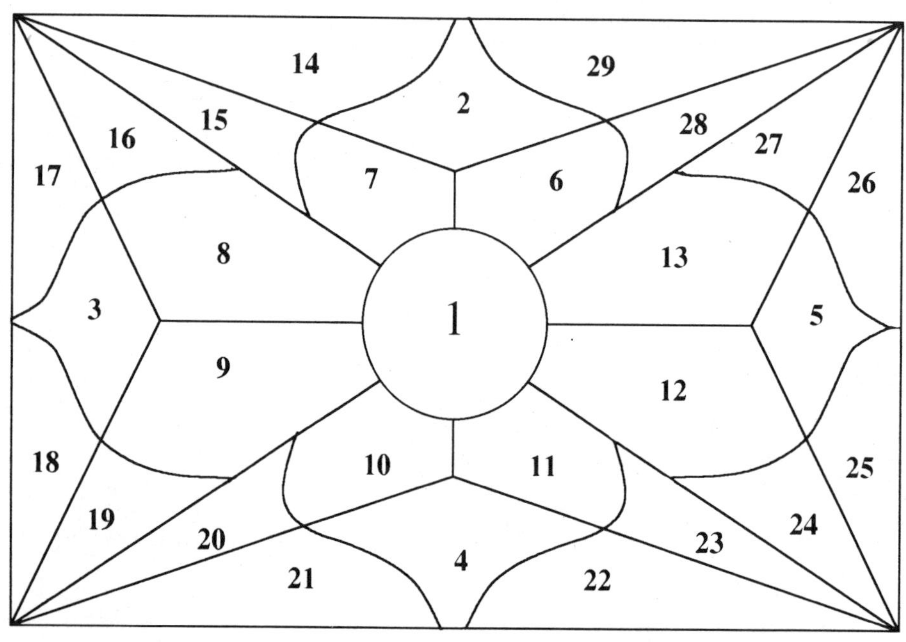

1. Five Wounds
2. Eagle of St. John
3. Bull of St. Luke
4. Angel of St. Matthew
5. Lion of St. Mark
6. Sacrifice of Isaac
7. Tower of Babel
8. Noah's Ark
9. Cain & Abel
10. Temple of Solomon
11. Altar of Ariel
12. Twenty Four Elders
13. Jacob's Ladder
14. Opening of the Fifth Seal
15. Plague of Locusts
16. View of Jerusalem
17. Vision of the Lamb
18. Measuring the Temple
19. Taking of the Dragon
20. The Beast from the Sea
21. Fall of Babylon
22. Christ with Seven Candelabra
23. Opening of the Seventh Seal
24. Woman of the Apocalypse
25. Four Angels of the Abyss
26. Opening of the Sixth Seal
27. Angel pointing to Book
28. Choosing of the Elect
29. Four Horsemen

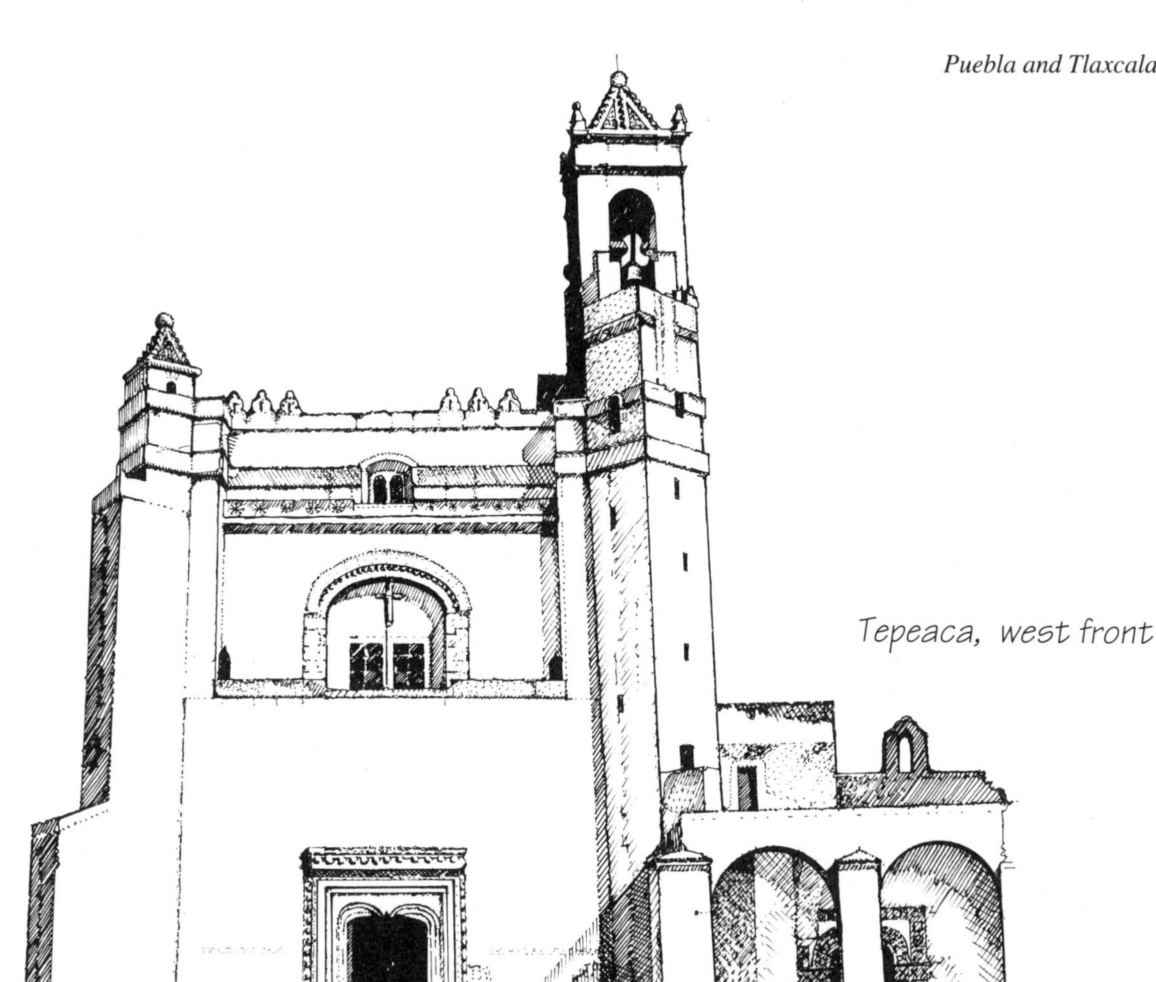

Tepeaca, west front

The Choir Paintings

Inside the church is a remarkable cycle of painted panels, illustrating scenes from the Old Testament and the Apocalypse of St. John, by the indigenous artist Juan Gerson. Long thought to be a Spanish or Flemish painter, he has recently been identified as a talented *tlacuilo*—a member of the native nobility who took the baptismal name of John Gerson, a medieval French preacher and theologian whose apocalyptic writings greatly influenced the Franciscans.

Gerson's paintings magnified intimate black-and-white engravings, probably taken from a medieval breviary, into a visionary and colorful pageant above the church entry, magically transforming it into the symbolic portal of the Celestial Kingdom. Painted on ovals of *amate* paper and mounted between the ribs of the vaulted underchoir, the compositions vividly depict people, supernaturals and surreal landscapes in radiant reds, blues and earth colors that seem to have faded remarkably little since they were painted in 1562.

At the center of the leaf-shaped vault is the emblem of the Five Wounds. The tips of the leaves enclose medallions of the Tetramorph—the symbols of the Four Evangelists. Old Testament scenes, including Noah's Ark, the Tower of Babel and Jacob's Ladder, fill the spaces between the inner ribs.

Sixteen episodes from the Apocalypse of St. John are squeezed into the sharper angles between the outer ribs. The artist clearly relished the dramatic subject matter, especially such scenes as the Taking of the Dragon and the Opening of the Seventh Seal.

A spectacular baptismal font, similar to that at Acatzingo, stands in the aisle beneath the elegantly vaulted nave. Its ample basin is carved with rosebuds, vines and gesticulating angels.

TEPEACA

Nose-Shaped Hill

Tepeaca's huge Sunday market draws vendors from as far away as Oaxaca and Veracruz. In early colonial times, its open-air bird market was famous. The Rollo, an imposing, six-sided, Moorish-style brick tower, erected in 1559 as the centerpiece of the market, still stands in the plaza.

Tepeaca's other colonial monument is the monastery of San Francisco, its fortress style appropriately reflecting the town's historic role as a frontier stronghold, both before and after the Spanish Conquest. Its roofline bristles with battlemented parapets and cannonball-fringed turrets like a medieval citadel.

The west doorway features a lobed *mudéjar* archway of white limestone, fringed by brown Isabelline beading. Complex star vaults cover the lofty nave and the narrow elevated sanctuary. The chief item of interest in the church is the wall painting of the Miracles of St. Francis on the south side. The intriguing possibility exists that it was painted by Simón Pereyns, who worked at Huejotzingo and Tepeaca in the late 1560s. If so, this is his only known mural to survive in Mexico.

The cloister is the oldest part of the monastery. Its archaic whitewashed arcades are decorated with rosettes, medallions and cannonball moldings.

Acatzingo, font angel

ACATZINGO

Where the Reeds Grow

While in the area, visitors may wish to take a look at Tepeaca's sister mission of **Acatzingo**, on the other side of the Mexico-Veracruz toll road.

The timeworn Franciscan monastery, now rarely used, stands across the plaza from the baroque parish church. Like Tepeaca, this is a classic fortress monastery, with elaborate battlements and a fine rib-vaulted nave. If the church is open, look for the primitive stone font, exquisitely carved with angels in flight and the prehispanic year sign Four Rabbit (1532) on the base.

TECALI

House of Onyx

In the dry hills west of Tepeaca, close by the famous onyx quarries of Puebla, stands the noble ruined monastic church of Santiago Tecali, a historic monument administered by INAH, with limited visiting hours.

Instead of a roughhewn fortress church, we find at Tecali an austere Renaissance basilica, its roofless nave divided by slender Tuscan colonnades. The only concessions to the fortress look are the nave buttresses and a narrow *camino rondo,* or defensive walkway, enclosed within the basalt walls. The lone south tower has a slender Florentine profile.

The pedimented porch highlights the broad west front. Based upon the triumphal arch, it is related to the doorways we have seen at Metztitlán (Chapter Two) and other Augustinian monasteries. The detailing of the porch is faultless, with cushioned Corinthian columns, elegant shell sculpture niches and relief panels of shells and pyramids around the entry arch. Heavily rusticated aisle doorways stand on each side.

Why this correctly classical building, completed in 1569, should have been erected in this rustic spot is far from clear, but its design has been attributed to Claudio de Arciniega, the Spanish architect who introduced the academic *purista* style into Mexico when working in this area in the mid-16th century.

Tecali, west front

Architectural decoration inside the church is limited to a few rosettes and diamond bosses, although vestiges of painted Renaissance coffering are still visible over the sanctuary vault.

The Altarpieces

Almost miraculously, some of the early colonial art and furnishings were rescued from the basilica before it was abandoned, and are now installed in the adjacent parish church.

The most precious of these relics is the Renaissance main altarpiece, dating from about 1580. At its center is the beautifully carved and richly clad figure of Santiago, the patron saint of the monastery, shown here as a pilgrim rather than as the usual militant horseman. Renaissance motifs of cherubs, swags, urns and grapevines adorn the spare framework and the shell niche housing the *santo*.

Four exceptional panels, once again of scenes from the life of the Virgin, occupy the outer compartments. Derived from Renaissance engravings, the formally posed figures are luminously painted in blues, crimsons and ochers by an unknown master with a keen eye for detail.

The glowing Annunciation is especially well observed, and along the base panels, the Four Doctors of the Latin Church recline in idealized Italianate landscapes, preoccupied with their studies. It is interesting to compare this *retablo* with the Plateresque altarpiece at nearby Cuautinchan.

A side *retablo* of the Miracles of St. Francis, also from the basilica, is contemporary with the main altarpiece. The central panel of the saint receiving the Stigmata is ringed by miniature scenes rendered in picturesque detail.

Other survivors from the old monastery include the rustic baptismal font, rimmed with a *tequitqui* frieze of thistles, medallions of the Stigmata and sacred monograms, flanked by robed neophytes. The original carved atrium cross of the basilica also now stands in front of the parish church.

CUAUTINCHAN

House of the Eagle Warriors

The nearby monastery of Cuautinchan is definitely worth a visit, for its authentic ambience and fine altarpieces.

The rugged, twin-towered church was built in the 1570s under the supervision of the Franciscan chronicler Fray Géronimo de Mendieta. It is girded by buttresses and braced by a massive bastion around the apse. Although the Renaissance west doorway is exemplary in its classical simplicity, the battered towers retain the flavor of medieval Tuscany.

The church contains an elegant Plateresque *retablo*, similar in form to the one at Huaquechula and possibly the oldest in Mexico. The altarpiece incorporates six large paintings, illustrating the early life of Christ, by the 16th century artist Juan de Arrué, painted in a charming but rather static Flemish style. Portraits of the Apostles line the base panels.

Other treasures at Cuautinchan include an ornate side *retablo* of San Diego, attributed to Simón Pereyns but more likely by Arrué, and a 16th century sculpture of the Virgin and Child with St. Anne, in the Andalusian manner.

A unique mural of the Annunciation survives in the partly ruined cloister. The biblical image, copied from a medieval woodcut, is deliberately juxtaposed with eagle and jaguar figures boldly painted in prehispanic codex style—a reference, we may speculate, to the town's pre-Conquest martial heritage proudly commemorated in its place name.

Cuautinchan, jaguar (mural)

Cortés and the Tlaxcalan Lords (Lienzo de Tlaxcala, 1550)

TLAXCALA

Hemmed in on three sides by the state of Puebla, Tlaxcala is a forgotten land, little changed since colonial times.

The natives of Tlaxcala played a key role in the Spanish Conquest of Mexico. They were a tough hill people, who had fortified their entire territory against their bitter enemies, the Aztecs.

After an initial skirmish, the Tlaxcalans joined with the Spaniards in their campaign against the Aztec empire. Without these native allies, Cortés would surely have failed in his venture. The Tlaxcalans continued to give him aid and sanctuary after his forced retreat from Tenochtitlán, and they participated in the final siege and destruction of the Aztec capital in 1521.

In fact, it was in Tlaxcala that the first conversions to the Christian faith took place. In 1519, the first cross was raised at Tizatlán, across the river from the present state capital.

As a reward for its aid during the Conquest, the Spaniards granted Tlaxcala the status of an "Indian Republic" under the Crown. Closed to Spanish settlers, it continued to enjoy a large measure of self-government under its traditional chieftains. Ironically, this special status contributed to a decline in Tlaxcala's fortunes. Its cool, dry highlands were poorly suited to agriculture and, without a strong Spanish presence, its influence waned. Before the end of the 16th century, political and economic power had shifted to the city of Puebla, surrounded by densely settled, warm and fertile valleys.

The City of Tlaxcala

The city of Tlaxcala is one of the oldest and best preserved colonial cities in Mexico. The main square is a typical provincial plaza of tree-shaded gardens, stone benches and sculpted fountains, bounded by arcades and handsome colonial structures. On its north side, the ornate Hispano-Moorish doorways of the 16th century government building are beautifully worked with *tequitqui* floral reliefs. Note too the intricate Hapsburg coats of arms cut into the facades on the west side.

From the main square it is only a few steps to the smaller Plaza Xicoténcatl, dominated by a heroic statue of this famous Tlaxcalan warrior-king. In the far corner of the square, a steep ramp lined with fragrant ash trees climbs up to the arcaded gateway of the rambling hillside monastery of San Francisco.

SAN FRANCISCO DE TLAXCALA

Following the fall of the Aztec empire, Franciscan friars spread out from the new capital to evangelize the countryside. The Tlaxcalans, as loyal allies, naturally were given high priority in the Spiritual Conquest.

The primitive mission of San Francisco was initially installed in the former palace of the native king Maxicatzin. After the colonial city was founded, in the flatlands across the Zahuapan river, construction of the permanent monastery began on a steep hillside south of the main plaza.

Why this precipitous site was chosen is not clear. Although it was surely not needed for defensive purposes, it was certainly healthier than the marshy riverside. A former pagan temple had stood on the hill—a sacred site perhaps deemed suitable for appropriation by the Christian church.

Since the building was finished in record time, it seems likely that the monastery was built upon an existing temple platform. The entire monastery seems to have been completed during a frenetic building campaign between 1537 and 1540, under the watchful eye of its first Guardian, the ubiquitous Father Motolinía.

The Church

Surprisingly, the Franciscans did not take advantage of the picturesque location, erecting an unassuming church and cloister instead of an impressive fortress monastery. The barnlike church, now the city's cathedral, presents a low profile unencumbered by belfries or battlements. Its simple classical porch is adorned only by the knotted cord of the Order.

Behind this plain facade is the richly ornamented interior, a storehouse of numerous priceless works of colonial art. Its outstanding feature is the magnificent 16th century wood-beamed roof by López de Arana, a Spanish artisan from Seville. Fashioned from dark inlaid woods accented with golden stars, the dazzling geometry of this beautiful *mudéjar* ceiling places it first among the few surviving examples in the New World.

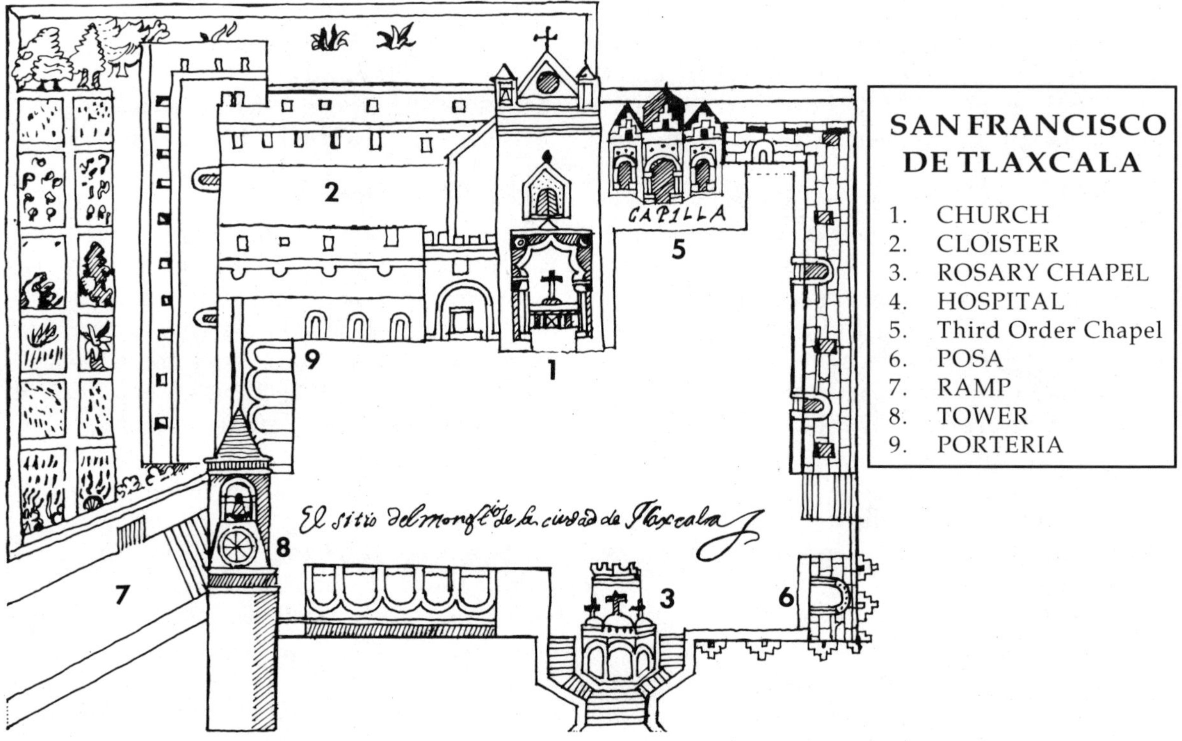

San Francisco de Tlaxcala, Rosary chapel

An array of ornate altarpieces lines the walls of the nave and the numerous side chapels of the church. The main *retablo* of the Assumption of the Virgin stands behind the high altar. Within a framework of Solomonic columns and cornices busy with cherubs and ornamental scrollwork, gilded niches hold elegant wooden statues of saints and friars. Large Renaissance paintings fill the outer compartments, some of them undoubtedly salvaged from an earlier altarpiece.

At the far end of the Chapel of St. Anthony, we can admire an even more luxuriant baroque *retablo*. Hollow wooden columns, entwined in a complex double helix, add a sinuous movement to the richly encrusted surfaces.

A series of naively carved archangels, dispersed in several *retablos* throughout the nave, also catch the eye. Another particularly interesting image is a painted crucifix made of cornpith—an ultra-light, prehispanic material adopted by colonial sculptors for processional images. Although scarred and bloody, the larger-than-life figure of Christ has a Gothic serenity.

The Third Order Chapel

More gilded *retablos* grace this large chapel on the south side of the church. On the main altarpiece is the unique figure of a kneeling St. Francis who holds up three spheres symbolizing the Franciscan Orders: the Friars Minor, the nuns of St. Clare, or Clarisas, and the lay Third Order, known as the Tertiaries. The powerful figure of the saint is finely carved, with expressive hands and face and a textured *estofado* habit.

The oldest items in this chapel are stone artifacts from the early years of the Spiritual Conquest. A simple basin by the doorway is supposed to be the original font in which the Four Lords of Tlaxcala were baptized. From the adjacent wall pulpit, it is claimed, the Gospel was first proclaimed in New Spain. If, as early documents indicate, this chapel occupies the site of the former open chapel of the monastery, then these artifacts may well merit these historical claims.

The Convento

The arcade of the *portería* is plain and provincial in its workmanship, the molded arches springing from corbeled capitals of eccentric design. The pink-painted cloister is also simple, as befits an early Franciscan house, its arcaded walks roofed with dark wood-beamed ceilings. Another beautifully crafted *mudéjar* ceiling covers the former *sala de profundis*, presently used as the regional office of INAH. The *convento* also houses a modest collection of ancient and colonial artifacts.

The pleasantly shaded atrium in front of the monastery extends beyond the church along a cut in the hillside. A single, free-standing *posa*, emblazoned with heraldic shields and carved with primitive reliefs of St. Francis, remains in the southwest corner of the atrium. The 17th century bell tower beside the main gateway, also freestanding, is a prominent landmark.

The Rosary Chapel

The most intriguing structure in the complex is the enigmatic Rosary Chapel on the western slope below the atrium.

The original function of this little hexagonal chapel is still a mystery. It was probably the first mission structure on the site, built as early as 1529, and was most likely set at the top of the stairway of the ancient temple. The chapel is arcaded with pointed Isabelline arches and massive bracketed cornices. The interior is spanned by an irregular Gothic rib vault, possibly the earliest to be constructed in the New World.

Formerly, the chapel overlooked a large patio at the foot of the ramp below, a space now occupied by the town bullring. In colonial times, popular outdoor masses were celebrated on special saints' days, especially August 15, the feast of the Assumption.

Two other historic Franciscan missions in Tlaxcala remind us of the close links of the Order to the momentous events of the Conquest. Both are located just north of the city of Tlaxcala: first, the extraordinary painted chapel at **Tizatlán** across the river, and further into the hills, the vast roofless monastery of **Atlihuetzía.**

Tizatlán, open chapel

TIZATLAN

Chalk Cliffs

Tizatlán was the hilltop capital of Xicoténcatl, "Man with a Bee at his Lips" one of the Four Lords of Tlaxcala. It was here, in 1519, that Cortés had his fateful encounter with the lords.

The *Lienzo de Tlaxcala,* a famous 16th century painted document, portrays them all gathered in front of a wooden cross. According to legend, the cross miraculously appeared amid mysterious clouds and heavenly light. The Devil was seen to scurry in fright from the nearby temple of Xochipilli, the festive god of flowers and song. Sections of the temple walls can still be seen, as well as the ruins of Xicoténcatl's palace, decorated with murals of warriors.

Spectacularly sited atop the western edge of the temple platform, the remarkable 16th century open chapel of San Estéban (Estéban was Xicoténcatl's baptismal name) commands a panoramic prospect of the valley below and the volcano of La Malinche to the southeast.

A tantalizing possibility exists that this may be the celebrated Bethlehem Chapel described by Father Motolinía in 1539:

For Easter, the Indians finished the patio chapel, a magnificent room they called Bethlehem. The chapel is well built and finely ornamented with arches. There are two choirs, one for the singers and the other for the orchestra. The Indians frescoed the walls in four days, with the Creation, the lineages of Jesse and Our Lady, our Father St. Francis, the Pope, the Emperor, cardinals, bishops, kings and knights. Spaniards who have seen it declare it to be as graceful as any in Spain.

If Tizatlán is indeed the Bethlehem Chapel, then it is the earliest Catholic building in Mexico to possess documented 16th century frescoes.

Although tucked behind the adjacent church, which it served for many years as a sacristy, the chapel is still a separate structure. Its striking but functional design features a projecting polygonal west front with open arcades, similar to the Rosary Chapel at San Francisco de Tlaxcala. Beyond the arcade stretches a lofty transverse nave, high enough to accommodate a pair of raised wooden choirs, as described by Father Motolinía. The chapel is covered by a substantial woodbeamed roof set on carved *zapata* brackets.

The Frescoes

Colorful religious murals glow on the chapel walls, painted in a vivid reds, yellows, indigo and earth colors. They display a blossoming of the indigenous artistic sensibility in the fertile field of Christian imagery, yet still resonate with the intensity of the Spiritual Conquest.

The oldest paintings decorate the high side walls of the apse and illustrate biblical and apocalyptic themes. On the south wall are scenes related to Last Judgment. At the top, in a graphic panel that may correspond to Motolinía's Creation scene, Adam and Eve, expelled from Paradise, gaze terror-stricken into the jaws of Hell. In the center, the stern figure of Christ seems to direct the legions of the damned towards the gaping mouth of Leviathan. Below, the partial figure of an archangel intercedes for the damned—or perhaps hastens them on their way.

On the opposite wall, Christ triumphantly brandishes the crimson banner of victory, in a sequence representing the Resurrection, the Descent into Hell and the Ascension.

A lively mural of God in Heaven, in the company of a celestial choir, spans the sanctuary arch. Painted a little later than the apse, this fresco has a more popular flavor. God sits at the apex like an oriental potentate, surrounded by naive angels, some swinging censers, others playing instruments. Incense burners, music stands, the sun, moon and clouds fill the intervening spaces. A profusion of flowers, medallions and cherubs' heads frame the archway and flow between the beam ends.

Down in the nave, remnants of large narrative murals explore familiar themes such as the Baptism of Christ and the Nativity. There is the exciting prospect that more may await discovery beneath the layers of whitewash.

ATLIHUETZIA

Falling Water

If you love moldering ruins, don't miss Atlihuetzía. Beside the spreading cedar in the plaza, allegedly planted by Cortés himself, looms the roofless monastic church, a gaunt local landmark.

In 1527, Axotécatl, ruler of Atlihuetzía and one of the Four Lords, sent his three sons to be catechized at San Francisco de Tlaxcala. On their return, the boys set about zealously smashing idols and reproached their father for his polygamy and excessive drinking. Enraged, Axotécatl beat and then burned to death the eldest son, Cristóbal. The two other boys fled, but continued their preaching and iconoclastic ways until they too suffered a martyr's fate.

The "Niños Mártires" as they are known in the pantheon of the Mexican Church, were a popular subject of colonial art. The most famous depiction of their martyrdom is a 16th century mural in the *portería* of **Ozumba**, near Tlalmanalco (Chapter One).

The vast brick and stone church at Atlihuetzía, once the largest in the region, is now a shell open to the sky. The great beamed roof that spanned the nave has gone and the choir has fallen, although the broad arcade that once supported it still stands. The plain stone wall pulpit remains in place, framing a view of the cemetery—the former site of the *convento*, now demolished. The antique bronze bell of the

Atlihuetzía, ruined nave

monastery, reputedly the first one to be cast in Mexico, now hangs in the tower of the parish church across the plaza.

The oldest part of the monastery is the shallow open chapel attached to the north side of the church. Almost certainly built in the 1540s, when Atlihuetzía was a humble *visita* of Tlaxcala, its arcaded front and primitive rib-vaulted sanctuary follow the same architectural style as the Rosary Chapel at San Francisco de Tlaxcala.

Visitors to the graveyard occasionally place a bunch of flowers against the rude tree cross in the sanctuary, the only remaining object in this deserted chapel.

Note: At **Atlihuetzía**, a new hotel overlooks the scenic waterfall that gives the village its name, and is a comfortable base from which to explore the region.

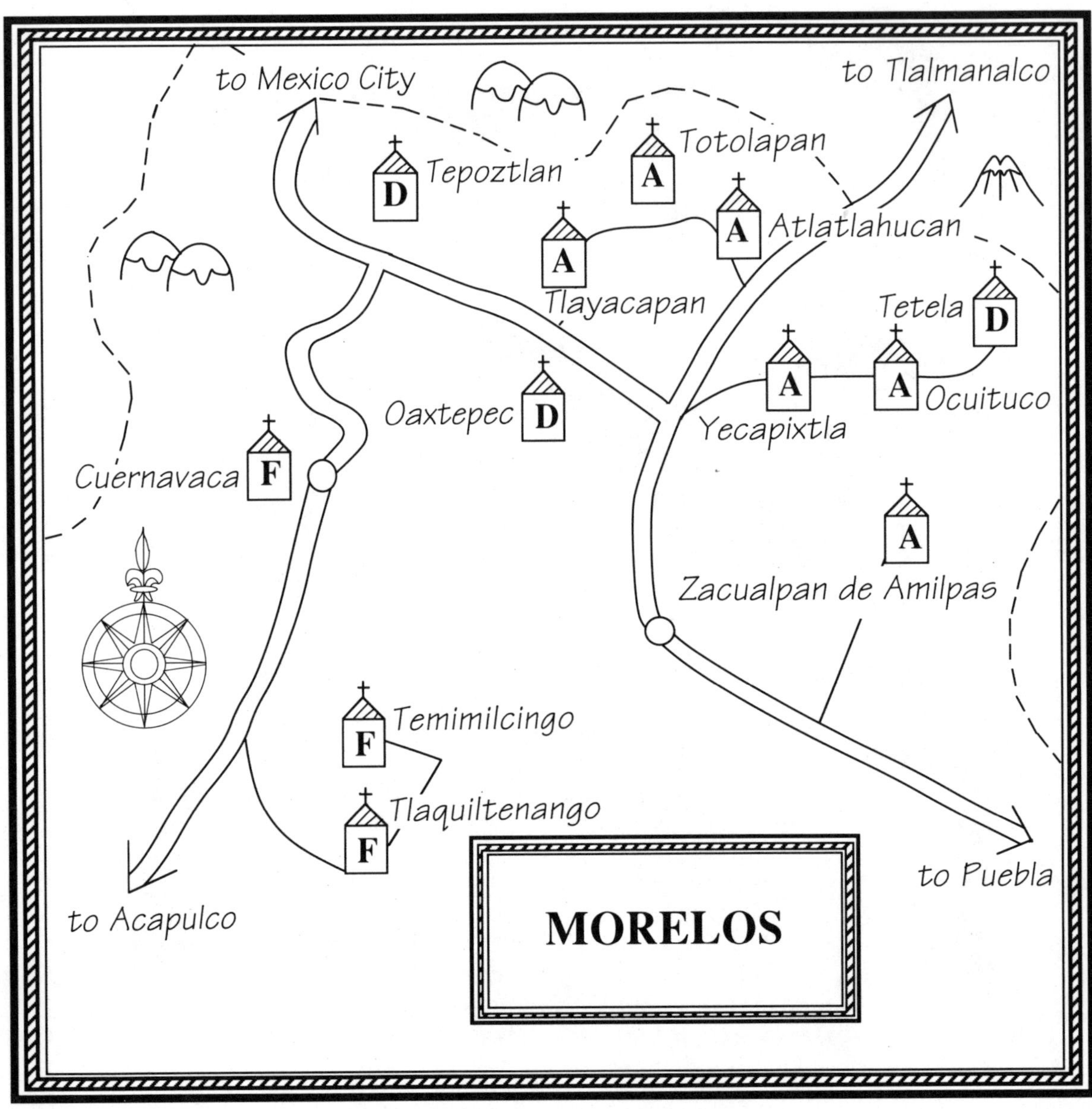
to Mexico City
to Tlalmanalco
Totolapan
Tepoztlan
Atlatlahucan
Tlayacapan
Tetela
Oaxtepec
Yecapixtla
Ocuituco
Cuernavaca
Zacualpan de Amilpas
Temimilcingo
Tlaquiltenango
to Puebla
to Acapulco
MORELOS

Chapter Four

In the Emperors' Gardens

The Monasteries of Morelos

The rich and powerful have always favored Cuernavaca and the foothill valleys of northern Morelos, a spring-like Eden ideally situated between the cold central highlands and the hot southern plains.

The Aztec emperor Montezuma maintained a celebrated menagerie and pleasure garden in Oaxtepec, still a popular spa. Later, the conqueror Cortés built his palace in Cuernavaca, as the focus of the Marquesado, his vast feudal estate. Prominent Spanish officials, viceroys and bishops established private retreats here on Crown lands and in the 1860s, during his brief, ill-fated reign, the Emperor Maximilian staged extravagant entertainments in Cuernavaca's lush Borda Gardens. Even today, numerous resorts, some occupying former haciendas, restore the flagging spirits of weekenders from Mexico City.

These lush valleys also had strategic importance. They straddled vital trade and communications routes that threaded through the mountain passes on their way south from the Valley of Mexico. Throughout history, the settlements of Morelos have been bitterly contested. The ancient Mexican kings constantly maneuvered to control the major towns.

Cortés, in turn, took care to secure the area before his final assault on the Aztecs. The region became a battleground during the War of Independence and served as both the cradle and the cockpit of the Mexican Revolution.

The Spiritual Conquest of Morelos

Like the rich and powerful, many friars, too, preferred a pleasant climate and idyllic surroundings, instead of pursuing arduous missionary work in remote places under harsh conditions. For them, the countryside seemed to be a New World paradise, the perfect place in which to build the New Jerusalem.

All three missionary orders—the Franciscans, the Dominicans and the Augustinians—staked out their claims to the area, each founding its own cluster of monasteries.

Under the personal patronage of Cortés, the Franciscans initially evangelized much of the region, but eventually confined their activities to Cuernavaca and a few subsidiary houses to the southwest. The Dominicans settled in the central part of Morelos, building major monasteries at Tepoztlán and Oaxtepec. Although late arrivals, the Augustinians successfully missionized the northeastern valleys, eventually building a ring of handsome fortress monasteries around their priory at Yecapixtla.

Art and Architecture

In Morelos, fortress churches are the rule. Plain, massive forms predominate, always heavily buttressed and crenelated, with tall, sheer facades. Many monasteries have Plateresque doorways, usually enlivened by *tequitqui* relief carving.

Open chapels abound. Despite a great range

of size and quality, they are all fundamentally derived from the colonnaded chapel at Cuernavaca.

Sixteenth century murals are another major legacy of the Morelos monasteries. They show exceptional diversity, from the colorful nave murals in Cuernavaca Cathedral to the sober frescoes in the *conventos* at Oaxtepec, Tetela and Tlayacapan.

The Monasteries

First, we visit **Cuernavaca Cathedral**, formerly the headquarters of the Franciscan Order in northwestern Morelos, and then we travel south to their primitive fortress church at **Tlaquiltenango**. Next we explore the two principal monasteries of the Dominican heartland, **Tepoztlán** and **Oaxtepec**, both famous for their early stonecarving.

Finally we look at the Augustinian houses of the "Ruta de Conventos" (Monastery Route), all noted for their monumental architecture and prolific frescoes: first a trio of imposing fortress monasteries at **Tlayacapan, Totolapan,** and **Atlatlahucan,** and then the great priory of **Yecapixtla**.

Lastly, we visit three hilltop missions in eastern Morelos, **Ocuituco**, **Zacualpan** and the painted *convento* of **Tetela del Volcán** on the upper slopes of Popocatépetl.

Cuernavaca Cathedral, open chapel interior

Cuernavaca Cathedral, nave mural (detail)

CUERNAVACA CATHEDRAL

In the time of the Aztec emperors, Cuernavaca was Cuahnahuac (Wooded Valley), a favorite playground of Montezuma.

When Cortés stormed through the area before laying siege to Tenochtitlan, he took an immediate liking to this garden city. A few years later, he returned here to build a palace for his new Spanish bride. This historic building is now the state museum, further distinguished by its exceptional 20th century murals by Diego Rivera.

Cortés entrusted the Spiritual Conquest of the populous region to the Franciscans. Barefoot and clad in ragged cloaks, the humble friars were a different breed from the rough Spanish soldiery, but just as determined. With single-minded devotion they ventured out from Cuernavaca, baptizing the Indians in their thousands and setting up rudimentary missions in the towns and villages.

The Monastery Site

In the winter of 1529, the first friars moved into their new monastery, founded on a hilltop site opposite the unfinished Palace of Cortés.

Four hundred and fifty years later, this religious landmark still serves Cuernavaca, now as a cathedral, its magnificent tower visible across the city. But despite its high, sunny location and attractive tree-shaded churchyard, the monastery retains a brooding 16th century aura. Medieval Franciscan images of sacrifice and death strike a chilling note throughout its precincts.

On one side of the battlemented atrium, between the open chapel and the baroque Church of the Third Order, stands the original monastery cross. At its base are a stone skull and crossbones, and beside them, a worn *cuauxicalli*—a ceremonial Aztec basin designed to hold the still beating hearts torn from human sacrificial victims.

The North Doorway

Passing through the northern gateway, the visitor faces the north doorway of the church across the atrium. As it was in the 16th century, this is still the main entry, always crowded with worshippers as well as vendors of books and devotional objects.

The doorway has an archaic simplicity. Unadorned columns with foliated Gothic capitals frame the plain molded archway. The steep triangular pediment encloses a Moorish niche,

Cuernavaca Cathedral, north doorway

flanked by hovering *tequitqui* angels with spread wings and windblown draperies. A heraldic monogram of Mary, dated 1552, was intended to remind the faithful of the *portiúncula*—the celebrated doorway of Santa Maria degli Angeli in Assisi, built by St. Francis himself.

The foliated calvary cross crowning the pediment stands over a skull and bones, set against the rocks of Golgotha—an arresting *memento mori*.

The Church Murals

In October, 1596, a rich Spanish merchantman, sailing from Manila bound for Acapulco, was blown off course by a typhoon and forced to take refuge in a Japanese port.

On board was a Mexican Franciscan, Brother Philip of Jesus. Seized by suspicious warlords, he was sent with 25 other local friars on a harrowing winter march to the court of the Emperor Hideyoshi. Interrogated and condemned as spies and heretics, the friars were taken to a hill outside Nagasaki to suffer the agony of crucifixion. Transfixed by a spear, Philip quickly succumbed. He became a celebrated martyr and the first Mexican-born saint, thereafter revered as San Felipe de Jesús.

In the 1950s, as workmen stripped the centuries of accumulated church furnishings from the cathedral, to prepare for its renovation, fresco fragments suddenly came to light beneath layers of dirt and whitewash. As the work proceeded, the scale and extent of the murals astounded the excited researchers. The discovery caused a sensation, creating almost overnight a national shrine to San Felipe.

Painted in the early 1600s—perhaps to commemorate the beatification of Philip in 1627—these magnificent murals retell the story of the twenty-six Japanese Martyrs, in grisly detail. These narrative frescoes are among the most ambitious, most complete and most original cycles of murals painted in colonial Mexico. They are also among the last, since by this date, altarpieces were replacing murals as the preferred medium for church embellishment.

Originally covering the entire length of the nave, 75 feet long by 25 feet high, the murals were painted by an unknown artist in vivid blues, greens and warm earth colors—a far richer spectrum than the monochromatic murals in the *convento*.

The striking compositions show a pronounced Japanese influence. The figures exhibit a flatness, strength of line and authentic costuming that suggest an oriental-trained artist, possibly even an eye-witness to the events portrayed.

Schools of fanciful sea creatures swim among the boats and around the arches of the doorway, lightening the grim imagery of the narrative scenes. These decorative details are certainly the work of a native artist, and would not be out of place in the pages of a prehispanic codex.

The dramatic circumstances leading to San Felipe's untimely end unfold on the walls in vivid detail. We see his arrival on the shores of Japan, the journey by boat and cart to the place of execution, and finally his crucifixion. The graphic source for this cycle of murals may have been the illustrated chronicle *Evangelization of the Philippines and Japan,* published shortly after the event.

But why should the story of San Felipe have been told here in Cuernavaca? By the end of the 16th century, the Spiritual Conquest of Mexico had been accomplished. The friars then turned their attention to more distant lands. The teeming islands of Asia and the recently explored Philippines presented new evangelical challenges.

The rambling monastery at Cuernavaca became the colonial gateway to the orient, the last staging post between Mexico City and the port of Acapulco. Here the friars prepared for the arduous missionary task, from which some would not return, including perhaps Philip himself. For the Franciscans, Philip of Jesus personified this spirit of selfless sacrifice, whose greatest reward was the martyr's crown.

The venerable stone baptismal font is the oldest remaining artifact of the early Franciscan era in the church and is now installed beneath the choir, in a sunken marble patio. A primitive Gothic wheel vault spans the choir arch above, at whose hub is a quaint relief of Our Lady of the Angels.

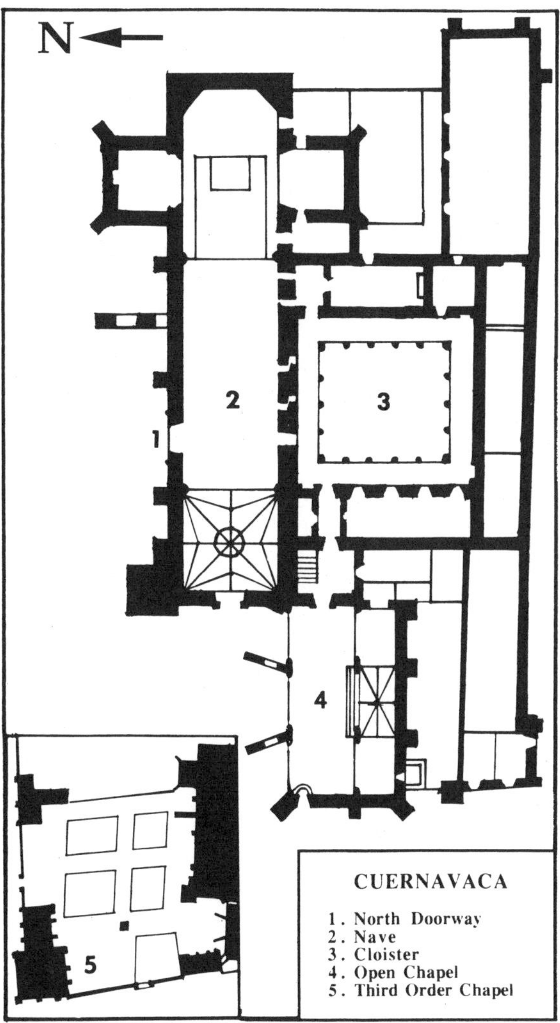

The Convento

A passageway beside the modernistic main altar leads into the old monastery and its cloister. As you pass through, turn to admire the 16th century Crucifixion mural beside the door jamb. Although the body of Christ has been partly effaced, Mary and John are still intact, their elegant Renaissance figures outlined in *grisaille* with red accents.

The cloister is a study in severity. Simple channeled arches on all four sides sit on squat pillars with plain ring moldings. Only vestiges remain of the frescoes that once covered the cloister walks.

The best preserved of these fragments is the delightful Spiritual Lineage of St. Francis. Rows of diminutive nuns and friars—each holding a name plaque—frame miniature scenes from the life of the saint, bordered by winged angels and the Franciscan knotted cord.

A few painted friezes of vines and pomegranates decorate the corner niches, now all sadly vacant except for an exceptional late 16th century statue of St. Christopher in the southwest corner. In this unusually expressive sculpture, the sinewy saint looks up in awe at the Christ Child upon his shoulder.

The Open Chapel

From this same corner of the cloister, another passageway leads into the open chapel, the architectural highpoint of the 16th century monastery. In the mural above the entry, St. Francis presents the Rule of his new Order to Pope Honorius.

In the early years of the monastery, even before the church was finished, the friars faced the vexing problem of how to minister to the countless new Christians. Their innovative solution was this great open-air chapel, described by John McAndrew, the distinguished art historian, as, "A dramatic design, strikingly ambitious and elegant, the most original work from the first half of the 16th century in Mexico."

From the raised sanctuary at the rear, the friars could preach and administer the sacraments in full view of the assembled Indians. In front of the sanctuary is a majestic transverse nave that soars to a height of over 60 feet, creating a truly Gothic sense of lightness and space. Tall slender pillars, capped by delicately carved medieval oak-leaf capitals, form the arcaded facade. This is supported by stepped flying buttresses that jut out at an angle, drawing the eye towards the sanctuary. Overhead, a diminutive preaching balcony has been cut into the crenelated parapet, which is inlaid with distinctive Crusaders' crosses of coarse black lava.

The center arch of the chapel neatly frames a vista across the atrium to the imposing shell porch of the 17th century Third Order Church, richly encrusted with folk baroque stuccowork.

Cuernavaca Cathedral, statue of St. Christopher

TLAQUILTENANGO

Within Burnished White Walls

Despite their success at Cuernavaca, the Franciscans erected few other monasteries within the boundaries of present-day Morelos. Their only other important house is located at Tlaquiltenango, in the tropical sugar country to the south.

Bankrolled by Cortés himself, the monastery was founded in the 1540s, in the precincts of the ancient temple for which the town was named. Floating like a black battleship in a sea of green canefields, the monastery is visible for miles around—a landmark rivaled only by the towering smokestack of the local sugar mill.

The monumental south side of the church is a windowless wall of irregular dark basalt, braced at intervals by narrow buttresses edged with white quoining. This rhythm is interrupted by the south doorway, a pedimented porch that is a country cousin of the north door at Cuernavaca, with skull and bones, and a calvary cross mounted on a simulated cairn of black boulders.

The *convento* is attached to the north side of the church, a configuration common in tropical regions of Mexico. We can still glimpse the archway of the elevated open chapel, set back above the entrance portico, framed by vines and archaic reliefs of the Five Wounds.

Inside the portico is a welter of early murals, some of them overpainted with Dominican subjects after the Order of Preachers successfully wrested control of the monastery from the Franciscans in 1570. A gaudy polychrome painting of St. Dominic in the company of Dominican saints and martyrs is the most prominent, but I prefer the black-and-white fresco of a friar confessing an Indian convert, from whose mouth sins stream forth in the form of little demons.

Tlaquiltenango, Calvary cross

TEMIMILCINGO

The dusty hills north of Tlaquiltenango shelter the quaint little monastery of Santa Maria Temimilcingo, a former Franciscan *visita* also taken over by the Dominicans.

The mission is no more than a 16th century open chapel, with a *convento* added. The formerly open portico of the chapel has been enclosed by a later facade, and the interior has been rather over-zealously renovated. The original preaching gallery, though, has survived and is accessible from the *convento.* A handful of *santos* and paintings are proudly displayed in the baptistery, including the remnants of a delicate miniature *retablo* of the Assumption.

Although the crumbling stonework of the disused *convento* has been recently stabilized, its spartan cloister and dark, bat-infested chambers conjure up a primeval feeling more appropriate to a Maya ruin than a Christian monastery.

The atrium cross, carved with crossbones and the symbols of the Passion, is a primitive relic of the Franciscan tenure of Temimilcingo.

The Dominicans in Morelos

Although the Dominicans arrived in Mexico in 1526, only two years after the Franciscans, they were plagued with problems and slow to establish mission towns.

At first they evangelized the lakeside villages around Mexico City, founding monasteries at **Azcapotzalco,** as well as **Coyoacan** and **Chimalhuacan** in the southeastern corner of the Valley of Mexico (see Chapter One).

From there, they moved into what is now northern Morelos, founding a modest house at **Oaxtepec** in 1528—the first in a chain of monasteries that ultimately extended southward through Oaxaca, as far as Chiapas and Guatemala. The Dominicans built another mission at **Yautepec**, followed by their main priory at **Tepoztlán**. Finally, they founded the little mission of **Tetela del Volcán** on the western slope of Popocatépetl.

Our journey begins at **Tepoztlán,** the largest and most elaborate of the Dominican monasteries, then continues to **Oaxtepec,** some 40 kms to the southeast. **Tetela** is described in the section on hill missions at the end of the chapter.

Tepoztlan, a cherub

Tepoztlan, rooftop garita

TEPOZTLAN

Cleft Hill

Walled in by the fantastical crags of the Sierra Tepozteca, locally called El Tepozteco, the tiny valley of Tepoztlán is charged with a mystical aura that resonates within the weathered precincts of the 16th century monastery.

In pre-Conquest times, Tepoztlán was the shrine of Ometochli, the god of *pulque,* whose bacchanalian rites attracted adherents from all over the region. In 1538, Dominican friars, led by Fray Domingo de la Anunciación, succeeded in baptizing the old king, Tepoztécatl, and so converted the natives to Catholicism—an event reenacted every September during the colorful Festival of the Virgin.

The friars toppled the great idol of Ometochli from its hillside shrine and carted away the shattered remnants to form the foundations of the monastery at Oaxtepec. Years passed, and in 1550, the Dominicans finally undertook to build a permanent mission here—the splendid monastery of Our Lady of the Nativity.

The design of the monastery has been attributed to the well-known Spanish Renaissance architect Francisco Becerra, who worked on Puebla Cathedral and other regional churches in the 1570s. However, only the *posa* chapels, and perhaps the outline of the west porch, give any indication of the sophistication to be expected from such an eminent architect.

The Atrium

From the busy marketplace, steep stone steps descend into the walled atrium, a vast field dotted with mossy stone crosses and giant cedars.

The western gateway sets the style for the monastery. Turreted *garitas* on each side of the archway sprout clusters of mushroom-like merlons capped with orbs, mimicking the eroded pinnacles of the mountain ridge behind.

Another orb stands at the apex of the northwest *posa* chapel nearby, where it supports an ornamental cross carved with the Dominican *fleur-de-lis.* This is one of the two remaining intact *posas*—the southeast and southwest *posas* are in ruins. The other surviving *posa* is ingeniously integrated into the *portería,* its long side now obscured by the monastery entrance and roofed by a ribbed vault. The elegance of this placement is matched by the decoration of the *posas*: Ionic columns and shell niches, artfully inset into the archways.

Tepoztlan, west porch

The Church

This is a church built for the ages. Squared wall buttresses and a massive flying buttress shore up the long nave. Tower bastions, mismatched because of frequent reconstruction following earthquakes and lightning strikes, firmly anchor the facade.

The remarkable west porch is one of the masterpieces of the Mexican Plateresque. The sophisticated framework combines Renaissance elements—fluted pilasters, paneled jambs and dentilled cornices—with Gothic details such as slender colonettes, and the sharply pointed pediment which echoes the north doorway at Cuernavaca.

In contrast, the relief carving bears the unmistakeable hallmark of the indigenous craftsman. The elongated, expressionless saints, the densely scrolled foliage, the patterned wings and drapery of the angels—all are excellent examples of native *tequitqui* work.

Iconographically, the porch links the cult of the Virgin Mary with the Dominican Order. A catalog of Marian symbols—the sun, the moon and the eight-pointed stars of piety and divinity—appear around the arch of the doorway. Medallions of the foliated Dominican cross alternate in the frieze with holy monograms of the Virgin, presented by fluttering angels.

Note the little dogs clenching torches between their teeth. The Dominicans were popularly known as the "Dogs of the Lord,"—a pun on their Latin name, *Domini cane*. The torch derives from a prophetic dream of St. Dominic's mother, in which she saw her son carrying the flaming brand of the Gospel to enlighten the world.

The pediment overhead is the sculptural centerpiece of the porch. The Virgin of the Nativity stands on the crescent moon in the center, cradling the infant Christ, whose halo resembles an Indian feathered headdress. On her left, St. Dominic stands in prayer, an eight-pointed star upon his forehead and his dog by his side. St. Catherine, a prominent Dominican saint, is on the right, wearing her martyr's crown and holding a heart to symbolize love and piety. Jars of lilies, emblems of purity, stand in the angles of the pediment.

Beside the porch is the stone baptismal font of the monastery. Juxtaposed on the fluted basin are the Dominican cross and a hill split by a copper ax—the ancient place glyph of Tepoztlán.

The Convento

From the *portería*, we walk down a dark passageway into the rambling *convento*, whose dimly-lit rooms are mottled with faded frescoes and lichen-covered stonework.

The former *sala de profundis*, a long vaulted room just inside the monastery entrance, retains vestiges of unusual multi-colored friezes: a red thorn-and-ribbon dado at chest level and a convoluted grotesque of entwined dolphins and dragons near the ceiling.

The cloister is starkly plain. Its beveled arcades lack any molding or carving, although the monotony of the long barrel vaults is relieved by red coffered ceilings with rosettes. Grotesque friezes of Dominican escutcheons, flanked by fantastic crowned and bearded figures, skirt the walks.

The refectory on the north side is noted for its splendid carved lavabo. Behind this, a stairway leads to the plain upper cloister, which is enlivened by rows of projecting *garitas*. The austere friars' cells are surprisingly spacious, some with inviting window seats facing the encircling bluffs.

Two other interesting architectural features are found on the upper level. To the northeast, an arcaded loggia commands a stunning vista of the entire valley. And isolated at the northwest corner is the "brothers' john", an elevated latrine block with an elaborate flushing system that drains discreetly beyond the monastery wall.

The Open Chapel

The ruined shell of the open chapel projects from the south side of the church. As wide as the church itself, the roofless chapel has a squared apse from which the sides flare forward to the gaping sanctuary arch. As at Cuernavaca, the sanctuary was originally fronted by an arcaded transverse nave, whose column bases still protrude from the weeds.

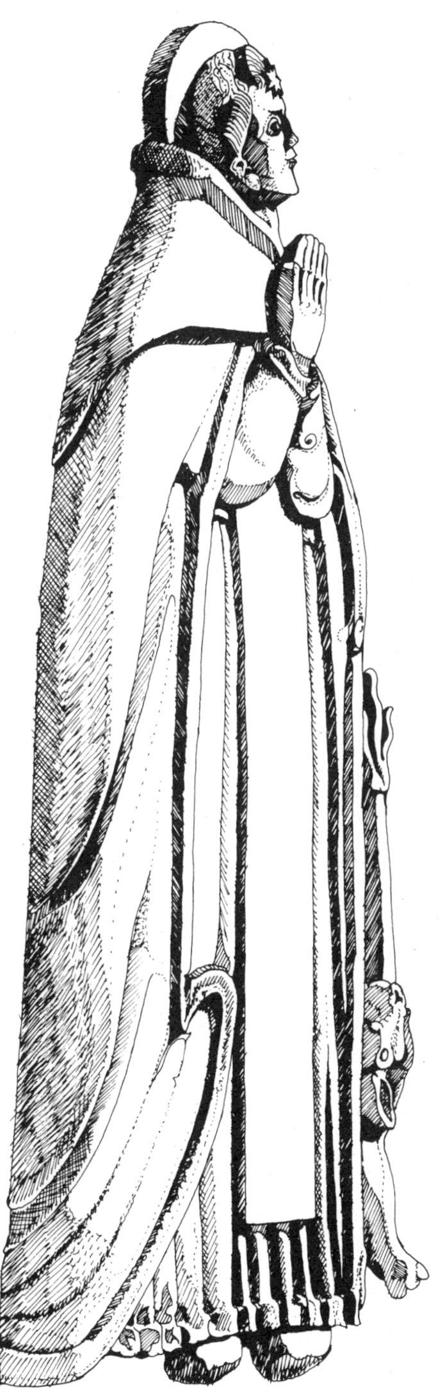

Tepoztlan, west front relief

The Festival of the Virgin

The links between ancient and modern Tepoztlán are renewed every year, on September 8, during the Festival of the Virgin, or "Altepehuitl," as it is called locally.

On the eve of the celebration, the townspeople make a torchlit pilgrimage up the mountain to the former shrine of Ometochli, to celebrate the conversion of Tepoztécatl to Christianity. Spectacular displays of fireworks follow, bizarrely illuminating the eroded pinnacles of the Tepozteco. Next morning, the baptism of Tepoztécatl is reenacted in the main plaza. The young man impersonating the legendary king enters the church, bearing a banner embroidered with the image of Christ, accompanied by dancers in Indian dress. Dancing and merrymaking continue in the atrium to the music of flageolets and a *teponaxtle*, the traditional Aztec drum.

In the afternoon, amid much flourishing of machetes, the townspeople perform the Battle of Moors and Christians—a colonial dance-drama that has been handed down from generation to generation since the friars first entered this enchanted valley four hundred and fifty years ago.

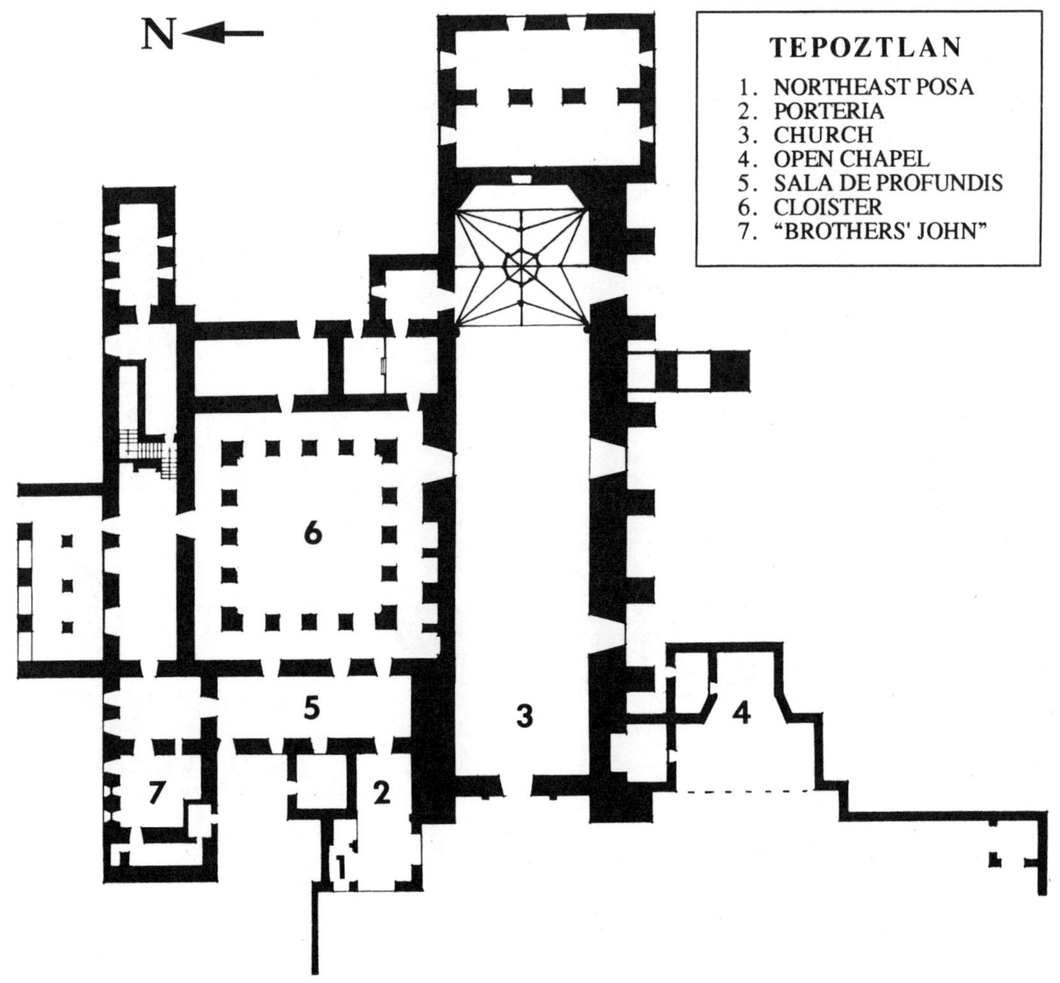

Oaxtepec, west front

OAXTEPEC

Calabash Hill

A land of hot mineral springs and lush, subtropical vegetation, Oaxtepec was a favorite retreat of the Lords of Xochimilco and later, the Aztec emperors.

When the Spaniards arrived, this idyllic spot was the exclusive preserve of Montezuma. Cortés, too, fell under its spell and named Oaxtepec as one of the four *villas*, or principal towns of the Marquesado. Today, the luxuriant gardens of the spa, dotted with pools, exotic plants and stands of ancient cypress, have been converted into a well-run public resort only an hour away from Mexico City.

The Dominicans chose Oaxtepec for their first monastery outside the capital. By the late 1530s, church and *convento* were under construction, founded upon an ancient pyramid. Stones from the ruins of the former temple were recycled for the monastery walls, as were the shattered remnants of the idol of Ometochli, hauled here all the way from Tepoztlán.

The Church

Threading a path through the crowded marketplace, past tables piled with squash and slabs of pungent *cecina* (the local cured beef), we reach a steep flight of stone steps. Climbing to the top, we confront the heavily buttressed west front of the 16th century monastery. The plain church facade is awkwardly provincial, with mismatched belfries and crude bull's eye windows.

But behind this unprepossessing facade we find a wonderful interior, skillfully fashioned from locally quarried, warm gray stone. The design is believed to be based on plans drawn up by the renowned Spanish architect Rodrigo Gil de Hontañón, who was closely associated with the Dominican Order. He designed the elegant New Cathedral at Salamanca, Spain, whose vaulting, completed by 1550, closely resembles that of the sanctuary here. Oaxtepec, in turn, may have been a model for the magnificent Dominican monasteries of Oaxaca (Chapter Five).

In a cruciform plan, rare for the 16th century, the long single nave opens out into narrow transepts. Arcaded niches on each side articulate the nave, which is ringed at the roofline by a deep running cornice, prominently punctu-

Oaxtepec, cloister

ated with large drum corbels. Panels of delicately carved rosettes outline the arches of the transepts and sanctuary, but the finest stonecarving is reserved for the exceptional Gothic vaults. The sanctuary vault is the most elaborate, its star pattern overlaid by a sinuous counterpoint of curved ribs, weaving an intricate wheel-and-leaf design.

Happily, few trappings clutter the church. Only in the transepts do we find a pair of late baroque gilded altarpieces—among the few examples remaining in Morelos. Above the north transept, a charming 17th century painted ceiling shows cherubs dancing in a circle, accompanied by angels playing lutes and violins.

The Convento

The *convento* is a gallery of early frescoes and its two-story cloister is one of the most attractive in the region.

A crude arcaded *portería* projects beyond the churchfront, its interior painted with colorful murals. At the north end, heraldic dogs flank the Dominican insignia, in a painted garden of fruits, flowers and birds. The hexagonal coffering of the *artesonado* ceiling is bright with reds and blues, in a design derived from Renaissance and Moorish patterns that is repeated inside the *convento*—and is a constant motif in all the monasteries of eastern Morelos.

Today, the *convento* is a student hostel, accessible only through a small doorway on the south side. The former refectory, now a small museum, branches off to the left, its long barrel vault adorned with another coffered ceiling.

On the far wall, appropriately, is a striking fresco of the Feeding of the Five Thousand, painted in warm charcoal tones flecked with faded blue and green accents. The classically robed figures of Christ and his disciples move with leisurely dignity through the Italianate landscape, distributing bread from baskets to a vast crowd, indicated by a phalanx of receding, rounded heads. The distorted figure sprawled in the right foreground seems to have migrated there from a painting by Michelangelo.

A patchy mural of St. Jerome, in red, blue and ocher, frames the arch of the stairway in the lobby. The saint kneels before the crucifix, a fanciful lion at his side—obviously the creation of an native artist who had never laid eyes upon a real lion, or even a picture of one.

The Cloister

A delightful space. Every architectural and sculptural element seems to blend in harmony. The simple, molded lower arcades are modulated by pointed prow buttresses that continue through projecting "apron" cornices to the upper level.

Elevated barrel vaults cover the lower cloister walks, which are also painted with coffered ceilings. Rib vaults embellish the corner bays. Panels of quatrefoil rosettes frame the corner niches, which contain a naive cycle of frescoes illustrating episodes from the Passion of Christ—the Arrest, the Scourging, the Way of the Cross and finally, the Crucifixion. Although poorly preserved, with muted colors and dim outlines, these powerful scenes once awed and inspired the friars as they walked around the cloister.

Fragmentary portraits of Dominican saints and martyrs decorate the pillars of the lower arcade, most prominently the forbidding black-robed figure of St. Dominic holding a skull. Nearby, a fresh-faced young friar apparently sprouts wings. The rooms around the cloister, now used as dormitories, contain numerous traces of murals, including one delightful frieze of running angels.

The arcades of the upper cloister are more ornamental than those below. The arches are trimmed with carved rosettes and fluting. Spiral cord moldings face the beveled corners of the piers, and edge the sharply faceted buttresses in between.

The murals here are confined to faded ceilings and a few lively friezes. Fantastic tritons—half man, half dragon—slink along the dado at waist level, wearing flowered and feathered headresses. Aztec speech scrolls protrude from their mouths. Similar motifs in the friezes at Tlayacapan and other Augustinian monasteries to the east suggest a band of itinerant muralists working in this area sometime in the 1560s.

A passageway at the northwest corner of the upper cloister leads to the church choir. The arch of the choir doorway is outlined by a painted thorn-and-ribbon border, surmounted by an ornamented calvary cross with a skull and piles of bones. At the end of the passage, a broad terrace opens out above the *portería*. An ornate Plateresque archway with paneled jambs and intricately carved rosettes indicates that a preaching balcony or perhaps even the open chapel of the monastery was located here.

Returning to the sunlit cloister, we may reflect on the hundreds of anonymous friars, who have trodden its shaded walks over the centuries. One of the few whose name has come down to us was Fray Gregorio López, a 16th century physician and botanist who labored in the mission hospital. In these placid precincts he compiled his famous *Treatise of Herbal Medicine*—the first such work to be published in the New World.

The Augustinian Monasteries of Morelos

As latecomers to the Spiritual Conquest, the Augustinians were often obliged to confine their missionary activities to remote or less attractive areas beyond or between those occupied by their Franciscan and Dominican rivals. However, the northeastern valleys of Morelos were an exception to this pattern.

During their trek to the Valley of Mexico, the first Augustinian friars had been enchanted by these green valleys clustered below Popocatépetl. Here in a land of eternal spring they envisioned an earthly Paradise, where St. Augustine's long-dreamed-of City of God might at last be realized.

In 1533, within a year of their arrival in Mexico, they founded a primitive mission at Ocuituco. The next spring, a second house was established at Totolapan and within the year, two more, at Yecapixtla and Tlayacapan. In the following decades, the building campaign continued, resulting in the chain of fortress monasteries that we admire today.

The Ruta de Conventos

Rising like castles out of the verdant foothill valleys, the crenelated Augustinian churches of Morelos still evoke the utopian dreams of the early friars.

Three imposing Augustinian monasteries, **Tlayacapan**, **Totolapan** and **Atlatlahucan**, nestle beneath the crags of the Sierra Tepozteca just north of Oaxtepec. They are readily accessible along a picturesque road that loops up from Oaxtepec and returns to the main Cuautla–Mexico highway north of **Yecapixtla**, the great Augustinian priory in the region.

Tlayacapan, "chinelo" dancer

TLAYACAPAN

Nose of the World

One of the most delightful lands in the world... an earthly Paradise. There are beautiful springs, wide rivers full of fish, the freshest of woods, fruit of every kind and the air is filled with the fragrance of a thousand flowers.

In these lyrical phrases, the early historian, Fray Diego Durán described Tlayacapan, regarded by the friars as a veritable Garden of Eden. A wild and romantic place, Tlayacapan is surrounded by the basalt bluffs of the Tepozteco, whose evocative shapes may have inspired its ancient place name.

During the Conquest, the inhabitants fiercely resisted the invading Spaniards. In a bloody battle, the native lords held Cortés' entire army at bay for two days before finally capitulating.

Fifteen years passed before the friars arrived, to the "great enthusiasm and devotion of the natives", according to the chronicler Juan de Grijalva. The Tlayacapan mission started out modestly, in 1534, as a little stone chapel. At that time it was a *visita* of nearby Totolapan, but twenty years later, San Juan Bautista Tlayacapan became a monastery in its own right, when the friars added a cloister to the chapel and began work on the church. Sited, as at Tepoztlán, to the south of the *convento*, the church was not completed until 1572.

Tlayacapan is an impressive structure, its great church and *convento* still enclosed by a spacious walled atrium. Noted for its wealth of 16th century murals, it is artistically the most rewarding to visit of the Augustinian monasteries in Morelos.

The Church

Confined between high flared buttresses and surmounted by a handsome *espadaña*, the facade achieves a dizzying verticality—an effect accentuated by its tall, multi-tiered west porch.

Fluted, paneled pilasters and narrow cornices outline the elongated classical design. The rounded arch of the doorway is echoed in the molded frame of the choir window. The pyramidal pediment brings to mind the lateral doorways at Cuernavaca and Tlaquiltenango.

The sparse carving has a naive charm. Stylized angels' heads alternate with starfish-like rosettes on the pilasters, while winged cherubs flap along the frieze carrying a swag of fruits and vegetables. The Latin inscription above the doorway, "John is his Name," refers to John the Baptist, the patron of the monastery.

The cavernous nave holds little charm. The gilded baroque *retablos* of yesteryear have been replaced, as everywhere else in Morelos, by stark neoclassical altars. Remnants of florid, late colonial murals mottle the walls and the barrel vault. Restoration in the 1960s uncovered a 16th century mural of the Mass of St. Gregory at the base of an altar on the north side of the nave. It depicts the various Instruments of the Passion and the sinister disembodied head of Judas, with the 30 pieces of silver hung in a purse about his neck.

The Open Chapel

Beside the church, a long, crumbling arcade stretches in front of the *convento,* terminating in the shell of a former *posa* at the north end. This portico fronted the former open chapel, the oldest section of the monastery. In the dark recesses behind its center arch lie the vaulted sanctuary and its two large side rooms.

Fragments of 16th century murals adhere to the walls of these somber chambers—the first in a series of remarkable frescoes at Tlayacapan. The best preserved of these paintings surround a doorway on the south wall, just beside the monastery entrance. Executed in the style of Renaissance engravings, from which they were freely adapted, the monochrome murals show episodes from the early life of Christ.

In the Visitation, Mary greets Elizabeth, the aged mother-to-be of John the Baptist. Over the doorway is the Dream of Joseph. An angel hovers in a cloud above the sleeping man,

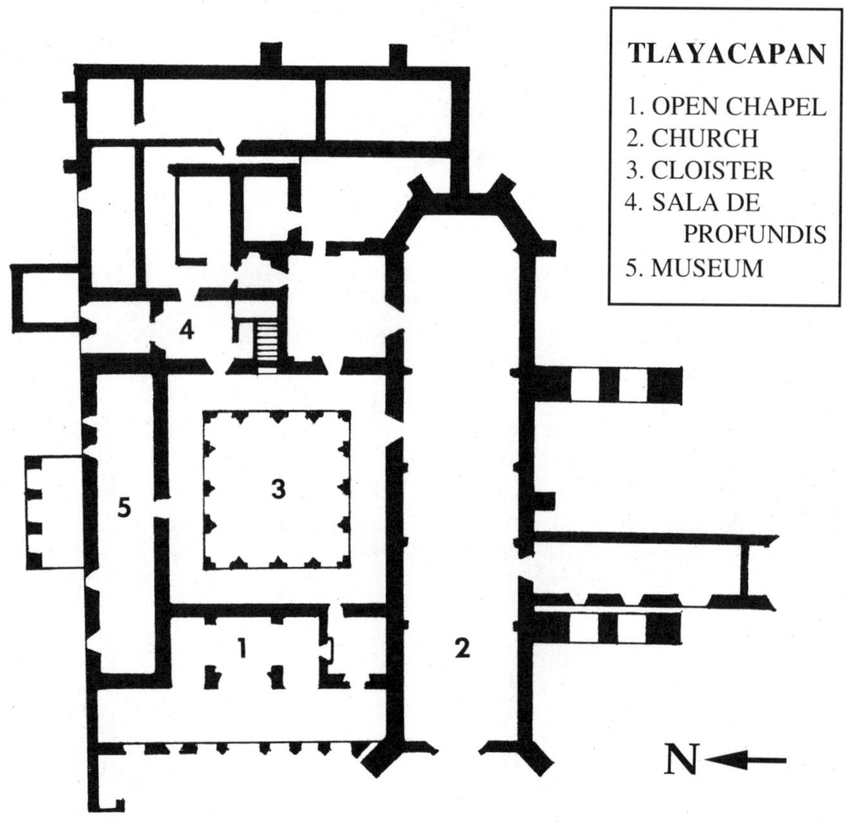

Tlayacapan, facade

Tlayacapan, cloister patio

warning him of the impending Massacre of the Innocents and urging him to flee. An inscribed philactery spells out the message, "Arise Joseph, son of David, do not fear to take Mary your wife." In the background is a monastery, presumably Tlayacapan itself.

The Circumcision of Christ, to the left, is drawn in precise detail, showing the infant Jesus in the arms of a sumptuously attired rabbi. To his right, Mary and Joseph pray, accompanied by a group of draped figures who crowd through the doors of the Temple.

Grotesque borders magnify the impact of the chapel murals. Bizarre creatures—part man, part lion, part fish and part plant—cavort along the walls, symbolizing life in all its aspects. Stylistically, the murals and friezes are similar to those at Oaxtepec, just down the road, and are, no doubt, the work of the same itinerant group of artists.

The Convento

Augustinian insignia above the doorway—prominently tasseled cardinals' hats with a calvary cross—mark the entry to the cloister.

The cloister arcades exhibit a refinement of design and craftsmanship lacking in many other Augustinian *conventos* of the region. The subtlety of the stonework is enhanced by the use of attractively multicolored local limestone, that ranges from pale gray flecked with white, to salmon pink and warm, reddish-brown.

High, fluted arches spring from compound piers, faced with prow pilasters and half columns with discus capitals. Vaulted bays with decorative carved ribs and corbels cover the walks and sacred monograms embellish the upper arcade.

An exquisitely carved Plateresque doorway in the southeast corner opens to the sacristy. A continuous floral chain frames the archway, fringed by bead moldings. Note the primitive crucifix of dark gray stone set in the wall overhead—the outsize hands and feet of the figure of Christ reveal its Indian workmanship.

The rooms surrounding the cloister are full of surprises. The sacristy, for example, is crowded with *santos*. On a recent visit I spotted an archaic Santiago in gilded armor, mounted on a prancing white carousel horse with a pig-like snout.

Sala de Profundis

Located in the northeast corner, this small room contains a bounty of elegant black-and-white murals with ocher accents.

The Four Evangelists and the Doctors of the Church preside over the room in Plateresque niches—a scheme recalling the painted stairway at Actopan (Chapter Two). St. Augustine writes diligently against a backdrop of weighty tomes, and the Virgin of the Immaculate Conception poses on the south wall in gracefully flowing draperies, attended by six fluttering angels that might have flown here from the facade of Tepoztlán.

Some of the most interesting mural paintings frame the recessed doorway on the north wall. St. Peter and St. Paul face each other on the inner jambs, while caryatids on each side of the archway "support" the mural above—an unusual Crucifixion that prominently features Christ's two crucified companions.

Most of the murals are bordered by fantastical friezes. The chimerical figures we saw in the open chapel reappear, this time sprouting wings and goat's horns.

The Museum

The old refectory on the north side has been converted into a local museum. A fascinating collection of prehispanic objects, colonial artifacts, local handicrafts and assorted religious relics and curiosities is gathered beneath its painted barrel vault.

The macabre main attractions are the mummies, recently unearthed from the church floor. A little boy dressed in a lace-trimmed jerkin holds a scepter. The girl beside him wears a crown of paper flowers and clutches in her hand three nails, symbolizing the Crucifixion. Two more bodies were laid to rest in ecclesiastical clothing—a common colonial custom. One teenage girl is robed as a Carmelite nun and a prosperous-looking middle-aged man is wrapped in the Augustinian habit.

An unusual altarpiece of the Twelve Apostles, dated 1737, stands on a dais at the end of the room. There is also a baroque canvas of the Virgin of the Light, attributed to the prolific 18th century painter Miguel Cabrera.

On display is an imposing masked *chinelo*, the famous regional folk dance figure, arrayed in a traditional flowing gown and feathered headdress. The name *chinelo* is thought to derive from "Punchinello", a character from the Commedia dell'Arte, overlaid in Mexico with prehispanic and Moorish traits.

Festive Tlayacapan

Carnival is the big fiesta in Tlayacapan, attracting revelers from all over the region. Every *barrio* fields a group of *chinelo* dancers, each with its unique costume and dance steps. Dressed in long cotton shifts, the dancers sport red or ocher masks with curled horsehair beards. Hand-painted and embroidered costumes are decorated with mirrors, feathers and flowers. All wear the striking *chinelo* headdress—an inverted cone with a fringed brim, crowned with extravagant plumes.

As Carnival comes to its tumultuous climax, the dance troupes vie with each other in the streets, weaving in and out of the crowd amid the din of fireworks, the blaring of brass bands and the deafening discharges of muzzle loading shotguns.

The ancient *barrios* of Tlayacapan maintain their own chapels—some 18 in all—many of which started out as hillside hermitages. The baroque chapel of Santiaguito, set against the bluffs on the east side of town, and the shrine of the Black Christ of La Exaltación, across the creek south of the monastery, are among the most elaborate and definitely worth a detour.

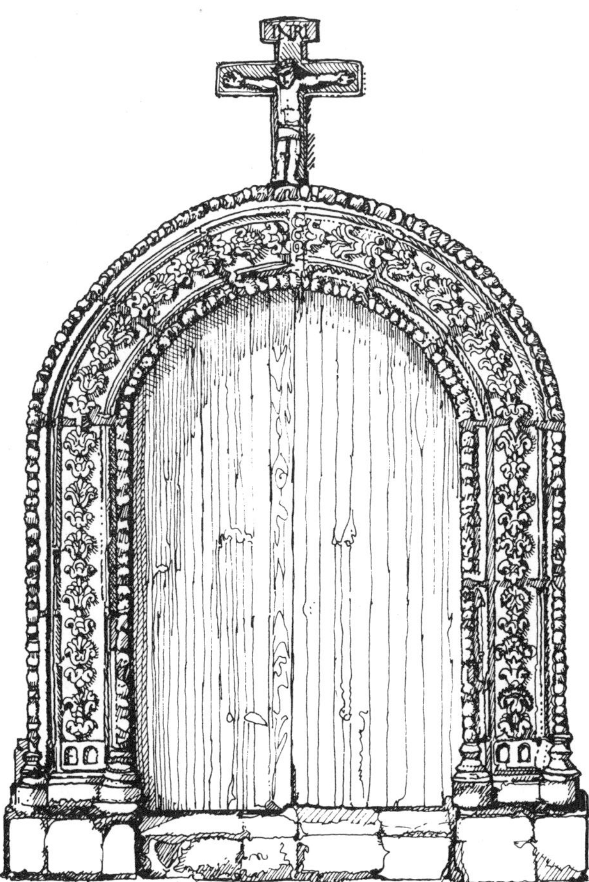

Tlayacapan, Isabelline doorway

Totolapan, Phillip the Apostle

TOTOLAPAN

Turkey River

San Guillermo Totolapan was the second Augustinian house to be built in Mexico, and it looks its age. In spite of partial restoration in the 1960s, today the monastery is in bad condition, its 450-year old fabric crumbling away. The neglected *convento* has been vandalized by squatters and its once splendid murals defaced.

Founded in 1534 by Fray Jorge de Avila, the Apostle of Hidalgo (see Epazoyucan, Chapter Two), the *convento* was enlarged in 1541 to accommodate friars who were forced to move here from Ocuituco. Totolapan, its prestige bolstered by possession of a miraculous image—El Cristo de Totolapan—briefly became the priory for the region. However, the crucifix was later removed to the Augustinian head monastery in Mexico City and soon after, Totolapan relinquished its preeminent status to the new priory at Yecapixtla.

Towering trees festooned with Spanish moss shade the spacious monastery atrium. Inside the battlemented walls, a processional pathway threads its way around, passing the last remaining *posa* chapel in the southeast corner.

The plain 16th century churchfront was remodeled in the 18th century, when its severity was softened by the curving lines of a new facade with a classical porch, a rose window and an undulating *espadaña*. The *portería*, long bricked up, has at last been reopened, giving access to the cloister.

The Murals

As at Tlayacapan, 16th century frescoes covered virtually every surface inside the *convento*. Although they are now in an advanced stage of deterioration, the surviving fragments still manage to convey some of the original sweep of the mural program, its excellent draftsmanship and vivid coloration.

The murals combine biblical scenes with ecclesiastical portraits. Of the cycle in the cloister, only a few scenes remain along the west walk, illustrating the Life and Passion of Christ. These include a scarred Crucifixion and, at the south end, two lunette murals. One is a delicately drawn tableau of an Augustinian nun, probably Santa Monica, sheltering members of the Order. The second depicts a haloed Christ, standing by the Sea of Galilee addressing two Apostles in a bright red canoe—presumably Andrew and Simon Peter.

Portraits of Augustinian saints and martyrs once adorned every pier around the cloister. Only vestiges remain, notably the commanding figure of St. Augustine on the west walk. He carries a church and crozier and the banderole over his head bears the Latin invocation, "Pray for us Blessed Father Augustine." On the corner pier, the freshly beheaded corpse of an unidentified martyr is dragged away by turbanned Turkish janissaries.

At one time, large medallions of the Four Evangelists graced the monumental west stairwell. Now, only St. Luke can be identified, accompanied by a rabbit—traditional scribe to the Aztec gods and the symbol of learning.

The Passion cycle continues on the ravaged upper level. In a scene based on a Flemish print, a fine, sad-eyed Christ, bound and crowned with thorns, is led away by another turbanned figure. One of the friars' cells contains a naive Holy Family by the same artist. The serenity and tender expressions of the figures are quite moving. An inventive assortment of decorative niches, friezes and ceilings, combining medieval, Moorish and Renaissance motifs, enhances the cloister murals.

Ornate foliated friezes along the walks are alive with dolphins and crested birds, enclosing medallions of Augustinian insignia, saints, martyrs and sacred monograms. Twisting strapwork and ribbon-and-vine panels border the archways, and an intricate geometry of stylized fruits and flowers covers the ceilings.

Atlatlahucan, open chapel

ATLATLAHUCAN

Place of Red Waters

The towering monastery of Atlatlahucan looks more like a medieval castle than a house of God. An enormous atrium with high crenelated walls, pierced only by a fortified western gateway, encloses the monastery.

The old processional path around the perimeter is marked off by an unusual inner wall. Two of the four original *posa* chapels have survived, in the southwest and southeast corners. Both have striking pedimented facades, with domed cupolas and huge merlons on each corner. A giant spreading fig tree stands like a sentinel in the middle of the atrium.

The Open Chapel

The earliest structure of the monastery is the open chapel, nestled beside the church on the north side. Related to the chapels at Cuernavaca and the nearby village of **San Juan Texcalpan**, (3 kms to the west of Atlatlahucan) it features a small raised sanctuary at the rear. Side walls flare forward to embrace an arcaded facade, framed by an exterior *alfiz*.

The low profile of this simple chapel has been dramatically altered with the addition of a tall, narrow archway in the center, capped by an *espadaña* to harmonize with the churchfront. Inside the chapel, the colorful ceiling is aglow with sun, moon, stars and whimsical cherubs, caught in a web of red and gold *mudéjar* strapwork that shimmers against the azure vault.

The Church

The severe west front is a study in verticality. Soaring angled buttresses topped with *garitas*, a crowning *espadaña* studded with merlons, long rainstreaks plunging like cataracts from the pinnacles atop the parapet—everything seems to accelerate the heavenward movement.

In vivid contrast to the plain exterior, the candlelit recesses of the nave are cluttered with folk altars and *santos*, draped with every manner of decoration: paper flags and streamers, plastic containers, even strings of fairy lights. Murky patches of devotional murals from every epoch flicker on the blue-tinted walls, including part of a Last Supper in the apse.

Unlike Cuernavaca Cathedral, San Mateo Atlatlahucan remains a bastion of pre-Vatican II Catholicism, where priests of the old school cling defiantly to the traditional trappings and rituals of the Church.

The Convento

The martial character of the monastery is evident in the portico and cloister, where serried ranks of merlons cap the plain arcades. In these spartan surroundings, the *convento* murals bring a welcome touch of color and ornament.

Sinuous arabesques, similar to those of the open chapel, weave like golden threads through the coffered ceiling of the *portería*. Spread across the south wall is a delightful early fresco of The Spiritual Genealogy of St. Augustine, painted in muted reds and earth colors against a background of celestial blue. The recumbent saint supports the Church, from which a tree extends. The Crucifix is placed at the top, and between the curving branches, saints and friars of the Order float on little clouds, resembling rubber dinghies.

A jumble of murals animates the walls and vaults of the cloister and its surrounding rooms. Although the quality is uneven and some passages have been clumsily retouched, it remains an impressive display. The refectory, for example, is covered by a multi-hued *artesonado* ceiling, in which Augustinian saints and religious insignia are transfixed in a swirl of strapwork. The triumphant figure of the Resurrected Christ holds his banner aloft on the end wall.

Looking across Atlatlahucan's battlemented parapets to the twisted gorges of the Tepozteco and the shining plain below, it is easy to feel like a feudal lord commanding his domain from atop the castle wall.

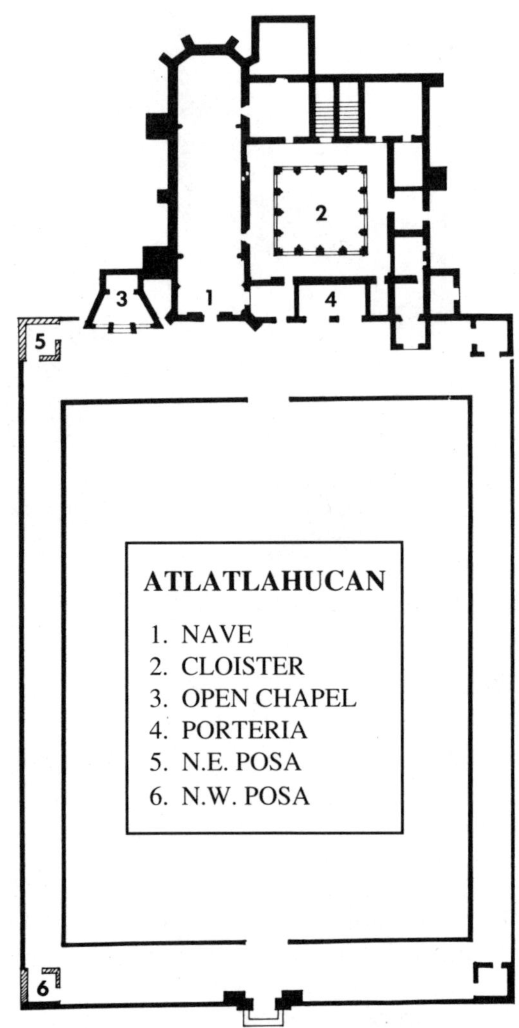

Yecapixtla, cherub and chimera (dragon)

YECAPIXTLA

Shining Nose

After ascending the 94 narrow stone steps of the dark spiral stairway, I emerged giddy and breathless into the midday glare atop the church roof. Santiago Aguilar, the 82 year-old sacristan, showing no ill effects from the climb, stepped into the *garita* perched precipitously at the apex of the facade and gestured towards the sweeping panorama.

A vast golden plain patched with green stretched away to the southwest, fading into an ash blue haze of smoking corn and sugarcane fields. The purple wall of the Tepozteco range faced us to the north, and to the east loomed the snow-capped cone of Popocatépetl.

"When the Federales came in 1914," Santiago reminisced as he gazed into the distance, "I was only nine. Most of the villagers left during the Revolution, but I stayed and hid. I saw it all." He turned and pointed to the battlemented walkways beside the roof parapets. "Cannon and machine guns were hauled up here to defend the town. Ah, the noise, the bloodshed, the destruction. How we all suffered!"

Yecapixtla is no stranger to violence and civil strife. Strategically placed on a fortified bluff between two deep gorges, this proud city doggedly resisted assimilation by the powerful Aztec empire. The aristocratic lords of Yecapixtla wore the jade noseplugs traditionally reserved for kings—a privilege proudly commemorated in the town's ancient place-name, "Shining Nose."

So when the Spaniards arrived in the spring of 1521, the independent townspeople put up a fierce struggle before finally succumbing to the superior numbers and weaponry of the invaders and their Tlaxcalan allies. "Such was the slaughter," Cortés later wrote, that "the river ran red with blood." Despite this fearful encounter, Yecapixtla retained its preeminence into colonial times and was chosen by Cortés as one of the four *villas* of the Marquesado.

Although Franciscans from Cuernavaca evangelized Yecapixtla and erected an adobe-and-thatch mission here, it was the Augustinians who built the magnificent monastery of San Agustín that stands here today. Fray Jorge de Avila, the builder of Totolapan, chose a site below the bluffs for a new priory, to be the axis of the burgeoning Augustinian presence in the region.

During the late 1530s, the great structure rose rapidly under the supervision of Fray Jorge, who hosted Cortés on his visits here. Although, according to tradition, both church and cloister were finished in Cortés' time, it is unlikely that the priory was anywhere near completion by 1541—the year the conqueror returned to Spain for the last time. Construction continued through the 1540s and 1550s and by 1580, the priory was finished.

The Church

Yecapixtla was a famous landmark even in colonial times. Tall flared buttresses, capped with *garitas,* anchor the gigantic west front. Merlons march across the crowning gable and parapets of the church, along the monastery front and atrium walls, and mark the corners of the *posa* chapels.

Despite its massive scale and rugged profile, Yecapixtla boasts two of the most handsome Plateresque doorways in the region. In their forms and details we can discern the hand of a master stonecarver.

The Renaissance framework of the pedimented west porch is spiced with Plateresque elements, like Gothic colonettes and niches. But it is in the details that the sculptor's skill shines brightest. He had a weakness for cherubs. Medallions of cherubs' heads entwine with rosettes, lilies and acanthus leaves on the door jambs and around the archway. Naive winged angels pose in the spandrels and high-spirited *putti* ride on fantastic dragons along the frieze.

Unusual cameos of a friar and a bewigged Spanish *hidalgo* are embossed on the column pedestals. A globe, superimposed with the cross—symbol of the Church Triumphant—projects from the center of the attic above. The globe is flanked by the Augustinian pierced heart and tasseled hat on one side, and the Stigmata of the Franciscan Order on the other. Imaginatively detailed egg-and-dart and heart-and-flower moldings enliven the arches and cornices.

Of special interest is the stone crucifix at the apex of the porch. The expressive body of Christ, with its foreshortened figure, enlarged extremities and stylized ribs, is undoubtedly a 16th century sculpture, carved by an indigenous journeyman rather than a Spanish master craftsman.

The understated north doorway is related to the west porch. Architectural highlights here include the cushioned candelabra pilasters, the elegant classical medallion busts and the pierced heart deftly woven into the doorframe.

The rose window is the most spectacular example of its kind in Mexico. It seems almost to float above the west porch, the sinuous *flamboyant* tracery rivaled in richness by the complex scrolls and ribbons of its circular frame.

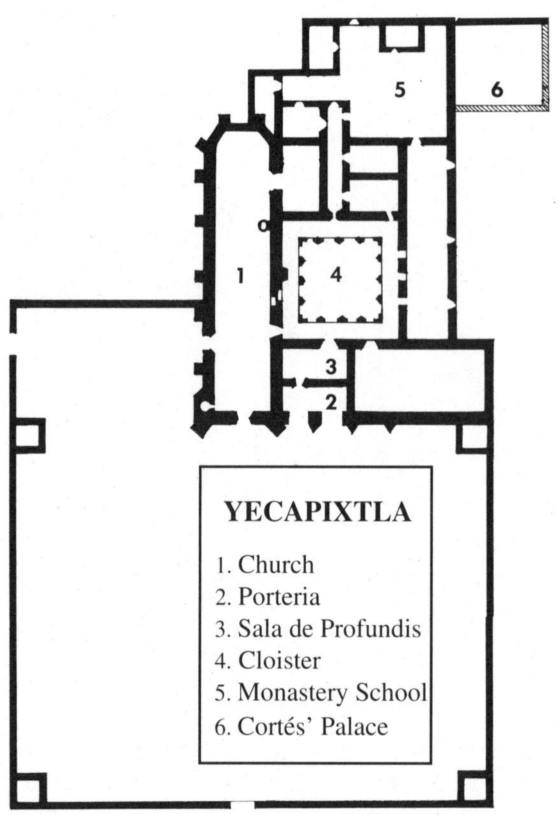

The Church Interior

An anonymous 18th century chronicler described the majestic church interior in glowing terms:

> *One of the most beautiful temples of this realm. Fashioned with such rare skill that the windows, the ribs of the vault, the pulpit and even the choir rail are all finely chiseled in stone in the same manner.*

Despite a facelift in the last century, when its gilded Baroque *retablos* were consigned to the flames and replaced by banal neoclassical altarpieces, the interior retains a certain grandeur.

Fortunately, most of the original stonework praised by the colonial writer is still intact—the flowing tracery of the sanctuary vault, and the sturdy ribs and bosses of the wheel vault under the choir. The pierced stone parapet along the choir is also unique, surmounted by spiky *fleurs-de-lis* and candelabra pinnacles.

But the most accomplished work of sculpture in the church is the ornate Isabelline pulpit,

Yecapixtla, west front

delicately carved with Augustinian insignia and monograms. Its curvilinear arches and Gothic finials are also clearly the work of a Spanish craftsman, as is the handsome processional doorway into the cloister—one of several similar portals in the monastery.

By contrast, the battered font is fringed by eroded lions' heads. Originally an outdoor fountain, it was pressed into service during the mass baptisms of the Spiritual Conquest and continues to fulfill the same role more than 400 years later.

Traces of monochrome figures and friezes, emerging from behind the 19th century overpainting along the nave, hint at a mother lode of 16th century murals still awaiting discovery.

The Convento

The outline of a bricked-up archway above the plain arcade of the *portería* may indicate the location of the old open chapel.

The *sala de profundis*, just inside the monastery entrance, is lined with faded 16th century murals. Painted arcades along the side walls frame portraits of Augustinian martyrs, outlined in black and highlighted with earthy reds and ochers. On the end wall is a splendid Resurrection, recreated from a medieval woodcut. The Risen Christ raises the cross in triumph above the overlapping haloes of a throng of saints and apostles.

The single-story cloister is surprisingly primitive, its heavy whitewashed arcades free of any carving. The cloister walks, on the other hand, are, or were, ablaze with color. Saints and founders of the early church look out from the arcade piers, many with scrolled name plaques. We can pick out the youthful St. Francis, and the imperious figure of Pope Gregory in his papal finery and triple tiara.

Red, blue and beige *artesonado* patterns cover the vaults, and lively grotesque friezes, studded with medallions, line the corridors. A few fragments of a mural cycle depicting Christ's Passion, unfortunately damaged beyond repair, cling to the corner bays.

Beyond the cloister, Isabelline portals lead to other rooms, including the sacristy, the Sagrario Chapel and the colonial monastery school. At the rear of the complex one can still explore "Cortés' Palace"—the quarters reserved for the conqueror on his visits to Yecapixtla.

The shadow of history falls into every corner of the monastery. As I was about to descend from the church roof, Santiago beckoned me to the rear, proudly pointing to an ancient timepiece hung in a small belfry. "This is the only thing that escaped damage in the Revolution. A wonderful old clock. German. Installed in the time of Don Porfirio and still keeping good time today."

Yecapixtla, facade cross

Three Hilltop Monasteries

To close out this chapter, we approach Popocatépetl to visit two smaller Augustinian monasteries, **Ocuituco** and **Zacualpan de Amilpas,** and then venture up on the slopes of the volcano to the painted Dominican monastery of **Tetela del Volcán**.

Ocuituco lies about 10 kms east of Yecapixtla, on the road to Tetela del Volcán, which is situated close to the Puebla state line.

Zacualpan is only 25 kms from Yecapixtla as the crow flies. Although it is accessible by a secondary road that branches south from Tetela, Zacualpan is best approached from MEX 140, an excellent highway that runs southeast across the state, from Cuautla towards Puebla. From the highway, at **Jantetelco**—noted for its restored church that was once the parish of Father Mariano Matamoros, a martyr of the struggle for Mexican Independence—a paved road winds up the Amilpas Valley, passing through several attractive small villages. Other local sights include the folk baroque churches of **Chalcatzingo** and **Tepalcingo**.

Ocuituco, fountain detail

OCUITUCO
Among the Gorges

Santiago Ocuituco was the first Augustinian mission in Mexico. Here in 1534, in a rude thatched hut, the friars gathered for their inaugural chapter meeting. When this primitive structure disintegrated after a few years, the Augustinians embarked on a crash program to erect a permanent monastery.

The normally compliant Indians complained bitterly about overwork to Archbishop Zumárraga. Condemning the building as "more sumptuous than the village could stand," he ordered the work halted. The Augustinians departed in a huff for nearby Totolapan, taking with them everything they could carry, even digging up the newly planted fruit trees !

Struck with the scenic beauty of the surrounding valley, Zumárraga chose Ocuituco for his personal *encomienda*. Construction of the monastery continued under his supervision, albeit on a lesser scale and at a slower pace.

The cloister dates from Zumárraga's time, about 1540, and is anything but sumptuous. It is the earliest and most primitive in the region, and the only part of the original monastery to survive. Built of heavy rubble and braced by ungainly squared buttresses, it has no ornamental stonework, apart from the lions guarding the archaic patio fountain.

A few years later, the Augustinians petitioned to return and by 1544 were back in residence. After a devastating fire, the church was rebuilt in the 19th century with an elegant gabled facade. The *portería,* however, has an unsightly modernized front, added to enclose a new chapel.

The atrium is the monastery's most attractive feature. From the carved basalt fountain in the plaza below, a flight of stone steps leads up to the baroque gateway. From here it is a pleasant stroll across tree-shaded terraces to the church, with a pause to admire the austere stone cross that still stands before it.

ZACUALPAN DE AMILPAS
Atop the Penitential Mound

This charming hill village of cobbled streets and rustic colonial houses is located off the beaten path, at the head of the scenic Amilpas Valley. The attractive monastery of La Concepción is planted high upon a rocky promontory on the southern slopes of Popocatépetl, overlooking the town and the surrounding walnut groves.

The modest 16th century Augustinian mission has been extensively rebuilt over the years. Ornate Moorish gateways invite the visitor into the atrium, whose unusual *posas* are set at angles in the corners and faced in exuberant baroque style.

The pink churchfront was also remodeled in

Tetela del Volcán
St. Catherine of Siena (mural)

the 18th century, silhouetted by a fashionable curvetted pediment. The Rosary Chapel was added to the north side in the same period, and elaborately outfitted with undulating cornices, *mudéjar* windows and a shining tiled dome. The rich interior of the chapel is also a decorative feast, in contrast to the sparsely furnished church. The ornate scrolled and gilded baroque altarpiece is one of the handful to survive in Morelos.

The elevated *portería* and open chapel, to the right of the church, also date from the 16th century. Blocked up for many years, they were opened up recently, bringing to light the painted vault of the open chapel—a bold hexagonal design inlaid with flowers and bordered by lettered friezes. The baptistery behind the *portería* contains a splendid shell font, raised on great carved scrolls of acanthus leaves.

In the cloister, the cut stone arcades are braced by prow buttresses in the regional style. Full-length black-and-white portraits of Augustinian saints and martyrs, some with hand-written biographies inscribed beneath their feet, embellish the piers of the lower arcade.

TETELA DEL VOLCAN

Village of Stone Roofs

Beyond Ocuituco, on the steep western side of Popocatépetl, perches the little mountain village of Tetela del Volcán. The narrow road twists up past fields and orchards, with spectacular views of the snow-capped volcano at every turn.

The unpretentious Dominican mission sits on a rise above the village plaza, commanding a panoramic vista of the volcano above and the Amilpas Valley below. An archaic statue of the monastery patron, John the Baptist, clad in animal skins, occupies a niche in the otherwise plain facade.

Built in the 1560s and recently restored, the handsome cloister arcades also display the prow buttresses and apron moldings typical of the area.

The Cloister Murals

The fresco cycle of the lower cloister is the most complete of its kind yet discovered in Mexico, giving us a unique insight into the monastic mural programs of the 16th century.

Uncovered in the 1950s by the Mexican scholar Carlos Martínez Marín, the frescoes are not in prime condition, but are fortunately free of the overpainting that has marred so many other early murals. Painted in blue, black and orange against a red background, the murals reveal a sure hand. The figures are elegantly drawn in an idealized Renaissance style, framed by ornamental Plateresque pilasters and borders of cherubs and garlands.

The frescoes fall into two main groups: the corridor murals around the walks, which include three important narrative scenes as well as the figures of penitents and martyrs, and the pier frescoes, which portray apostles and saints associated with the monastic orders.

The Corridor Paintings

Three narrative murals in the corners of the cloister link John the Baptist to important episodes in the life of Christ. The most compelling of these are the Baptism of Christ and a fragmentary Visitation of St. Elizabeth, in which the blonde, long-haired Mary touches hands with Elizabeth, already pregnant with John the Baptist.

Delicately drawn portraits of female martyrs and penitants are interposed between the corner frescoes, among them a willowy Santa Lucia and the reclining Mary Magdalene.

The Pier Frescoes

Framed by painted Plateresque niches on the inner faces of the arcade piers, this series of twenty religious portraits is the most comprehensive sequence to survive in any monastery.

The founders of the mendicant orders—St. Francis, a youthful St. Dominic and the venerable St. Augustine—appropriately occupy three of the corner piers—the main supports, physically and symbolically, of the building. The Twelve Apostles appear on the smaller intermediate piers. Like the martyrs, they are sensitively depicted, with almost feminine features. St. Catherine of Siena, conspicuous in her black and white habit, is the best preserved of the Dominican saints.

The Miracle of the Rosary

A notable curiosity at Tetela is the large mural of the Miracle of the Rosary, in the upper cloister. Unlike the other murals, this visionary scene has an unmistakably indigenous flavor, reminiscent of the early Mexican codices.

The painting commemorates a celebrated incident in which Fray Domingo de la Anunciación, the Apostle of Tepoztlán, resurrected an Indian by reciting the Rosary. The portrayal of the miracle is dramatically enhanced by the apocalyptic imagery of the scene.

The body of the Indian lies stretched out on a platform, surrounded by mourners in native dress. His earthly possessions, which include a chest, a feather headdress and a rosary, hang in front of the bier. His soul, in the form of a naked child, issues from his mouth, only to be seized by a devil with a wolf's head and protruding tongue. Below on the right, fearsome demons with claws and wolves' tails set upon a nude woman, while blindfolded Indians are thrust by Satan's minions into the infernal regions.

This modest Dominican house of Tetela serves to whet our appetite for the feast of great Dominican monasteries that awaits us in Oaxaca, the subject of our final chapter.

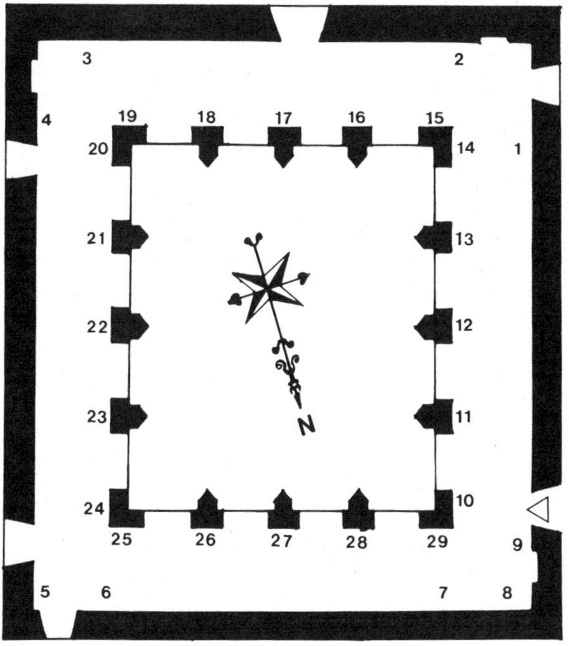

TETELA MURALS

Corridor Murals

1. St. Barbara
2. St. Ursula
3. Baptism of Christ
4. Mary Magdalene
5. The Resurrection
6. St. Jerome
7. The Visitation
8. St Lucia
9. St. Catherine

Pier Frescoes

10. St. Dominic
11. St. Peter
12. St. Andrew?
13. John the Evangelist
14. St. Thomas Aquinas
15. Catherine of Siena
16. Santiago
17. St. Phillip
18. St. Thomas
19. St. Vincent Ferrer
20. St. Anthony of Florence
21. St. James Minor
22. St. Paul
23. Apostle?
24. St Francis
25. St . Augustine
26. St. Judas Thaddeus
27. St. Matthew
28. Apostle?
29. St. Peter Nolasco

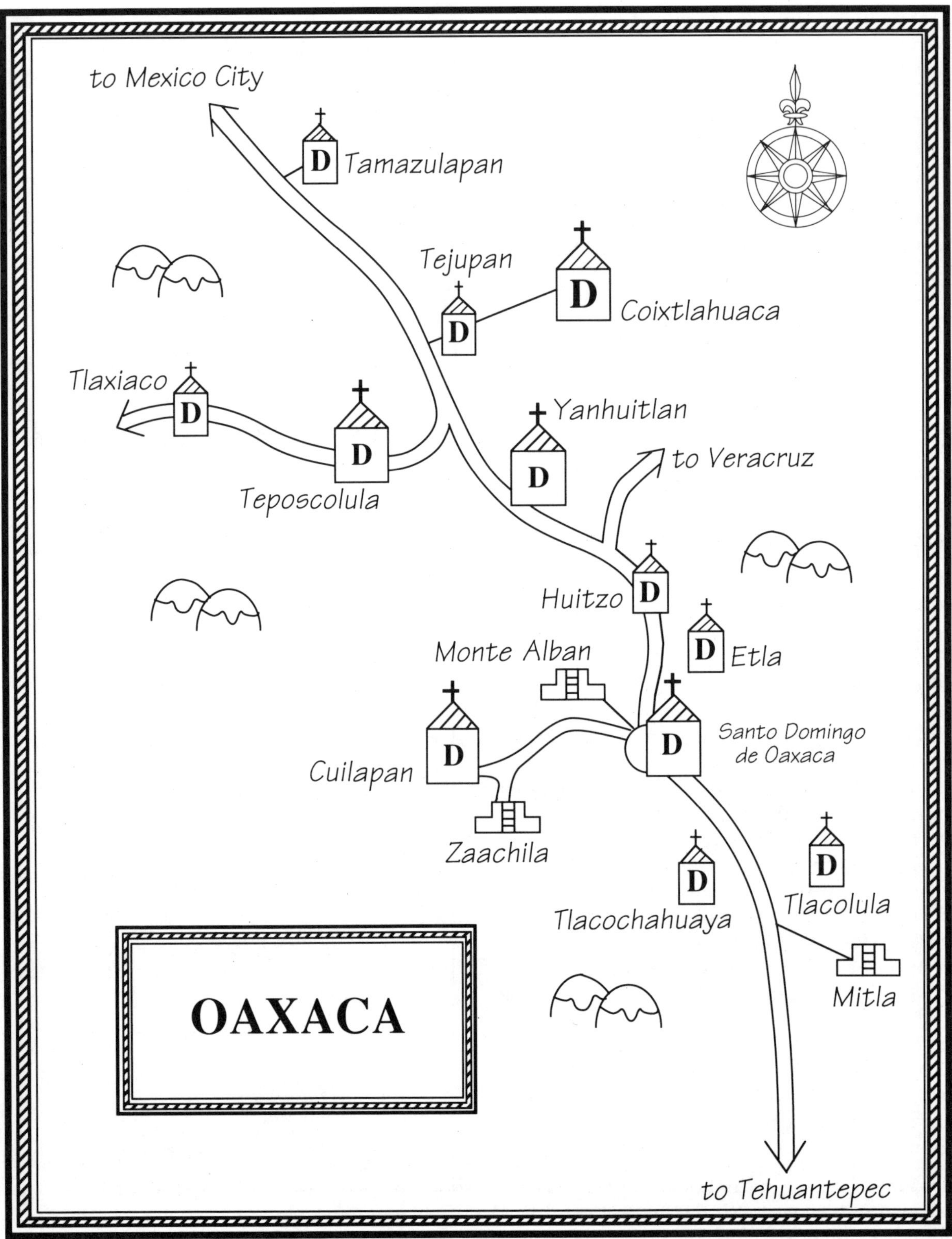

to Mexico City
Tamazulapan
Tejupan
Coixtlahuaca
Tlaxiaco
Yanhuitlan
to Veracruz
Teposcolula
Huitzo
Etla
Monte Alban
Santo Domingo
de Oaxaca
Cuilapan
Zaachila
Tlacochahuaya
Tlacolula
Mitla
OAXACA
to Tehuantepec

Chapter Five

Golden Temples

The Monasteries of Oaxaca

Oaxaca is a magical land. The stark beauty of its sierras and valleys, the pervasive presence of the Indian people and their traditional ways, and not least, the ancient ruins that recall a lost civilization—all these combine to fascinate the traveler.

And then there are the churches. From the baroque temples of the City of Oaxaca, a colonial city built on a human scale, to the glistening domed chapels that grace even the smallest village, they are a source of endless pleasure and surprise to those ready to explore them.

From ancient times, people have settled in the highland valleys of the Mixteca Alta and the fertile basin of the Oaxaca Valley—areas that were even more attractive in early colonial times, before deforestation and depopulation took their toll. It was here, too, that the native peoples, the Zapotecs in the Oaxaca Valley and the Mixtecs in the north, attained high levels of civilization prior to the Spanish Conquest. Several important ceremonial centers attest to their achievements over the centuries, among them the hilltop city of Monte Alban and the mosaic-walled necropolis at Mitla.

By the time the Spaniards arrived, however, they found only warring city states pitted against each other and the encroaching Aztec empire. Following the Conquest, which encountered only scattered local resistance, the Spaniards rapidly colonized the region, in most cases with the cooperation of the native lords, who were allowed to enjoy many of their former privileges. Cortés, impressed with the beauty and fertility of the area as well as its large native population, reserved a large part of it for the Marquesado, his own personal fiefdom.

The Dominicans in Oaxaca

The City of Oaxaca, a garrison town established by the Aztecs during their brief occupation of the area, was chosen as the site for the Spanish regional capital. As it grew and prospered, the bishop, López de Zarate, invited the Dominican Order to evangelize the region and establish a chain of missions.

Virtually all of the monasteries in Oaxaca were built by the Dominicans. During the 1540s, they founded monasteries in every major settlement. With the help of native labor, they launched an ambitious building program that continued through the 1550s and 1560s, financed by revenues from the new silk and cochineal dye industries.

By the end of the 16th century, as elsewhere in Mexico, the combination of soaring Indian mortality and economic decline brought a halt to missionary expansion. Curtailment of Dominican activities in Oaxaca by the colonial authorities slowed the building of monasteries. Nevertheless, in 1592, with 42 active missions in the region, the Order felt justified in creating the new Dominican province of St. Hippolytus in the Oaxaca Valley.

Art and Architecture

Oaxaca is earthquake country—which helps to explain its robust buildings. A fortress-like architecture of massive buttressed walls and apses, monumental facades and squat towers was designed to withstand the frequent shocks—not always successfully. Many of the monasteries we see today—Yanhuitlan, Santo Domingo de Oaxaca and Teposcolula, among others—have been reinforced or rebuilt over the centuries because of repeated tremors.

Unlike the austere Franciscans, the Dominicans built on a lavish scale and spent freely on the embellishment of their monasteries. Facades, cloisters, interiors and, above all, the open chapels show a breadth of scale, sophistication of design and richness of finish, to such a degree that the Dominicans were frequently criticized for the "unseemly extravagance" of their buildings.

It is among the Oaxacan monasteries that a truly Dominican style flowered in Mexico. Based upon the designs of several Dominican churches in the province of Salamanca, Spain, and the earlier monastery of Oaxtepec in Morelos (Chapter Four), a distinctive style was developed in the 16th century by a few talented friars, assisted by a handful of European craftsmen.

This Dominican style confidently fused Renaissance forms with Gothic and *mudéjar* elements of the Spanish Plateresque style to create a bold, monumental architecture. Characteristic features include ornamental paneled doorframes, flattened arches, candelabra columns, ribbed vaulting and heavy drum corbels set in prominent running cornices.

The high quality of the stonework is one of the most attractive aspects of the Oaxacan monasteries. Locally quarried fine grained limestone, in pink, brown, green and gold, was skillfully transformed by native masons into the fine architectural and sculptural detail that distinguishes virtually every building. Superb 17th century stuccowork, much of it executed by artisans from Puebla, is another feature of many Oaxacan monasteries. It can be admired at Santo Domingo de Oaxaca, Yanhuitlan and Etla.

Mural painting was undoubtedly as widespread in the Oaxacan monasteries as elsewhere in Mexico, but relatively few frescoes have survived the triple onslaught of time, neglect and earthquakes. The Tree of Friars at Cuilapan and the St. Christopher in the stairwell at Yanhuitlan are two outstanding examples that remain.

Finally, the Oaxacan monasteries are well endowed with exceptional colonial altarpieces, some as early as the 16th century. Large, beautifully crafted *retablos* are still in place at Yanhuitlan and Coixtlahuaca; the lavishly recreated altarpieces of the church of Santo Domingo de Oaxaca are especially magnificent.

The Monasteries

There are two main monastic clusters, those in the Oaxaca Valley, in the center of the state, and those of the Mixteca Alta to the north.

We start with **Santo Domingo de Oaxaca**, the opulent mother house of the Dominican Order, located in the City of Oaxaca. We then explore the surrounding valleys, visiting first the great unfinished monastery of **Cuilapan**, in the shadow of ancient Monte Alban, and afterwards, the folk baroque temple and hermitage of **San Jerónimo Tlacochahuaya** in the Tlacolula Valley.

Next we ascend to the mountain valleys of the Mixteca Alta, where we visit a quartet of major monasteries: **Yanhuitlan**, queen of the Mixteca missions, **Coixtlahuaca** and **Teposcolula**—both acclaimed for their magnificent open chapels—and lastly, the imposing early Dominican house at **Tlaxiaco**.

THE OAXACA VALLEY

The Valley of Oaxaca is located at the convergence of three lesser valleys that descend from the surrounding ranges to form a fertile basin.

As the largest and richest of the regional population centers, it naturally became the focus of Spanish colonial life and development.

The City of Oaxaca

From thence, we came to the city of Oaxaca... a fair and beautiful city to behold. There are six cloisters of nuns and friars, all of them exceedingly rich, but above all is the cloister of the Dominican friars whose church is worth millions.

With these words, the English Dominican friar Thomas Gage, who journeyed through Mexico in the mid-17th century, left us a rare glimpse of this prosperous city at its zenith.

Oaxaca is a city of churches—29 by a recent count. Because of constant earthquakes, many of the 16th century buildings have crumbled. Most of the churches we see today date from the 17th and 18th centuries—a period that marked the apogee of church wealth in Oaxaca. The energetic Bishop Maldonado spent freely on an ambitious building campaign that gave birth to a unique regional style, the Oaxacan Baroque.

In a break from the austere, fortress-like churchfronts of the 16th century, elegant *retablo* facades blossomed, inaugurating an inspired architecture of classical columns and cornices, crowded with statuary, opulent reliefs and a profusion of ornate carving.

Locally quarried stone—luminous greenish-gold building blocks and easily worked, fine grained brownstone for sculpture and architectural detail—also helps to unify these distinctive buildings.

One of the earliest and most influential of the city churches was the Dominican priory of Santo Domingo de Oaxaca.

SANTO DOMINGO DE OAXACA

From the cathedral square at the heart of the city center, a pedestrian promenade, lined with ornamental street lamps and attractive colonial houses, leads north for several blocks to the noble priory of Santo Domingo, newly restored upon its terraced plaza.

Santo Domingo is first among the Dominican monasteries of Oaxaca. It stands beside the Plaza del Rosario, the former atrium, now planted with rose gardens. The monastery complex is dominated by its imposing church, beyond whose tall towers and sculpted facade lies the most sumptuous baroque interior in Mexico. The former *convento* now houses the Oaxaca State Museum, a major tourist attraction famous for its pre-Columbian and colonial art treasures.

The early years in Oaxaca were difficult ones for the Dominican Order. A handful of friars arrived here in 1529 and quickly built a rude adobe chapel, dedicated to St. Paul (San Pablo), not far from the main square. But because of poor construction and frequent earthquakes, the building soon fell into disrepair.

By 1550, the Dominicans had decided to build a new priory on a large tract of land situated on the heights above the city. Although the monastery was dedicated in 1575, construction dragged on until the end of the century. The lavish scale of the project and its enormous expense strained Dominican resources and stirred complaints against the Order.

Then, on the last day of the year 1603, just as the friars were about to move into the newly finished buildings, a catastrophic earthquake struck the city. Both the old mission of San Pablo and the new monastery were severely damaged. The friars were forced to seek refuge in the monastery of Cuilapan, outside the city.

Finally, in 1610, they were able to move into their new quarters. Even so, the church was not finished until almost fifty years later.

Santo Domingo de Oaxaca, west front

The Church

The building of it [is] the fairest and strongest in all those parts. The walls are so broad that when I was there I saw carts driven upon them loaded with stone.
Thomas Gage, 1648

Santo Domingo's impressive west front is a handsome sight in the afternoon sun, the amber glow of its stonework contrasting with the blue mountains behind and the white glare of the flagstones in front.

Imposing twin towers, set on massive bases, are surmounted by giant merlons and bulging tiled domes. The towers frame the tall, narrow *retablo* facade—an innovation that sparked a new fashion among the colonial churches of the city.

The facade is transitional in style, although the basic form is firmly within the Renaissance tradition. Fluted Corinthian columns, a few with bulbous candelabra shafts, subdivide the four main tiers, while classical friezes of cherubs and acanthus foliage decorate the cornices. But baroque touches have crept into the facade; the ornate "eared" frame of the central relief and the decorative broken pediment in the top tier are two examples.

The relief shows St. Dominic and St. Hippolytus the Martyr holding up the church. Hippolytus was the patron of the 17th century Dominican province of San Hipólito de Oaxaca, and he wears the traditional garb of a Roman soldier, with a plumed helmet between his feet.

An ornate baroque cartouche in the upper tier frames the Dominican Cross of Alcantara, flanked by the Dominican dogs, brandishing torches, and the giant reclining figures of Faith, Hope and Charity. Statues of saints occupy the scalloped sculpture niches, some of them squat frontal figures with large, awkward hands—possibly survivors from an earlier facade destroyed by a quake.

To the right of the church is the baroque portal of the Rosary Chapel. Another eared frame encloses a relief of the Virgin giving the Rosary to St. Dominic. From their cloud throne, Mother and Child gesture graciously towards the half naked figure of the saint, who kneels penitentially in the lower left hand corner. A cherub hovers, displaying the Rosary. Again, an elaborately framed Dominican cross appears in the broken pediment above the doorway, with the Marian monogram and Dominican dogs holding torches.

The Interior

The spare symmetry of the facade hardly prepares us for the radiant church interior, now fully restored to its colonial elegance.

Most of the original decoration dated from the 17th and early 18th centuries. With the dissolution of the priory in the mid-19th century, however, the church was converted into an army barracks. The interior was vandalized and the altarpieces destroyed. When the church was returned to the Dominicans at the beginning of this century, an ambitious program of restoration began, spearheaded by the energetic Father Estéban Arroyo and completed in 1976.

The earliest work of art in the church is the The Genealogy of St. Dominic, adorning the underchoir. Based on the medieval motif of the Tree of Jesse, this spectacular painted relief spreads out across the vault in the form of a branched grapevine.

Springing from the reclining figure of Don Félix de Guzmán, the patriarch of the family, it traces the earthly lineage of the noble founder of the Dominican Order. Members of the family, real and imaginary, emerge like blossoms from buds set among the tendrils and bunches of grapes. These diminutive, fresh-faced figures exude a charm and directness that establish this ceiling as one of the most appealing masterpieces of Mexican popular art. The Virgin is a later addition, placed like a Christmas ornament at the top of the tree.

Possessed by a *horror vacui*, all the other surfaces in the church—walls, vaults, domes and niches—are encrusted with ornament. Paintings, polychrome reliefs and statues are enmeshed in a sparkling web of white and gold, exemplifying the exuberant Pueblan Baroque style of stuccowork.

Above the choir, amid a swirl of gilded shells, foliage and strapwork, the Virgin shelters St.

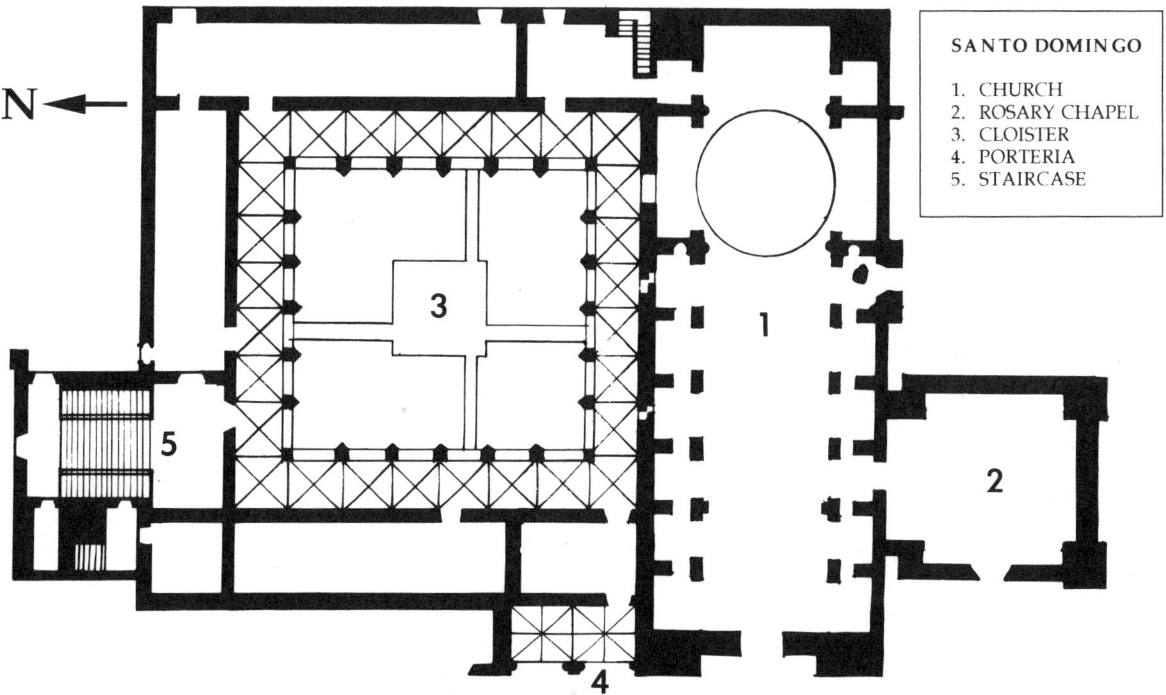

Santo Domingo de Oaxaca,
Lineage of St. Dominic

Dominic and St. Rose of Lima beneath her outstretched cape. Saints and martyrs of the Order radiate in bands around the dome, diminishing in size as they ascend towards the dove of the Holy Spirit at the apex.

The Marian mysteries along the nave vault—the Annunciation, the Conception and the Assumption—are framed by oval cartouches in a field of gilded arabesques. Above the crossing, a company of Dominican popes, saints and patriarchs is woven into a design of undulating *mudéjar* strapwork studded with angels and rosettes—an eye-dazzling tour-de-force in red, blue and gold against the white stucco dome.

The altarpieces are modern reproductions of the original baroque *retablos* destroyed in the 19th century. The sumptuous gilded main altarpiece, together with the ornate pulpit and altar rail, were reconstructed on the basis of old descriptions and surviving examples from the period—notably the main *retablo* at Yanhuitlan. The baroque framework of twisted Solomonic columns, curvetted cornices and scalloped niches provides an elegant showcase for the 17th and 18th century paintings and statuary.

The Rosary Chapel

The Cult of the Rosary was zealously promoted by the Dominicans. In the later colonial period especially, wealthy individuals and religious fraternities were encouraged to endow opulent

Rosary Chapels. Erected and decorated in the 1720s, this chapel is covered by a large octagonal dome. The Virgin of the Rosary appears at its apex as the protectress of the Dominican Order. Nuns and friars kneel piously beneath her ample blue cloak. The large gilded Crucifixion over the west doorway is flanked by the Franciscan saints, St. Anthony of Padua and St. Francis himself.

The emotional power of the chapel is somewhat dissipated by its excessive ornamentation. The pantheon of saints and apostles is almost overwhelmed by a profusion of angels, shells, arabesques and overlapping scrolls.

The Monastery

The former monastery is now the Oaxaca State Museum, housing a prime collection of ancient and colonial sculpture and artifacts, as well as priceless Mixtec goldwork and jewelry. There are also excellent permanent and changing ethnographic and historical exhibits.

The plain double archway beside the church marks the old *portería* of the monastery. Its ribbed vault and walls were once covered with multicolored murals, of which only fragments remain—notably the eroded figures of Saints Peter and Paul on either side of the entry. The classical pedimented doorway is boldly emblazoned with the Dominican insignia and the date 1575, recording the dedication of the original priory.

Beyond the entry vestibule, now the museum bookstore, lies the spacious two-story cloister. Expertly crafted from brilliant white limestone, its arcades establish the distinctive architectural detailing found in Dominican cloisters throughout Oaxaca. To minimize earthquake damage, the substantial stone piers were faced with "prow" buttresses, so-called because of their resemblance to the bow of a ship. Half columns with simple cylindrical capitals are attached to the sides of the piers, and bold matching drum corbels are mounted in the walls along the walks to support the heavy rib vaults.

The large flat panels on the inner faces of the piers at one time displayed full-length portraits of popular Dominicans, but are now mostly blank. Only a few partial figures and friezes, in the corners and around the doorway, suggest the former glory of this painted cloister.

A modestly framed doorway in the north walk opens onto the elaborate baroque double staircase. Its ornamental stuccoed interior, also carved and painted in the plush Pueblan style, is unrivaled in Mexico. Ceilings and side walls contain enormous reliefs of Dominican saints and insignia, framed by stucco scrolls and ornamental strapwork.

The arcades of the upper cloister are more Renaissance in feeling, with rusticated buttresses and elaborately dentilled cornices. The large surrounding rooms house the exhibits. Displayed along an inner corridor on the west side is a small but high quality collection of 17th and 18th century wooden statues and reliefs of special interest to admirers of Spanish colonial art.

At the end of this corridor, raised high above a stairway leading to the church choir, is the carved and painted stucco dome of the former friars' chapel. At its center is La Purísima, the Virgin of the Immaculate Conception, ringed by an amazing variety of ornamental moldings—chains, beads, rosettes, chevrons and stylized acanthus leaves.

Santo Domingo de Oaxaca, facade relief

On the western outskirts of the City of Oaxaca, a side road is posted to Zaachila, a Zapotec site famous for its ancient tombs. Winding through the rolling Zimatlan valley, the road passes the Dominican monastery of ***Santiago Cuilapan****, the largest in the Oaxaca Valley, situated within view of the hilltop ruins of Monte Alban.*

date plaque in the Basilica

CUILAPAN

Coyote River

Every July 25th, during the fiesta of Santiago, a troupe of plumed dancers, resplendent in giant disc-like headdresses, gather in the monastery atrium to perform the Dance of the Conquest. In this colorful dance-drama, preserved at Cuilapan since the 16th century, the townspeople reenact Cortés' epic defeat of the Aztecs.

The ritual has its roots in pre-Conquest times. When the Spaniards arrived, Cuilapan was the sole remaining Mixtec enclave in this predominantly Zapotec region, and proud of its links with the aristocratic Mixtec kingdoms to the north. Each year, according to a Dominican chronicler, the inhabitants had celebrated, in an elaborate ceremony, an ancient triumph over their Zapotec enemies.

Here, in 1550, the Dominicans decided to build a monastery, on a mesa just outside the village. It was to be a large priory, with its own seminary to prepare the friars for mission work in the Mixteca Alta.

Fray Domingo de Aguiñaga, the forceful prior of Santo Domingo de Oaxaca, was also the founder of Cuilapan, responsible for its design and for marshalling the vast resources of labor and material necessary for its construction.

He gave impetus to the arduous first decade of building and was succeeded in 1559 by Fray Bernardo de Albuquerque, another energetic prelate with long experience in the supervision of church construction. Assisted by a Portuguese master mason, Antonio de Barbosa, Father Albuquerque oversaw the architectural detailing of the monastery.

With the introduction of wheat into the fertile valley, as well as fruit and walnut plantations, the community grew in size and wealth. Construction continued intermittently into the 1570s, but in 1580 work abruptly halted. Whether because of a lack of funds and labor, a dispute with the Cortés estate, or growing official criticism of the ambitious building program, we do not know for sure, but the great church remains unfinished to this day.

Within its enormous enclosed atrium, the priory of Cuilapan consists of three main structures: the main church, the *convento* and the enigmatic arcaded "Basilica" projecting from the north side of the church.

The Basilica

Once inside the atrium, the visitor is immediately impressed by the broad facade of the Basilica, so called because of its long, narrow nave and arcaded side aisles. One of the most original buildings in the Americas, it was conceived as the nave of an open-air church, a primitive pole-and-thatch *ramada* designed to shelter the large Indian congregation.

When this perishable structure deteriorated, a permanent stone building was erected with walk-through arcaded walls and a wooden pitched roof. While the main church remained unfinished, the Basilica served for many years as the monastic church. Late in the 1500s, its arcades were blocked up and the elaborate facade added.

With the abandonment of the Basilica in the last century, the wooden roof burned and collapsed. Although the roof is still missing, the arcaded walls have recently been opened up again, restoring the Basilica's original open character.

The facade is a Plateresque fantasy, crisply carved from local green and gold stone. Conceived as a Roman triumphal arch with triple entries, it is curiously flanked by a pair of conical turrets that might have graced a medieval French chateau.

The main doorway is imposing, with fluted jambs and Corinthian-style columns. In the attic above, Faith and Hope recline against an elaborate escutcheon of a *fleur-de-lis* cross flanked by torch-bearing dogs. The scallop shells are symbols of Santiago (St. James), the patron saint of the monastery.

Clean lines and monumental stonework characterize the interior of the Basilica. Two Tuscan colonnades once stretched the entire length of the building, although only one stands today. Just inside the main doorway, a pair of battered holy water stoups is surmounted by crucifixes. The two original side entrances (the fourth bay from the east end) are also marked by large relief crosses.

Recessed midway along the east wall is the wall pulpit with its built-in stairway. Although its paneled parapet has been mutilated, the overhanging shell canopy and powerful scalloped bracket beneath attest to the pulpit's massive forms—a monumentality that distinguishes much of the monastery's architectural sculpture.

The Dominican eight-pointed cross, with stars and *fleurs-de-lis*, is boldly carved on a plaque over the narrow stair entry, along with crossed keys and maces, books, a pierced heart and a crown of thorns.

Time and the elements have erased most of the vivid murals that once colored the now naked walls of the Basilica. A few naively drawn

Cuilapan, the Basilica

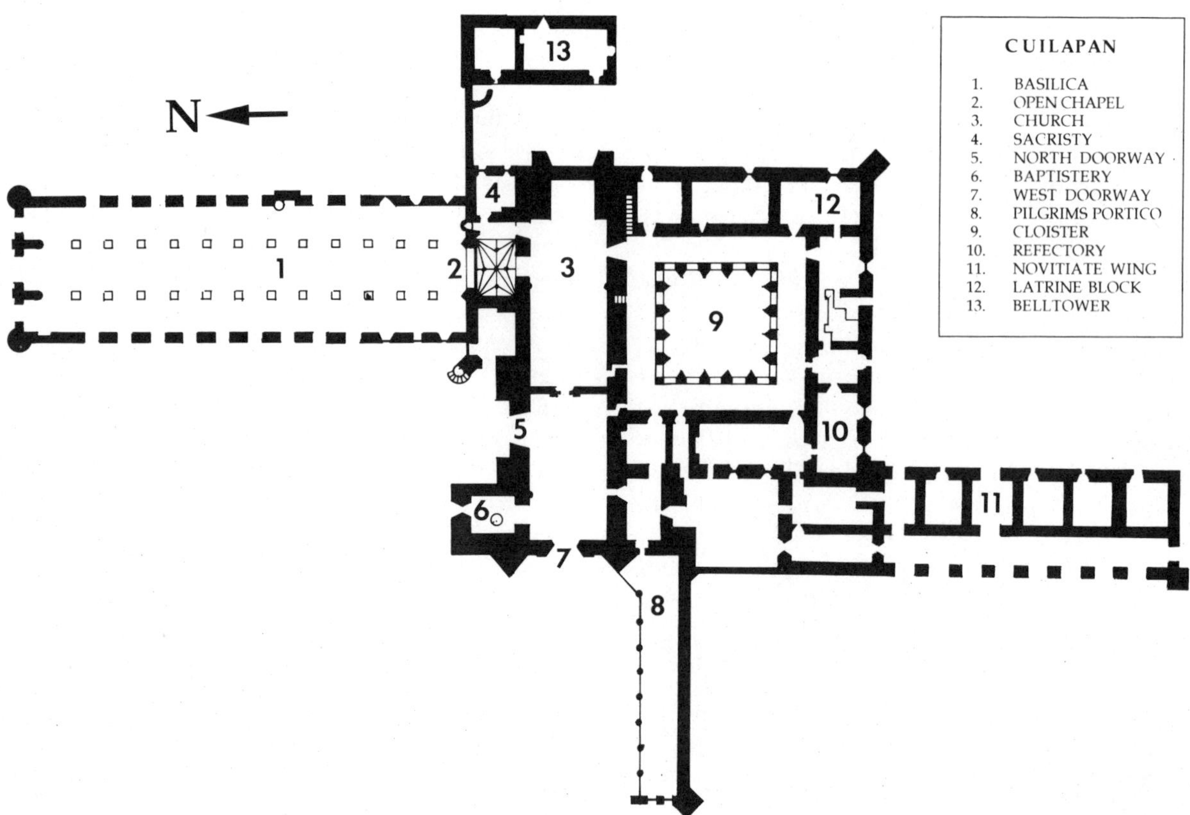

fragments of scenes from Christ's Passion cling to an inner archway along the east wall—the Road to Calvary, a Crucifixion with the figure of Mary, and a spirited Triumph of Christ Resurrected.

On the end wall, we can recognize the blocked-up sanctuary arch of the former open chapel. Beside it is an intriguing relief, dated 1555 and inscribed with Mixtec date glyphs, which may be the original foundation stone of the monastery. On the other side of the arch, a small doorway leads into the main church.

The Church

The former open chapel and its two side rooms, now incorporated into the church, are the earliest part of the monastery. The chapel has been remodeled in pseudo-Moorish style, but happily retains its original Gothic vault.

The sacristy beside the chapel still serves its original purpose. Its main feature of interest is a 16th century mural of the Calvary, still in excellent condition. Behind the kneeling figure of the Dominican saint, Peter Martyr, his head cloven by an axe, we see a turreted building—an early representation of the Basilica. An elaborate grotesque frieze of birds and animals, fruits, flowers and vines borders the fresco.

Although built on a huge scale, the church is simple in plan. Facing the broad nave, a handsome coffered vault covers the apse—a distinctive feature of the Dominican style. Enclosed within the ten-foot-thick south wall are the shell of a wall pulpit and two tunnel-like wall confessionals.

The unfinished nave was never vaulted in colonial times, although it may have been partially covered by a wood or thatch roof. Even today, only the two easterly bays have been crudely roofed for use as the parish church. The giant half columns that divide the two bays are carved with spiraling foliage and rest on rosette-studded bases with unusual globe-and-chain feet.

In stark contrast to its imposing architecture, the interior reveals a poverty of furnishing. There are remnants of at least one respectable colonial altarpiece and a striking folk sculpture of a dark-complexioned Santiago mounted on a splendid white steed. But the most interesting monument inside the church is the Isabelline tomb of Princess Donaji, set into the floor in front of the sanctuary. The inscription memorializes the star-crossed romance between the Zapotec princess, a 16th century convert to Christianity, and her lover, the Lord of Tilantongo, a Mixtec town near Yanhuitlan.

The two westerly bays are open to the sky. Into their cliff-like elevations are set the monolithic drum corbels and rib haunches intended to support the great vaults of the church and raised choir, which were never completed. The doorways to the choir are isolated in the upper walls, elegantly framed with pointed arches and ashlar jambs.

The spacious former baptistery was completed. We enter through an Isabelline doorway on the north side. In the center of the floor, beneath the high ribbed vault, stands a charming baptismal font embossed with rosettes, urns and water-spouting imps.

The roofless section of the church boasts two Plateresque porches, on the north and the west. Both display the elegant sobriety that characterizes 16th century Dominican architecture in Oaxaca.

The unfinished north entry is the more sophisticated of the two, closely related to the monumental north doorway at Yanhuitlan. The design utilizes a door-within-a-door motif. The paneled inner doorway has fluted Ionic pilasters and a dentilled entablature topped by candelabra finials. This scheme is repeated on a larger scale in the outer frame, whose flanking quarter columns push skyward, terminating in giant baluster pinnacles.

The west doorway was evidently designed to maximize the sharp *chiaroscuro* effects of the strong afternoon sun. The multi-faceted archway is flanked by cylindrical double columns that thrust through the entablature into the pediment overhead. The wall above the porch is pierced by two windows, side by side—a rare configuration also used in the old west front at Yanhuitlan.

Cuilapan, church facade

The Convento

The pointed archway of the monastery door is almost lost behind the grand loggia of the "Pilgrims' Portico,"—a long colonnade like the one inside the Basilica.

The stately two-story cloister was a model for many other superb Dominican cloisters in Oaxaca. Five rib-vaulted bays line each side, and like those at Santo Domingo de Oaxaca, the sturdy piers of the arcades are faced with prow buttresses, Tuscan half columns and heavy drum corbels on the corridor side. The inner panels of each pier were originally painted with figures of saints.

As we walk counter-clockwise around the cloister, the rhythm of the architecture becomes insistent. At every corner, the tunnel of receding arches and columns impels the eye towards the painted niches at the far end. Now vacant, these niches formerly held devotional images to inspire the meditating friars.

On the west side of the cloister we pass through the refectory, noting the wall lectern reserved for reading the scriptures during meals. Beside the refectory lies the rambling kitchen complex with its vast open hearth and beyond that, the disused latrine block.

An impressive *sala de profundis* occupies the south side, its walls veiled with faded murals of Dominican saints. At the far end, Christ and his disciples are seated around a circular table for the Last Supper.

The adjacent lobby contains the most interesting mural at Cuilapan, a 16th century Tree of Friars. A tree sprouts from the figure of St. Dominic and spreads into several branches. Settled on each branch are rows of diminutive black-robed saints and martyrs, like starlings, some clutching their own severed heads.

The main stairway also opens off this lobby. The worn steps remind us that generations of friars passed up and down, no doubt often glancing up at the angels' heads carved on the bosses of the vaulted stairwell.

The sunlit upper arcades are much like those of lower cloister, with the addition of paneled stone parapets and half columns instead of prow buttresses. Only the corner bays are vaulted, and beamed ceilings cover the walks, eliminating the need for stone corbels. Sixteen cells open off the shaded inner corridors on three sides of the cloister. Stripped of their furnishings and bereft of murals, they are now bare and forlorn, apart from angled window seats that offer bright vistas of the Zimatlan Valley.

A final item of interest is the novitiate wing that extends from the southwest corner of the *convento*. Arcaded on one side, the wing was probably added in the 1560s when the friars fled here from the quake-devastated City of Oaxaca.

Although Cuilapan saw its glory days in the 16th century, later events have kept it in the history books. In February 1831, Vicente Guerrero, a hero of the War of Independence and the second president of Mexico, was briefly imprisoned here before facing the firing squad. His dismal cramped cell stands in sharp contrast to the grandiose marble monument erected to his memory across the patio outside.

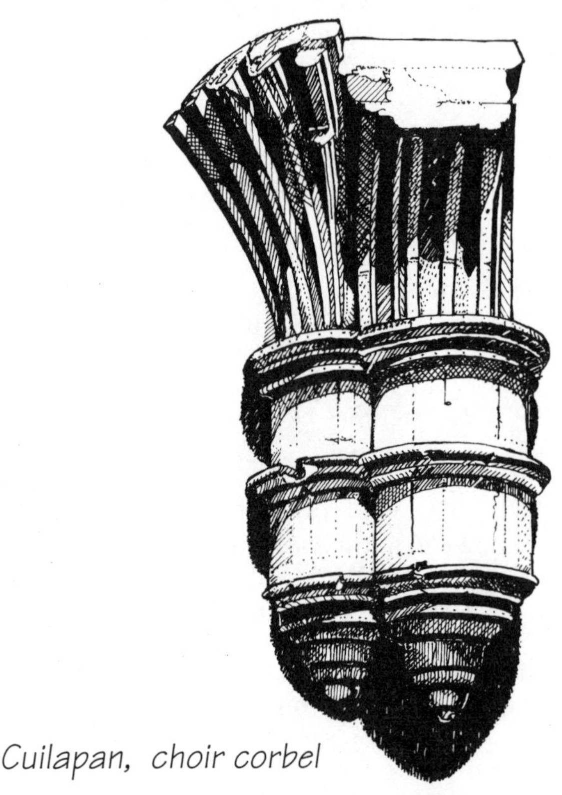

Cuilapan, choir corbel

The Tlacolula Valley

The southeastern arm of the Valley of Oaxaca is called the Tlacolula Valley after its principal settlement, the bustling town of Tlacolula, well known for its colorful Sunday market.

The Pan-American highway (MEX 190) is the main artery of the valley, passing close to the Zapotec ruins at Yagul, Dainzú and Lambityeco, as well as the weaving village of **Teotitlan del Valle** and **Tlacolula** itself. As the valley narrows and becomes more arid, a secondary road turns off to the prehispanic necropolis of Mitla and the 17th century church set atop its ruins.

Our main destination in the valley is the folk baroque monastery of **San Gerónimo Tlacochahuaya**.

Tlacochahuaya, St. Jerome

TLACOCHAHUAYA

Night Fighter

Nestled in a foothill valley only 20 kms from downtown Oaxaca and nowadays readily accessible from Highway 190, Tlacochahuaya was quite remote in early colonial times. It was for this reason that, in 1558, Fray Jordan de Santa Catalina, a Dominican ascetic, chose this spot as an isolated retreat for prayer and meditation, and duly dedicated it to St. Jerome (San Gerónimo), the patron of hermits and penitents.

Although the early hermitage was intentionally spartan, it was transformed during the 17th century into a substantial monastery, designed to serve the nearby Zapotec communities.

The newly restored church is probably the best known example of folk baroque architecture and decoration in Oaxaca. Imposing whitewashed gateways admit the visitor to the spacious paved atrium—a quiet precinct of giant shade trees enclosed by battlemented walls. Domed *posas* mark the corners and an eroded sundial stands in front of the north portico. Embedded in the north wall of the church are slabs of ancient Zapotec stonecarving.

The massive churchfront again reminds us that we are in earthquake country. Heavy bastions support squat, single-stage towers typical of country churches throughout Oaxaca, with fluted pilasters, undulating pediments, and high, tiled cupolas. Note the delicate wrought-iron crosses atop the lanterns.

Sandwiched between the tower bases is a pink stucco *retablo* facade in popular baroque style. Simplified scrolls, broken cornices and plain molded pilasters frame two tiers of sculpture niches, and the crowning pediment is accented with vestiges of blue and red paint.

The statuary is primitive and direct. Over the doorway, St. Jerome kneels in penitence before the Crucifix, one hand clutching a rock and the other resting on a skull. The saint strains in ecstasy to hear the Word of God emanating from the trumpet beside his left ear. The hieratic figures of St. Augustine, St. Thomas Aquinas and St. Francis occupy the surrounding niches. In the middle tier, two masculine archangels escort the pious Virgin, who is enfolded in voluminous robes. A wild-looking God the Father, with flowing hair, beard and mustache, watches over her.

The Church Interior

Inside, the church is a delight of colorful frescoes, old colonial altarpieces and regional folk

Tlacochahuaya, west front

art. Walls, ceilings and domes are ablaze with decorative murals painted in brilliant reds, blues, greens and gold. Patterns of rosettes, winged angels' heads, giant urns, floral bands and braided moldings frame the celestial company of figures around the domes, including the Holy Trinity and numerous archangels.

The Four Evangelists on the pendentives above the crossing seem poised to fly heavenwards, their fingers delicately raised in gestures of benediction. Although much has been made of the "Indian" look of the murals, the iconography is conventionally Christian, rooted in European Renaissance and baroque pictorial traditions. The native contribution lies in the forthright draftmanship and freshness of vision—all characteristic of authentic folk art.

The church furnishings are extraordinarily rich and varied. The first item that catches the eye is a sculpture of the Trinity, near the entrance. A richly attired Padre Eterno wears the triple coronet of the Trinity and holds up an orb and crucifix. His sumptuous robe, rippling beard and wide-eyed visage give him an unmistakably Byzantine aspect.

By the north door hangs a cornpith crucifix. The emaciated body of Christ, with its twisted limbs, seems gruesomely incongruous against the cheery floral backdrop. But my favorite piece in the nave is the naive figure of Christ entering Jerusalem on his misshapen donkey.

The paneled pulpit is decorated with stylized rosettes, supposedly derived from the Zapotec glyph for "earthquake." Atop the canopy is a diminutive St. Jerome, enshrined in a tabernacle. Look for the ornamental 18th century painted organ case in the choir loft.

The Altarpieces

A row of old altarpieces lines the nave. On the south wall, the *retablo* of St. Hyacinth (San Jacinto), a popular Dominican saint, illustrates episodes from his life in a series of charming miniatures. The painting of the Virgin of Guadalupe, in an adjacent *retablo*, is signed by the noted regional artist Joseph Nabarro and dated 1689.

Most of the altarpieces in the sanctuary and transepts date from the 17th and early 18th centuries and are executed in a provincial style transitional between Renaissance and early baroque. Many incorporate large paintings set in ornamental gilded frames with fluted or spiral columns. Several paintings appear to predate the *retablos*, and some are even mounted directly on the wall without frames.

The kneeling statue of St. Jerome, accompanied by his lion, appears in the main *retablo*, which also features paintings by Juan de Arrué, a well-known Oaxacan painter and student of Simón Pereyns and Andrés de la Concha, the 16th century masters who worked in the Mixteca Alta. The dramatic central subject of the Descent from the Cross reveals a strong Mannerist influence in its unnatural lighting and the restless movement of the drapery.

The *retablos* in the transepts and beside the sanctuary arch stand on old wooden bases carved with Dominican symbols and sacred monograms. A serene Virgin of the Rosary, holding a doll-like infant Jesus in her outstretched arms and framed by the Mysteries of the Rosary in miniature roundels, occupies pride of place in another incomplete altarpiece nearby.

The humble *convento* behind the church is the only surviving part of the original hermitage, its plain whitewashed cloister contrasting with the decorative richness of the church.

San Pablo Mitla

TLACOLULA

Place of the Crosses

Sunday is market day in Tlacocula. Bustling stalls and colorful vendors of local handcrafts overflow from the street into the churchyard. Zapotec Indians from the surrounding villages crowd into the church of Santo Cristo to pay their respects to El Señor de Tlacolula, a venerated image safeguarded inside a sturdy wrought-iron screen behind the altar.

Originally a Dominican mission, it looks much like a hundred other provincial Oaxacan churches, with its stuccoed facade and tiled dome. The interior contains a wealth of beautifully wrought metalwork by local artisans, notably in the Rosary Chapel on the south side of the narrow 17th century church. Saints and biblical characters throng the walls, ceilings and door frames. Stucco statues, exuberantly carved and painted in red, white and gold, display an extraordinary range of expressions and gestures. My favorite is the decapitated figure of John the Baptist, stoically holding out his severed head.

Known locally as La Capilla de Plata (Silver Chapel), this little chapel is a gem of the folk baroque style. It is interesting to compare this triumph of popular art to the more sophisticated Pueblan style of the Rosary Chapel at Santo Domingo de Oaxaca.

MITLA

Place of the Dead

The recently renovated church of San Pablo Mitla stands squarely atop the platform of a pre-Conquest structure. On its foundations are carved several of the intricate geometric motifs unique to this necropolis of the Zapotec and Mixtec kings.

Hard-edged, blocky forms distinguish the 17th century church. Its plain geometry was clearly intended to rival the stonework of the ancient buildings that surround it. Stark rounded doorways and niches, simply framed by half columns and prominent cornices, articulate the triumphal arch of the facade—features designed to dramatize the play of brilliant southern sunlight and deep shadow. Hexagonal tiled domes with slender lanterns cluster like beehives above the building, creating a serpentine silhouette against the bare hills behind.

Several painted colonial *santos* are displayed in the plain whitewashed interior, which also contains a handsome painting of the Baptism of Christ.

Bounded by high walls and empty corner chapels, the bare cobbled precinct of the atrium remains apart from the daily life of the village, as befits this ancient resting place of kings.

THE ETLA VALLEY

The northwestern arm of the Valley of Oaxaca is actually the Etla Valley, a fertile region of large haciendas that was once the breadbasket of colonial Oaxaca.

St. Peter and St. Paul Etla and **Santa Caterina Huitzo** are two 16th century monasteries typical of the smaller Dominican houses in Oaxaca. Located just off the Pan-American highway, both are easy to visit en route to the Mixteca Alta.

ETLA

Spectacularly sited on a terraced ridge with a panoramic view of the valley, the cut stone church of St. Peter and St. Paul stands in a large atrium paved with green flagstones. The elegant facade is one of the widest in Oaxaca, a model of classical simplicity.

A slender colonnade of smoothly rounded arches frames the *portería,* which also doubled as an open chapel. The handsome two-story cloister follows the pattern set by Santo Domingo de Oaxaca, its tall vaulted arcades faced with half columns and prow buttresses.

The ornamental ceiling in the northeast corner—a riot of painted baroque stuccowork in the Pueblan style—comes as a surprise in the otherwise sober cloister. Scrolled and scalloped cartouches, emblazoned with *fleur-de-lis* crosses and strapwork, radiate about a luxuriantly foliated central pendant.

HUITZO

The monastery at Huitzo still retains its modest 16th century character. The soft white limestone facade has a classic Dominican look, with its beveled doorway outlined by paneled jambs and arch. Note how the drum capitals of the flanking half columns extend through the entablature—a quirk we also saw in the west porch of Cuilapan.

A crude *bas-relief* of St. Dominic, accompanied by his dog and bishop's miter, is set over the monastery entrance. Inside, the low arcades of the single-story cloister have a medieval weightiness. Heavy stone vaults rest on sturdy pillars and massive drum corbels.

Primitive fish swim through carved waves on the water stoup halfway up the stairway to the upper cloister, and eroded Zapotec glyphs are still visible in the ancient stones of the patio fountain.

Huitzo, St. Dominic

THE MIXTECA ALTA

This less traveled region of rugged mountains and highland valleys is dotted with Dominican monasteries, large and small.

The grandest of them all, the priory of **Santo Domingo Yanhuitlan**, is conveniently located on the Pan-American highway that winds north through the Mixteca Alta on its way to Mexico City.

Three other imposing monasteries also lie within reach of the highway north of Yanhuitlan: **Coixtlahuaca** to the east; **Teposcolula** and **Tlaxiaco** to the west.

YANHUITLAN

Wide and Spacious Valley

At about two in the afternoon, the rain lifted. From the far side of the atrium, a ragged line of mourners slowly approached, the women's faces obscured by black *rebozos*.

A small coffin swayed on the shoulders of the four pallbearers as they rounded the corner of the church. Carefully, they lowered their burden onto the top step before the barred church door and removed their rain-stained *sombreros*. A young woman stepped forward and tenderly placed a bunch of lilies on the plain coffin lid. There was no funeral band, or even a priest to administer a final blessing. Someone lit a candle and a low murmur of prayer rose from the company. After a few moments silence, the coffin was hoisted once more and the melancholy little group filed down the steps and away to the walled *camposanto* across the highway.

Isolated atop an ancient temple platform, the magnificent priory of Santo Domingo Yanhuitlan was singled out by art historian John McAndrew as, "the handsomest sixteenth century church in Mexico." This extraordinary architectural monument is also a unique treasure house of Spanish colonial art.

Ancient Yanhuitlan had enjoyed wealth, power and prestige for hundreds of years before the arrival of the Spaniards. As one of the leading kingdoms of the Mixteca Alta, its influence extended beyond its local boundaries, as far south as the Oaxaca Valley. This independent tradition cost Yanhuitlan dearly when it refused to pay tribute to the Aztecs and murdered Montezuma's ambassadors. The outraged emperor immediately launched a punitive expedition. Yanhuitlan was sacked and a thousand of its leading citizens were taken to be sacrificed to the vengeful gods at Tenochtitlan.

With the fall of the Aztec empire, Yanhuitlan submitted to Spanish rule virtually without protest. The leading Spanish settler and *encomendero* of Yanhuitlan was the *conquistador* Francisco de Las Casas, a relative of Cortés by marriage.

He established a close alliance with the native lord, who took the Christian name Gabriel de Guzmán and continued to enjoy much of his former wealth and influence.

The Dominicans at Yanhuitlan

Although a Dominican mission was established here as early as 1538, Las Casas and Guzmán resented the friars' presence and refused to give them assistance. In the face of this hostility, the Dominicans left Yanhuitlan and for the next ten years devoted their energies to building the monastery at nearby Teposcolula. During this time, Gabriel de Guzmán was accused of idolatry and imprisoned, no doubt at the instigation of the disgruntled friars.

It was not until 1548, two years after the death of Francisco de Las Casas, that the Dominicans returned to Yanhuitlan. In spite of his antipathy to the friars, the concern of the *encomendero* for his eternal soul prevailed, and in his will he provided generously for the construction of a splendid new church. His devout son and heir, young Gonzalo de Las Casas, enthusiastically embraced the project, sending to Spain for artists and skilled artisans.

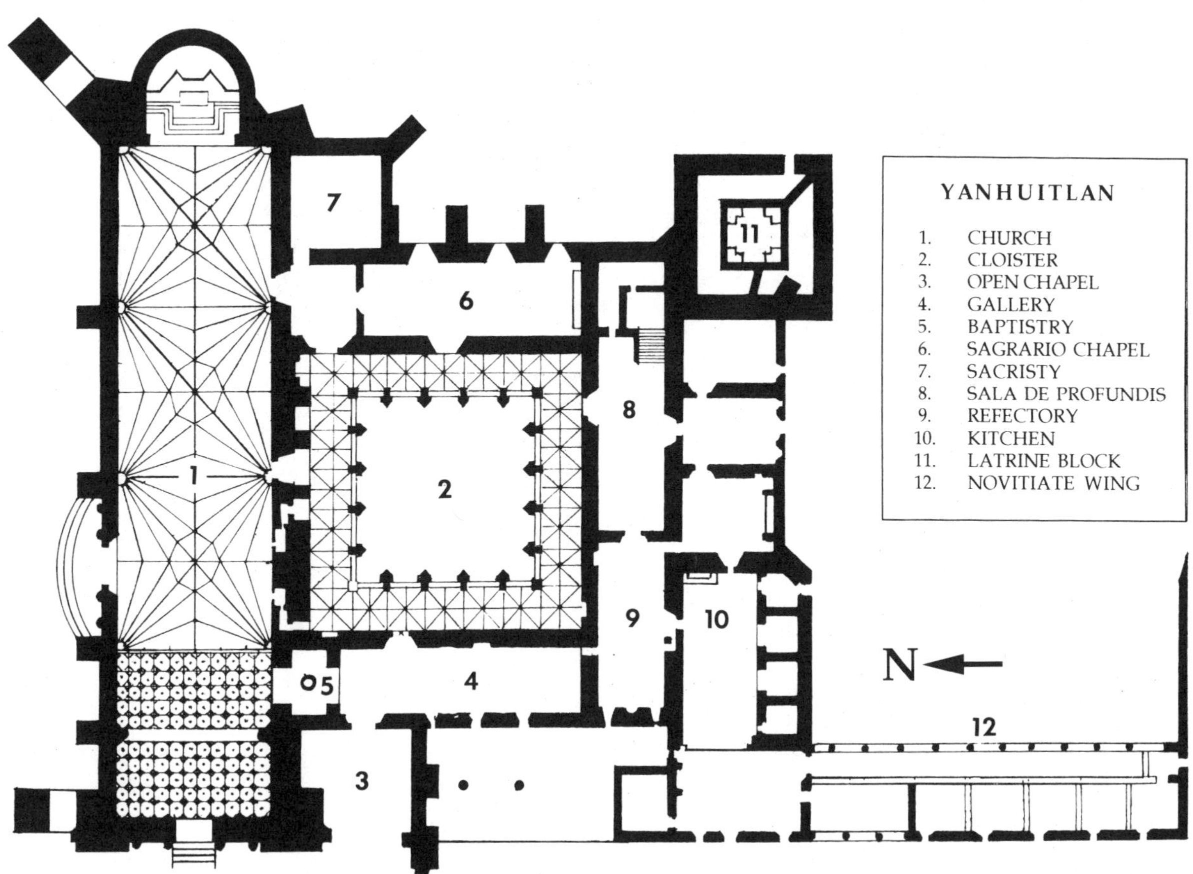

The design and construction were supervised by two talented friars, Fray Antonio de Serna and Fray Francisco Marín, both men of culture with a talent for administration and architectural planning. Assigned to Yanhuitlan in 1550, these peripatetic friar/architects also worked at Teposcolula and Coixtlahuaca during the critical periods of planning and early construction.

The foundation stone at Yanhuitlan was ceremoniously laid by Gonzalo de Las Casas himself, amid a throng of kneeling Indians. Friars inscribed crosses on the stones, and reportedly placed gold and silver objects and precious stones into the foundation. The arduous tasks of quarrying and laying the stone were performed by Indian workmen, which buoyed local pride in the great priory.

Construction continued for more than twenty years, with crews of 400 to 600 workers. The *convento* was completed in time for the 1558 Dominican chapter meeting. The church seems to have been roofed by 1570, when the magnificent main altarpiece was being assembled and installed.

As the only permanent priory in the Mixteca Alta, Yanhuitlan was the main focus of Dominican activity in the region. A Mixtec language center was established here to prepare the friars for their missionary tasks. Its school for training Indian craftsmen, modeled on Fray Pedro de Gante's famous Franciscan school of San José in Mexico City, may account for the high quality of workmanship in the area—in woodcarving and painting as well as stoneworking. The school was used as a workshop by the Spanish artist Andrés de la Concha for producing large altarpieces for churches and monasteries throughout the region.

The early colonial period was a golden age for Yanhuitlan. Dominican influence was unchallenged. In the mid-17th century, the Dominican chronicler Father Burgoa extolled the clear air, healthy climate and agricultural riches of the valley, praising its inhabitants as docile, civilized and peaceful.

However, with economic reverses and the decline of the native population, hard times came. Dominican influence waned as the power of the civil authorities and the secular religious hierarchy grew. With Independence, the priory was buffeted by a series of violent and destructive blows. When royalist forces occupied it from 1812 to 1821, the church was used as a stable and soldiers were quartered in the choir. In 1866, the priory was occupied by French troops, who were finally ousted after two years by General Porfirio Diaz, later to be president.

Despite the suppression of the monastic orders in 1859, the Dominicans contrived to stay on at Yanhuitlan until 1889, confidently casting a new set of bells in 1877. The last Dominican to preside over the mission was a pugnacious one-armed friar who unsuccessfully attempted to incite the local population against his successor, a secular priest.

The Monastery Plan

The deliberate siting of the monastery on a pre-Columbian temple platform dramatized the triumphant ascendancy of the Christian religion over this citadel of the former religion.

Three flights of steps, on the east, north and west, convey the visitor up to the vast atrium. Originally surrounded by a high wall, it measured 350 by 500 feet. Here, Father Burgoa witnessed the stirring spectacle of several hundred Indian youths dancing in green-plumed headdresses.

The priory follows the customary plan for monastery buildings in Mexico: a massive fortress church with a *convento* attached to the south side. Yanhuitlan has no separate open chapel. Although there is plenty of space in the atrium on the north side of the church, it seems that no chapel was ever built there. Most likely, the spacious arched *portería* functioned as an open chapel in the early years.

As might be expected in a building that took almost a century to complete, the monastery is a fascinating stylistic mix. The main influence is that of the later Spanish Plateresque, an inspired fusion of Renaissance forms with late Gothic and Moorish elements, leavened at Yanhuitlan with baroque additions.

The mercurial stonework seems to change color with the weather and the time of day, sometimes pinkish white, at other times greenish gold.

The Church

The formidable exterior has the look of a medieval citadel, fortified against the ever present risk of earthquake. The rugged walls and the

Yanhuitlan, west front

great rounded bastion of the apse are braced by stepped, pierced buttresses. Arched windows with Gothic tracery are cut into the lofty nave, which is covered by handsome ribbed vaults.

The west front is not the first one. The present *retablo* facade was superimposed on an earlier Plateresque front after an earthquake, sometime in the early 1600s. Part of the original facade was recently discovered still in place behind the present one, and can be glimpsed from the elevated choir. Two arched openings, also belonging to the earlier facade and now visible only from the choir, flank the choir window—an arrangement perhaps copied from the west front at Cuilapan.

The present facade follows the sober baroque pattern set by the west front of Santo Domingo de Oaxaca. Confined between the two plain tower bases, the three carved tiers are cleanly articulated by classical orders of columns and pilasters with sharply projecting cornices. The center section is emphasized in each tier, with sculpture niches in the flanking compartments. The decorative sculpture is also simplified—even stilted—although it contributes to the classical restraint of the facade.

The main doorway is outlined by a diamond-paneled arch with *fleurs-de-lis* and an ornate keystone carved with a book symbolizing the Gospel. Dominican dogs, with stylized curly ears and tails, brandish torches on the pedestals of the flanking Tuscan columns. St. Francis and St. Catherine of Siena occupy the side niches. The intervening spaces are carved with shells and bands of intricate scrolls and tendrils.

Above, an engaging relief in a bold cruciform frame depicts the Virgin of Mercy with the Christ Child, sheltering a Dominican friar and a nun beneath her ample cloak—probably St. Dominic and St. Catherine. Chubby cherubs, above and below, add to the naive charm of this tableau. Paneled Ionic pilasters and elaborate sculpture niches with diminutive statues frame the large choir window on the third level. The facade terminates in an ornate curvetted pediment in the Flemish style. The recently strengthened bell tower is an 18th century addition.

The North Doorway

The elegant 16th century north portal is the most sophisticated Plateresque doorway in Oaxaca. Now beautifully restored, it is closely related to the north doorway at Cuilapan. Although much larger and more ambitious, it may be the work of the same architect.

The "door-within-a-door" design is again skillfully manipulated, using a limited but highly effective vocabulary of forms. Candelabra columns of giant urn-like sections piled one upon another and capped with medieval capitals frame the portal, pushing through the upper cornice to embrace the nave window in a crowning arrangement of curved moldings and obelisks.

The inner doorway restates the outer pattern. On each side of the coffered and paneled doorway, fluted Corinthian columns rise to support a plain entablature and attic. The scalloped pediment above, flanked by candelabra pinnacles, artfully echoes the crowning motif of the outer frame. Although the medallions in the spandrel are blank, the escutcheons beside the pediment overhead are intricately carved with the Instruments of the Passion, surmounted by heraldic plumed helmets.

The Church Interior

The scale of the Yanhuitlan nave is audacious for earthquake country. It is over 200 feet long, almost 60 feet wide, and soars to a breathtaking 100 feet in height.

These cathedral-like dimensions are complemented by a sequence of majestic Gothic vaults covering the three main bays of the nave and the choir. They are supported on clusters of ribs springing from huge drum corbels that are embedded in a deep running cornice encircling the nave. A coffered half dome of Roman proportions covers the apse. Each coffer contains an eight-pointed golden star—the celestial symbol of St. Dominic—shining forth against the dark blue of the vault.

The broad triumphal arch framing the sanctuary is exuberantly ornamented with ornate stucco reliefs, probably executed in the early years of the 17th century by same Pueblan artists who created the lavish painted ceilings at Santo Domingo de Oaxaca. The painted figures of Peter, Paul and the archangels step out from a web of interwoven strapwork.

The vast raised choir dominates the west end of the church. Beneath the choir is one of the most treasured fixtures in the church, an exquisitely crafted wooden *artesonado* ceiling. Recently restored to its original condition, it is one of the few surviving 16th century examples in Mexico—and the largest.

The *mudéjar* design is carved entirely of cedar and is composed of alternating hexagonal and diamond-shaped modules, or *casetones*. Each recessed module is built up from richly carved and painted moldings, creating a densely textured allover pattern. Carved pineapple pendants in the form of delicate rosettes hang from the center of each hexagon.

The rib-vaulted baptistery below the choir contains a font of striking design. Its stone basin is conventionally carved with leaves and Dominican rosettes and stands on a fluted shaft supported by four corner legs in the form of plumed serpents devouring each other. This pre-Conquest motif refers to the four cardinal directions of ancient cosmology and is rendered even more Indian by the serpents, feathery scales. Why such pagan imagery was tolerated by the friars is a mystery.

Two doorways on the south side of the nave are related stylistically to the north porch. The portal beside the sanctuary, leading to the sacristy and Sagrario Chapel, is surmounted by candelabra pinnacles and a gilded shell relief. The door to the cloister, now closed, more closely resembles the outer frame of the north doorway. The classical shell niche in the pediment contains the crowned figure of St. Catherine of Alexandria.

Note the ornate baroque organ case standing on a giant pillar beside the choir.

The Altarpieces

Yanhuitlan is a virtual museum of gilded altarpieces, in styles spanning the entire colonial period. The lofty main *retablo* is one of the great heirlooms of Mexican art. It rises over 50 feet to fill the apse, almost touching the coffered vault. The altarpiece takes the form of a folding screen with lateral wings thrusting out towards the nave.

Gilded columns across the four main tiers divide the *retablo* into seven vertical bands, or *calles*, in which paintings and sculptures alternate. The framework of the altarpiece was remodeled in the 17th century in the Solomonic style, with spiral columns of twisted vines, shell niches, ornate baroque scrollwork and all manner of carved foliage.

The paintings and sculptures are earlier, dating from the 16th century. The paintings have been identified as the work of Andrés de la Concha, a celebrated Sevillian painter who traveled to Mexico in 1568, under commission from Gonzalo de Las Casas, to supervise the construction of the altarpiece.

After completing the Yanhuitlan altarpiece in the early 1570s, he worked on *retablos* at Coixtlahuaca and other area missions, in collaboration with the Flemish artist, Simón Pereyns.

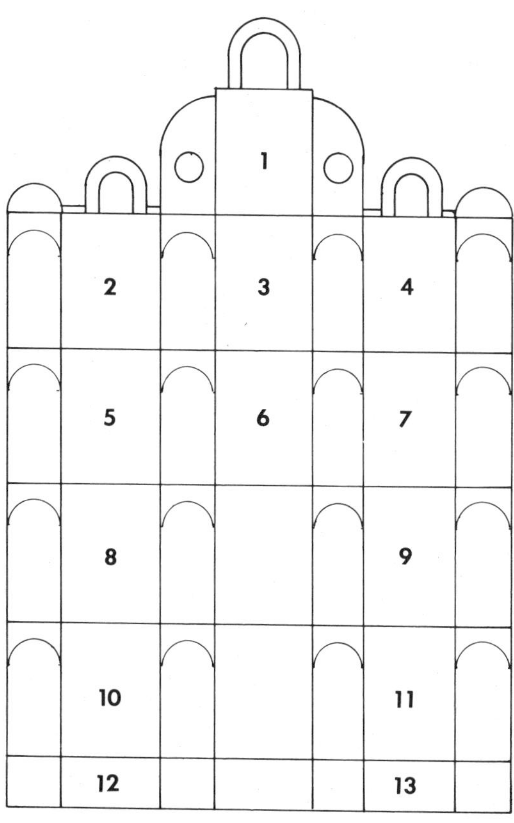

YANHUITLAN

The Retablo Paintings

1. Descent from the Cross
2. Virgin of the Rosary
3. Coronation of the Virgin
4. Last Judgement
5. The Ascension
6. The Resurrection
7. Pentecost
8. Three Kings
9. The Circumcision
10. The Annunciation
11. Adoration of the Shepherds
12. Mary Magdalene
13. St. Jerome

De la Concha painted in the Mannerist style of the Andalusian school, using a mellow but subtle palette. The paintings at Yanhuitlan are considered the earliest, the most complete and the best of his Mexican oeuvre. The classical lines of the compositions are enlivened with passages of baroque fire, tempered by traditional Spanish realism.

The subjects are compelling and easily read. The figures are dramatically grouped but attention is always paid to facial expression and graceful gestures. The artist painted familiar scenes from the lives of Christ and the Virgin. There are 16 panels in all, some of which are in urgent need of cleaning and restoration.

On the first tier, the Annunciation contrasts an energetic Archangel Gabriel, bedecked in flying drapery, with the meek figure of the Virgin Mary at prayer. The Adoration of the Shepherds, on the right, effectively captures the awe of the rustics, who gaze fixedly upon the Christ Child floating ethereally in the foreground. The leading shepherd wears Indian sandals. The Adoration of the Magi, on the other hand, portrays splendid personages in luxurious dress.

Because of their height and soiled condition, the paintings in the upper tiers are difficult to make out, but on the fourth level, there is an interesting Virgin of the Rosary, surrounded by 15 miniatures of the Mysteries of the Rosary. Among the pious worshippers at her feet are Gonzalo de Las Casas and his family—the benefactors of Yanhuitlan—whose remains rest in wall niches behind the *retablo.*

A Michelangelesque Last Judgment, opposite, shows Christ and his disciples amid the cowed company of the Damned. The sinuous Descent from the Cross, at the top of the altarpiece, is another masterly composition.

Sixteen handsome statues, set in shell niches, complement the paintings. Monumentally carved in dignified frontal poses, the hands and faces are expressively detailed. Although they have been attributed to Pereyns, they were in all likelihood produced in De la Concha's workshop. The brilliant *estofado* treatment of the draperies may be the result of later retouching.

The figures come in fours: the Four Evangelists, the Four Founders of the religious orders, the Four Doctors and the Four Fathers of the Latin Church. Only St. Dominic, the patron saint of Yanhuitlan, stands alone at the top.

The careful preservation and restoration of this magnificent altarpiece for future generations should be a national project of the highest priority.

No less than ten side *retablos*, many incomplete, line the nave, running the gamut of colonial styles, from Plateresque to "Churrigueresque." The altarpiece of La Soledad (the Virgin of Sorrows) contains a large portrait of the Virgin, also thought to be the work of De la Concha.

The Sagrario Chapel

Another artistic treat awaits the visitor before leaving the church. Beyond the sacristy lies the Sagrario Chapel, formerly part of the *convento.* At the far end of this long dimly-lit chapel is an altarpiece carved entirely from onyx, a work unique in Mexico.

Framed in the Dominican fashion with slender baluster columns and a baskethandle arch ornamented with rosettes, the central relief depicts the Descent from the Cross. John and the Three Marys mourn the dead Christ, whose limp body is gently lowered by turbanned figures.

Despite its two-dimensional aspect, a quality of the Italian engraving from which it was derived, this tableau achieves great expressive power through the fresh approach of the anonymous native sculptor.

The Convento

A huge basket-handled archway, set at the top of a broad flight of stone steps, frames the *portería.* This arched portico to the *convento* may have functioned as the open chapel of the monastery in the early years. From its stagelike platform, the friars preached to the outdoor congregation.

At the rear of the *portería* is the rectangular entry to the *convento*, framed by foliated panels and surmounted by a Dominican cross emblazoned with the motto of the Order, "Therefore we preach Christ Crucified."

The long gallery to the right of the entrance foyer displays an extraordinary collection of religious artifacts. Painted wooden angels, belonging to the *barrio* chapels of Yanhuitlan, are arranged along the sides. On Good Friday and other feast days, these figures, wearing wings and crowns, are borne in procession through

Yanhuitlan, cloister walk

the town, carrying the Instruments of the Passion.

The most evocative of the processional figures in the gallery is the macabre image of Death Enthroned. Fashioned in part from a human skeleton, it is a powerful artifact of the folk imagination.

Mounted on the end wall is a worn relief of St. Dominic, once the centerpiece of a major *retablo.* Arms outstretched, the saint shelters the friars and nuns of his Order. In its present condition, the original crisp carving and painted detail can only be imagined.

The Cloister

At the heart of the *convento* is the delightful two-story cloister. Recently restored by INAH, it radiates a peaceful monastic atmosphere. Built around an ancient cypress that still shades the patio, its flagged walks provided a secluded haven for meditation and prayer.

Fine stonework in the Dominican style distinguishes the elegant lower cloister. The molded arcades rest on compound piers of Doric half columns faced with sturdy prow buttresses. Ribbed vaults cover the five bays on each side, increasing in complexity above the corner compartments. As in the church, the vaults spring from rounded corbels set in a running cornice. The diminutive roof bosses are carved with traditional Dominican emblems like the eight-pointed star.

Recessed into the end of each walk are large, rosette-studded niches which contained sacred images for the friars to contemplate as they perambulated the cloister. Embedded in the north walk, linking church and cloister, are two wall confessionals, their openings also outlined with bands of rosettes. On the east walk is a noble pedimented doorway, with unusual spiral pedestals, that originally opened into the Sagrario Chapel.

Another square Plateresque doorway opens into the former *sala de profundis*, on the south side of the cloister. The doorway is framed by broad coffered bands with incised, diamond-point decoration and surmounted by the Dominican cross. Here, the friars paused to pray for their departed brethren before breaking bread in the adjacent refectory.

The vestibule beside the *sala de profundis* is lit by a dramatic open-work Maltese cross cut into the wall above an outer doorway. From here, a monumental stone staircase winds around the stairwell, its heavy stone rail topped with *fleur-de-lis* finials. A huge fresco of St. Christopher stands above the stairs—the only mural to survive in the *convento.* The saint strides from the water carrying the Christ Child on his shoulder, observed by a diminutive friar in the lower right hand corner, holding out a lantern. The awkward proportions and rigid folds of Christopher's drapery and pantaloons give the mural the force of an icon.

The upper cloister provides a good vantage point for viewing the rugged tower and south wall of the church. Built of brick, the walks have wood beamed ceilings instead of stone vaults. Friars' cells open onto corridors behind the cloister walk. Dominican insignia are carved on the lintels of each cell doorway and include such esoteric emblems as the hand of St. Catherine of Siena holding the heart of Christ, St. Thomas Aquinas holding a church and book, and the Five Wounds of Christ superimposed on the Cross of Alcantara. Although the partitions between the cells are gone, the picturesque window seats remain.

Another fascinating adjunct to the *convento* is the latrine block, located across the roof at the southeast corner. Its simple but practical design incorporates 16 stalls, four on each side of a square, amply ventilated by large windows and a central shaft. An ingenious flush system, fed by piped water, disposed of the waste.

Back in the atrium, a long flight of steps leads down to the village plaza. At the foot of the stairway, embedded in the wall of a small domed springhouse, we can trace an ancient carving of a Mixtec warrior in full regalia—a reminder that this impressive Christian monument was built upon the foundations of an older and very different culture.

Note: Because Yanhuitlan has no resident priest, the church is only sure to be open on Sunday mornings, just before and during midday mass.

TEJUPAN

The village of Tejupan, on the Pan-American Highway, marks the junction with the road to Coixtlahuaca. The little mission of Santiago Tejupan, beside the plaza, faces away from the town across a vast cemetery.

Remodeled with a huge bell tower and baroque dome, the mission retains a few characteristic Dominican features, notably the elaborately paneled west doorway, flanked by floating candelabra pilasters. The *portería* is also classic, its sturdy Doric arcade inset with a medallion of the Dominican cross. The coffered arch of the sanctuary echoes Yanhuitlan.

Take a moment to walk through the ornate cemetery gateway into the graveyard—a fantasy of broken colonial headstones and modern tombs like miniature churches, crafted of whitewashed concrete and wrought ironwork.

The road to Coixtlahuaca starts from the northwest corner of the plaza.

COIXTLAHUACA

Plain of the Snakes

In February 1926, chilled to the bone after a long night on horseback, Manuel Toussaint, the champion of Mexican colonial art, breasted the final ridge. There he caught his first glimpse of the magnificent monastery of Coixtlahuaca on the far side of a narrow valley, eerily illuminated by the pale dawn light. Today, no horse is necessary. The once remote monastery is accessible by a paved road—a scenic ride through wooded ravines and arid badlands.

Now a poor and sparsely populated village, in prehispanic times Coixtlahuaca was an important religious center, the site of a celebrated temple of Quetzalcoatl, the "Plumed Serpent," from which Coixtlahuaca derives its name.

When the Dominicans arrived here in the 1540s, they appropriated the elevated temple site for their new monastery. The friar/architect Fray Antonio de Serna drew up the plans, and construction was under way by the end of the decade, although the complex was not completed until 1570.

The monastery stands apart from the village atop the ancient platform, which was laboriously carved into the east side of the hill and built up on the west. The elongated atrium fills the entire site, although the monastery buildings are grouped together at its south end. Following a sandy, tree-lined pathway that cuts across the atrium from the inconspicuous northern gateway, the first structure we come to is the elegant open chapel, set back from the church.

The Open Chapel

The chapel is the earliest part of the monastery, built soon after its founding in 1546. A forerunner of its more elaborate cousin at Teposcolula, the chapel is separate from the church. Raised on its own base, it comprises an elaborate vaulted sanctuary and adjacent sacristy. A broad archway frames the chapel front like a proscenium, creating a dramatic stage for religious ceremonies and outdoor masses.

As at Teposcolula, the chapel is braced in front by flared flying buttresses. Unfortunately, the graceful fluted columns that supported the arched buttresses have been filled in with rough masonry, so that the soaring effect of the original chapel has been greatly diminished.

The majestic polygonal vault that once crowned the sanctuary has fallen, its broken ribs jagged against the open sky. Although on a more modest scale, the recently renovated ceiling of the adjacent sacristy gives us an idea of the original grandeur of the sanctuary vault.

In contrast to its classical architecture, the relief carving of the chapel has a strong indigenous flavor. Here at Coixtlahuaca, we find the only significant use of prehispanic themes and indigenous artistic conventions in Oaxaca.

Native *tequitqui* stonecarving—deeply undercut flat relief—predominates in the sculptural detail. A curving frieze of spreadwinged eagles entwined with plumed serpents rims the entire archway—images that bring to mind the Indian cult of Quetzalcoatl, whose inner sanctum may have stood on this very spot. Primitive angels, wearing crowns and medieval robes, head the supporting capitals, while medallions emblazoned with the Cross of Alcantara decorate the spandrels.

The Church

Indigenous touches carry over into the sculpture of the fortress church, which is otherwise thoroughly European in its design and iconography. The monumental walls, buttresses and tower abutments are plain, unrelieved by windows, parapets or decorative detail. Ornament is strictly confined to the west front and the north portal—but what magnificent ornament!

Although both facades are classically compartmented with large paneled doorways and rose windows, their sculptural programs are different and their overall effects quite distinct.

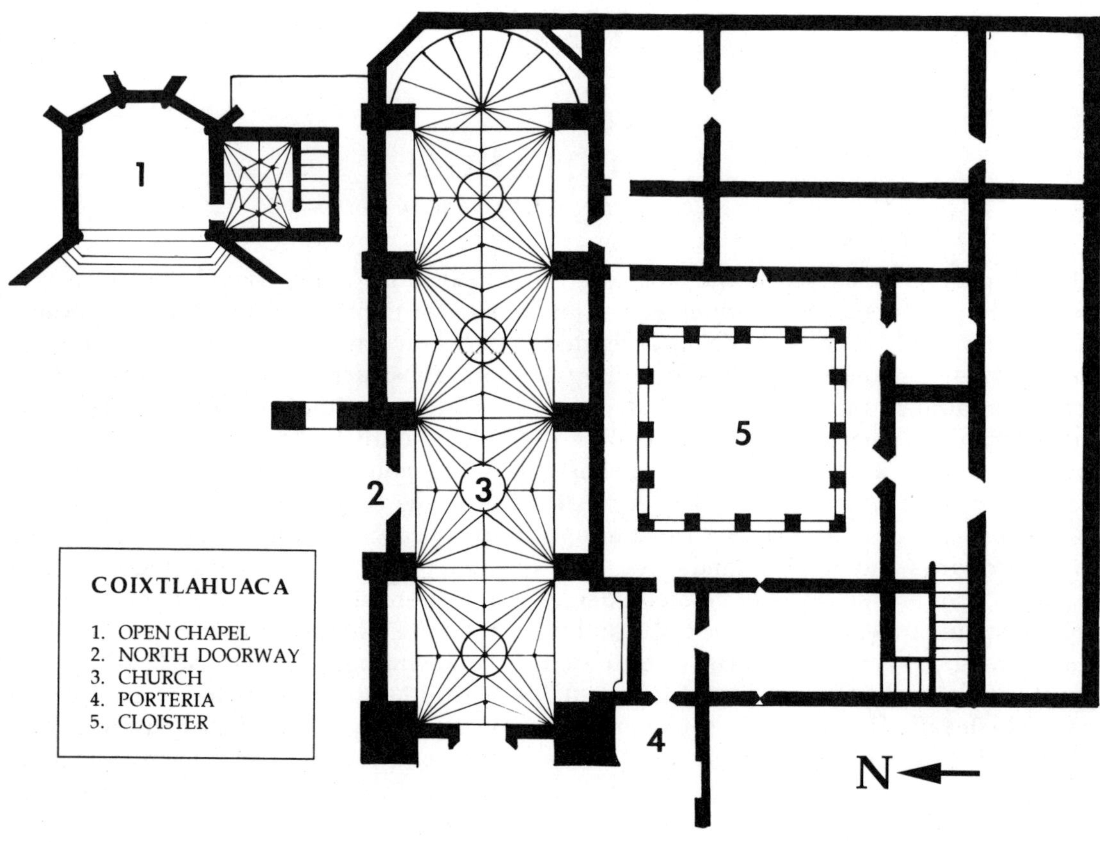

Coixtlahuaca, church facade

The North Portal

This is the earlier and the more original of the two portals—a Plateresque tapestry in stone, woven by skilled native stonecarvers.

The lofty doorway is conventionally Dominican, its beveled arch outlined by diamond-point paneling. *Fleur-de-lis* crosses, identical to those of the adjacent open chapel, stand out in high relief from the spandrels.

A trio of unusual relief figures occupies the pediment above the doorway. John the Baptist, with an inscription identifying him as the patron saint of Coixtlahuaca, is in the center; St. Peter and St. Paul stand on either side. The rigid stance, stylized drapery and floppy feet flexing forward over the supporting brackets, give the figures a medieval cast, recalling the reliefs of the north door at Huaquechula (Chapter Three). This may reflect their common origin in Flemish prints.

The rose window in the top tier of the portal is a rarity in Mexican churches. Here, the basically Gothic form has been transformed by geometric detailing into a classical motif. Rosettes in coffered bands ring the opening and stud the twelve outer petals of the design.

But the most interesting features of the north facade are the reliefs that flank the rose window. They represent the Instruments of the Passion, arranged in a flattened, codex-style composition. The sun, moon and stars surround the central crucifix with a full complement of objects associated with the Crucifixion: the crown of thorns, the scourge, the ladder, the cockerel, Veronica's veil and less frequently portrayed items, like the 30 pieces of silver spread in a band at the top. Speech scrolls issue from the mouths of two Roman soldiers.

The West Front

While it shares many Plateresque motifs with the north portal, the west front is more assertive. Based on the designs of the Renaissance architect Sebastiano Serlio, the bold forms of this *retablo* facade have a classical authority, especially when thrown into sharp relief by the intense sunlight of the Mixteca Alta.

A coffered archway and pilasters, richly embossed with rosettes instead of diamonds, frame the imposing doorway. The Latin inscription on the frieze is dated 1576—probably to commemorate the completion of the facade. The triangular pediment above encloses a superb bas-relief of the quadripartite Spanish imperial coat-of-arms, framed by the two-headed Hapsburg eagle.

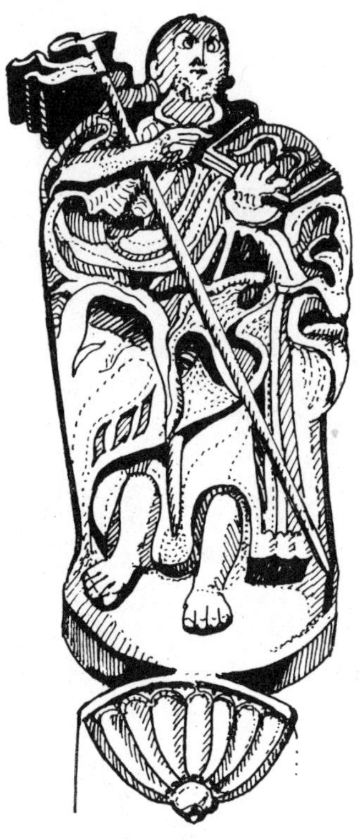

Coixtlahuaca, John the Baptist

The rose window overhead is virtually identical to that of the north portal and is divided by slender colonnettes from the massed tiers of shell niches that extend upwards on both sides of the facade. Each niche is carved with winged cherubs and knotty tree crosses in several variations, greatly enriching the texture of the facade.

The top tier may be a later addition. The decapitated statue at center represents St. Dominic holding up the church. Above the saint soars the dove of the Holy Spirit, now also headless, whose spread wings recall the eagles around the chapel archway. Outsized Renaissance medallions with stylized busts of eminent Dominicans fill the outer compartments.

The single-stage south tower is typically Oaxacan, ornamented with a tiled dome and applied pilasters in folk Ionic style.

The Church Interior

The spacious interior at Coixtlahuaca is a match for the grandeur of Yanhuitlan. Magnificent wheel vaults cover the four main bays. Their radiating ribs—molded, incised and painted with floral designs—create a colorful canopy high above the long nave. The bosses are delicately carved with black-and-white Dominican crosses, saints and diminutive scenes of the Crucifixion—details best viewed from the raised choir.

The vaulted underchoir is easier to examine. Here we can admire the festive baroque doorway to the Chapel of the Virgin of Guadalupe (formerly the baptistery), its painted archway set atop an extravagant pair of spiral columns.

Instead of the narrow coffered sanctuary we saw at Yanhuitlan, Coixtlahuaca boasts a broad apse roofed by a vast segmented rib vault, providing an ideal setting for the magnificent main altarpiece.

The Main Altarpiece

The dazzling main *retablo* is the artistic and religious focus of the church. Its ornate white-and-gold baroque framework rises through five tiers, each encrusted with luxuriantly carved foliage and scrolled cornices, and is divided into five vertical *calles* by complex *estípite* columns.

As at Yanhuitlan, the altarpiece is a showcase for several paintings and sculptures from an older 16th century *retablo.* A few surviving Renaissance columns from the earlier frame can be identified by their swagged, fluted shafts and Ionic capitals.

Of the fourteen painted panels, eleven are attributed to the 16th century master, Andrés de la Concha. Despite their neglected condition, these are major works, considered to be among the finest group of Mannerist paintings in the New World.

Occupying the outer compartments of the three lower tiers, they illustrate many of the same episodes from the life of Christ that we saw at Yanhuitlan: the Annunciation, the Adoration of the Shepherds, the Adoration of the

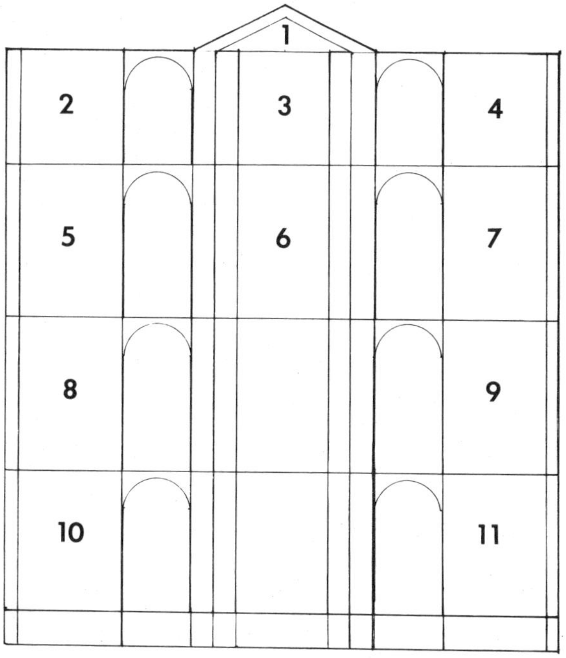

1
2 3 4
5 6 7
8 9
10 11

COIXTLAHUACA

The Retablo Paintings

1. God the Father
2. St. Anne
3. Trinity
4. St. Joachim
5. Ascension
6. Crucifixion
7. Resurrection
8. Presentation in the Temple
9. Three Kings
10. Adoration of the Shepherds
11. Annunciation

Magi, the Presentation in the Temple and the Resurrection.

The compositions are striking, with animated figures in the style of Tintoretto, enhanced by a cool palette of blues, greens and violets.

The Annunciation in the lower right panel is particularly appealing: a lithe Archangel Gabriel inclines intimately towards the graceful Virgin, who modestly lowers her eyes. In the Ascension panel, the imposing figure of Christ in Glory stands before the Virgin and the Apostles—a scene made more dramatic by the angular black and purple background.

Simón Pereyns, the Flemish master who collaborated with De la Concha at Yanhuitlan and created the Huejotzingo altarpiece (Chapter Three), may have carved several of the figure sculptures at Coixtlahuaca. Various saints, apostles and Doctors of the Church are portrayed in magisterial poses with eloquent faces and luxurious draperies. John the Baptist, in the center, is a muscular saint of heroic bearing and expressive features.

When properly cleaned and restored, this altarpiece will assume its rightful place of honor among Mexico's finest artistic treasures.

Several other *retablos* of interest rest in large side niches along the nave. Near the sacristy, on the south side, is a rare altarpiece in a style transitional between the Renaissance and the Baroque. The Virgin of the Rosary is paired with Passion scenes in a classical frame of fluted Corinthian columns.

Note also the boldly paneled red and gold wall pulpit, mounted high on a molded, corbeled base.

The Convento

From the unassuming *portería* a carved entry admits us into the rambling *convento*. Although more modest than its counterparts at Cuilapan or Yanhuitlan, the cloister has a satisfying simplicity. Only the lower level is intact, its fluted arches resting on heavy piers with plain squared buttresses and attached half columns. Long spine moldings run along the the tunnel vaults of the cloister walks, joined at intervals by powerful ribs springing from huge drum corbels.

A variety of decorative doorways, some framed with *alfiz* moldings and pointed Isabelline arches, are scattered throughout the *convento*. One cloister doorway is carved with intricately patterned relief scrolls and foliage. Its companion portal, at the top of the stairway to the choir, is surmounted by a bold candelabra *alfiz* enclosing a sinuous thistle pattern. Note the fine linenfold door.

Although the arcades of the upper cloister are missing, the visitor can still explore this level by climbing the baronial stairway on the south side. Much of the rest of the monastery is in ruins. To the south, nothing remains but catacomb-like chambers beneath crumbling arcades. Of all the Oaxacan monasteries, Coixtlahuaca is the least altered,despite its neglected interior. Like Manuel Toussaint, the visitor will be well rewarded, without having to endure such an arduous journey.

Coixtlahuaca, open chapel—pelican relief

A few miles south of Tejupan, the Pacific coast road branches off the Pan-American highway to the west. As it winds through the narrow Teposcolula valley on its way across the Sierra de Tlaxiaco, it passes through the town of ***San Pedro y San Pablo Teposcolula****.*

TEPOSCOLULA

Place of the Carved Copper Axes

When the Dominicans moved here in 1538 from Yanhuitlan, they infused new life into this rainswept valley. They relocated the mission town, and from the dark red soil leveled an atrium for the new monastery of St. Peter and St. Paul.

The friars introduced highly profitable silk raising, exploited salt mining and developed cochineal dye production. By mid-century, Teposcolula had become the richest and most populous town in the Mixteca Alta. After 1580, however, the collapse of the silk industry and the spread of devastating epidemics among the natives brought about a rapid decline in the community's fortunes—a decline from which the town has never fully recovered.

The Open Chapel

The only lasting monument to Teposcolula's brief golden age is the monastery, especially its magnificent open chapel—one of the great masterworks of Spanish colonial architecture.

This unique outdoor temple displays an audacity of design unique in 16th century New Spain. The apogee of Dominican architecture in Oaxaca, it surpasses all other open chapels in Mexico, including those at Cuernavaca, Tlalmanalco, Cholula and even the Basilica at Cuilapan.

An impressive double loggia, 140 feet in length, faces the atrium. The front arcade, set on the fluted shafts of giant Doric columns, reaches the commanding height of 40 feet. The rear colonnade, much lower to allow for an

upper story, creates an impression of great depth.

Projecting angled buttresses focus attention on the hexagonal sanctuary—the dramatic centerpiece of the design. Although the spectacular rib-vaulted dome over the chapel has collapsed, the few remaining fragments give some indication of its former grandeur.

The elegance of the detailing matches the awesome scale of the chapel. Its geometrical forms—coffered paneling, sparely ornamented with fluting and diamond-point decoration—manifest a classical nobility and sobriety. There is no sign of the decorative flora and fauna that adorn its sister chapel at Coixtlahuaca.

The doorway at the rear of the chapel is typically Dominican, with a flattened arch, candelabra finials and the *fleur-de-lis* escutcheon of the Order. A concealed staircase in the rear wall ascends to the elevated choir gallery.

Construction of the chapel began around 1550,

Teposcolula, west front

probably under the supervision of Fray Francisco Marín, the friar/architect who worked at other major Dominican monasteries throughout Oaxaca. Whether it follows Father Marín's own design we do not know, but this remarkable building is clearly the product of a audacious and original talent.

The Church

Compared to the open chapel, the rest of the monastery seems provincial in design and workmanship.

Perhaps as a result of earthquake damage, the 16th century church was extensively altered in the 18th century with a cruciform plan and domed east end. The uneven finish of the west front suggests a local rebuilding effort, with limited funds and without benefit of an architect.

The unusual tower bases, divided by crude pilasters and pierced with sculpture niches, are a radical departure from the usual plain bastions of most Dominican facades and may be a rustic recollection of the baroque basilican front of La Soledad in the City of Oaxaca.

The facade sculptures have a primitive vigor, particularly those of St. Anthony and the Virgin. The large, scrolled stone brackets beneath the lower niches are the most original feature and may have been part of an early arcade demolished by tremors. Helmeted angels, looking remarkably like Indian warriors, clutch the Instruments of the Passion.

The west doorway is framed with reliefs of stylized vines, braided with fruit, leaves and rosettes. The baroque pediment atop the facade encloses the statues of St. Peter and St. Paul.

The interior has been remodeled with tiled walls and floors, and decorative wrought ironwork. The single remaining *retablo* is a gilded late baroque work with a naive polychrome relief of the Descent from the Cross. Other notable furnishings include a pair of rococo wooden confessionals with elaborately carved arms, arching foliated backs and scalloped canopies. A matching vestment chest is kept in the sacristy. A large painting of the Virgin of the Rosary in the sanctuary shows what may be the old church in the background.

Sadly, the celebrated *retablo* by Simón Pereyns and Andrés de la Concha, completed in 1581

Teposcolula, facade sculpture of the Virgin

for the princely sum of 4300 pesos, has vanished, although seven crudely overpainted but still imposing wooden saints in the *convento* may belong to this lost altarpiece.

The Convento

In stark contrast to the Renaissance splendor of the open chapel, the *convento* has a confined, medieval ambience. The recessed double archway of the *portería* rests on archaic capitals, carved with rosettes and acanthus leaves and clearly related to the facade brackets.

Beside the *portería* is the curious little chapel of St. Gertrude. Since the friars were reputedly buried here, the crypt-like arrangement of groin vaults set on massive, stubby spiral columns may be intentional. On the far wall, the altarpiece of St. Barbara appears to be an assemblage of pieces from several old *retablos*. The central image of the saint is framed by painted portraits of John the Baptist, St. Francis and St. Jerome, which may date from the late 16th century.

The cloister is a disappointment. Its rude arcades and rough brick vaults show little of the architectural styling and accomplished stonecarving that distinguish most other Dominican cloisters in Oaxaca.

Several large 18th century paintings fill the bays of the cloister, illustrating scenes from the life of St. Dominic. The sentimental Birth and Baptism of St. Dominic is crowded with figures and anecdotal incident in the baroque fashion. In another panel, St. Dominic receives the Rosary from the Virgin, as well as a stream of milk from her breast.

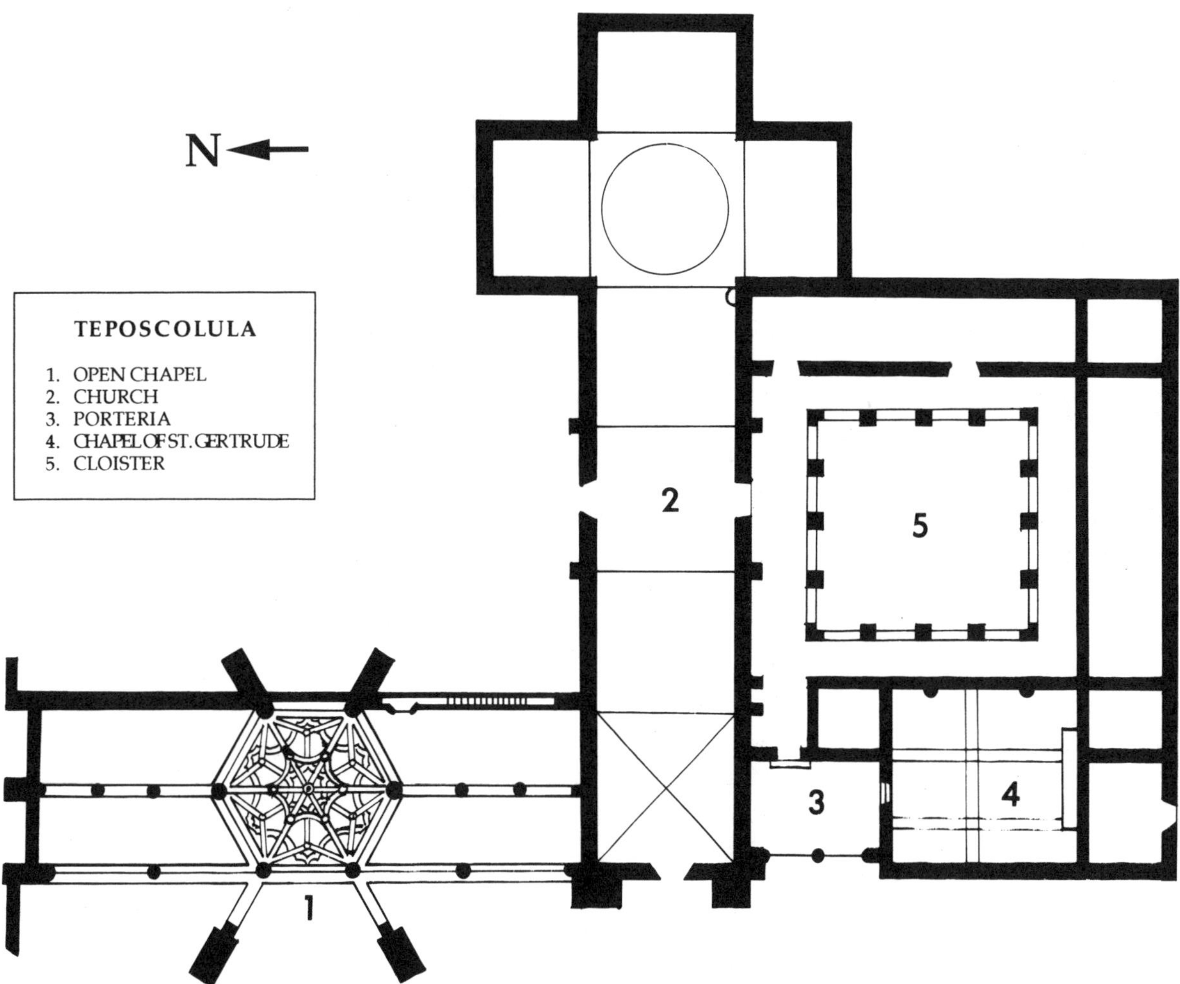

Hidden in the remote valleys of the Mixteca Alta are numerous village churches, many of which are former Dominican missions. The largest and most accessible of these is the monastery at Tlaxiaco, a market town on the winding main road about 50 kms west of Teposcolula.

TLAXIACO

Bloodstained Ballcourt

From prehistoric times, Tlaxiaco has straddled the main trade route to the Pacific coast, controlling access to the surrounding highlands. Recognizing its strategic location, the Aztecs established a garrison here in the 15th century, in order to keep the communities of the Mixteca Alta in subjection.

Following the collapse of the Aztec empire and the subsequent Spanish settlement, a Dominican mission was founded here in the 1540s by Fray Gonzalo de Lucero—the first one to be established in Oaxaca.

The mighty church looms above the tree-shaded square in front—originally the monastery atrium. The austere lines of the west front recall the landmark Dominican mission at Oaxtepec in Morelos (Chapter Four), its immediate predecessor. Braced by angled buttresses, the soaring ashlar stonework of the facade shows off the handsome pedimented doorway to advantage. Like the Renaissance doorways at Tula and Tepeji in Hidalgo (Chapter Two), it is framed by diamond-faceted coffering, flanked by fluted half columns on paneled pedestals and capped by a trio of bulbous candelabra. This assertive entry may have been the model for Dominican doorways throughout Oaxaca.

A simple bull's-eye window and a small Dominican cross pierce the cliff-like expanse of the upper facade, whose severity is softened by a curvetted baroque parapet that undulates across the top and around the towers.

Four Gothic vaults cover the nave, springing from huge drum corbels set in a running cornice in the classic Dominican manner. But the best preserved vault in the church is under the choir, which still retains its original carved bosses.

A giant coffered arch covers the three-sided apse, possibly the first of its kind in Mexico and the precursor of the majestic sanctuary vaults at Cuilapan and Yanhuitlan.

Tlaxiaco, west doorway

This is the end of our exploration of the fortress monasteries of Mexico, in all their variety. It is difficult not to stand in awe of these 400 year old buildings, situated for the most part in provincial towns and poor villages across the republic.

Whatever the social costs of their construction, the 16th century monasteries endure as impressive monuments to the determination and religious faith that moved their builders, men who shaped the material as well as the spiritual worlds of Spanish colonial America.

GLOSSARY

(S) = Spanish (N) = Nahuatl

Acanthus. Large-leafed plant with thorny foliage, the basis for classical architectural ornament.

Ahuehuete *(N)*. Type of Mexican cedar tree.

Alfiz *(S)*. Decorative rectangular molding over a doorway. *See also* **Mudéjar**.

Almagre *(S)*. Orange/ocher earth color.

Amate *(N)*. Mexican bark paper, usually made from the fig tree.

Arabesque. Elaborate ornamental pattern of Islamic origin.

Archivolt. The inner curve of an arch, a soffit.

Artesonado *(S)*. Intricate coffered ceiling design, usually of joined, inlaid wood.

Ashlar. Rectangular cut stone facing.

Atlantean. Type of column or building support in the form of a male figure.

Atrium. Enclosed churchyard or monastery forecourt.

Banderole. Inscribed pictorial banner, a philactery.

Barra *(S)*. Ceramic or building clay.

Barrio *(S)*. Quarter or district of a Mexican town.

Bas-relief. Low relief, a sculptural technique.

Biretta. Ecclesiastical cap or beret, worn by Catholic prelates.

Camino Rondo *(S)*. Passageway enclosed within the walls of a church.

Calle *(S)*. 1. street 2. vertical band of an altarpiece.

Camposanto *(S)*. Cemetery, burial ground.

Cantera *(S)*. Stone used for contruction, usually fine-grained and easily worked.

Cavetto. Molding with a concave cross section.

Cenobite. Monk, especially of the early Christian church.

Chichimec *(N)*. Nomadic indigenous peoples of prehispanic and early colonial northern Mexico.

Chiluca *(N)*. Fine-grained white limestone quarried in the Valley of Mexico.

Chimalli *(N)*. Aztec war shield.

Codex. Prehispanic or early colonial document in indigenous pictorial style

Coffer. Geometric sunken panel used in architectural decoration.

Cofradía *(S)*. Religious fraternity or brotherhood.

Convento *(S)*. Monastery residence that includes the cloister.

Copilli *(N)*. Aztec plumed warbonnet.

Cordon *(S)*. Knotted cord.

Crozier. Bishop's crook or staff of office.

Cuauxicalli *(N)*. Aztec ceremonial vessel for holding the hearts of sacrificial victims.

Dado. Ornamental border on the lower part of a interior wall.

Dentils. Tooth-like rectangular blocks used to ornament classical cornices.

Diamante *(S)*. Diamond, diamond shaped.

Encomendero *(S)*. Holder of an encomienda.

Encomienda *(S)*. Grant of native labor made to Spanish colonists by the Crown.

Escudo *(S)*. Decorative shield or escutcheon.

Escutcheon. Heraldic shield or coat-of-arms.

Espadaña *(S)*. Wall belfry, usually atop the church facade.

Estípite *(S)*. Column or pilaster incorporating an inverted obelisk.

Estofado *(S)*. Decorative technique for imitating clothing on religious statuary.

Flageolet. Archaic flute or pipe.

Flamboyant. Architecture of the French/Flemish High Gothic, featuring ornate, flamelike stone tracery.

Fleur-de-lis. Decorative emblem based on the lily.

Fluting. Vertical grooves decorating the shaft of a pilaster or column.

Fray *(S)*. Medieval fraternal greeting used by Spanish friars as form of address.

Fresco. Technique of painting on wet or dry plaster.

Garita *(S)*. Ornamental pinnacle or battlement in the form of a sentry box.

Grisaille. Gray monochrome used in drawing or painting.

Grotesque. Style of ornamental frieze based on classical designs, depicting fantastic birds, beasts and foliage.

Halberd. Ax-like pike or staff.

Hidalgo *(S)*. Gentleman or minor noble; from *hijo de algo*, son of somebody.

Huarache *(N)*. Native Mexican sandal.

Huerta *(S)*. Cultivated garden or orchard.

Isabelline. Hispano-Flemish Gothic architectural style, named for Queen Isabella of Spain.

Lavabo. Basin for ritual handwashing.

Lunette. Crescent-shaped space above a doorway or beneath a vault.

Macana *(N)*. Obsidian-edged Aztec sword.

Maguey *(N)*. Agave plant, cultivated in arid regions for its juice, flesh and fiber.

Mannerist. Sophisticated artistic and architectural style based on exaggerated or distorted classical forms.

Manueline. Highly ornate late Gothic architectural style, developed in Portugal, incorporating Asian and African decorative motifs.

Merlon. Decorative pyramidal battlement.

Mudéjar *(S)*. Spanish architectural style based on Moorish forms. Also called Hispano-Moorish.

Nahuatl *(N)*. Language of the Aztecs, still spoken by Indians of central Mexico.

Obsidian. Volcanic glass, sharp when chipped and used for cutting.

Ogee. Curved, pointed arch.

Pantli *(N)*. Aztec war banner.

Phylactery. *See* **Banderole**.

Pila *(S)*. Font or water basin.

Pilaster. Flattened column used as decorative architectural element.

Pinjante *(S)*. Glove-shaped pendant, a decorative device popular in 18th century Mexican architecture and design.

Pochteca *(N)*. Aztec merchant.

Portiuncula. North doorway of a Franciscan church.

Portería *(S)*. Entry portico to a monastery.

Posa *(S)*. Covered shrine or processional chapel in a monastery atrium.

Predella. Base panel of an altarpiece.

Pulque *(N)*. Native Mexican beverage made from fermented maguey sap.

Purista *(S)*. Severe, academic Renaissance style of architecture, originating in 16th century Spain.

Quetzal *(N)*. Tropical bird with brilliant red and green tail feathers.

Rebozo *(S)*. Long shawl worn around the head and shoulders.

Recinto *(S)*. Extremely hard and coarse black basalt.

Retablo *(S)*. Carved and painted wooden altarpiece.

Sala de Profundis *(S)*. Monastery chapter room.

Santo *(S)*. Popular religious statue or image.

Soffit. Underside of an arch, lintel or cornice.

Solomonic. Column with spiral decoration, often in the form of a grapevine, derived from biblical descriptions of the Temple of Solomon; term used to describe 17th century Mexican baroque altarpieces.

Spandrel. Triangular space between an arch and the rectangular surrounding frame.

Stigmata. Marks of Christ's wounds.

Tecali *(N)*. Translucent onyx, also called Mexican alabaster.

Teponaxtle *(N)*. Aztec wooden drum.

Tequitqui *(N)*. Early Spanish colonial sculpture of European forms using pre-Conquest stonecarving techniques.

Tezontle *(N)*. Porous, lightweight reddish-black volcanic stone.

Tlacuilo *(N)*. Indigenous Mexican artist or scribe.

Tlauhquechol *(N)*. Ceremonial Aztec plumed headdress.

Visita *(S)*. Non-residential church or mission, visited by a priest from a distant monastery.

Zapata *(S)*. Wooden roof beam, often decoratively carved.

Yanhuitlan, Dominican dog

BIBLIOGRAPHY

English Language

Baird, Joseph A. *The Churches of Mexico, 1530–1810.* Berkeley: University of California Press, 1962.

Braunfels, Wolfgang. *Monasteries of Western Europe.* Princeton: Princeton University Press, 1980.

Burke, Marcus B., and Linda Bantel. *Spain and New Spain.* Corpus Christi: Art Museum of South Texas, 1979.

Edwards, Emily. *The Painted Walls of Mexico.* Austin: University of Texas Press, 1966.

Kubler, George. *Mexican Architecture of the Sixteenth Century.* New Haven: Yale University Press, 1948.

McAndrew, John. *The Open-Air Churches of Sixteenth Century Mexico.* Cambridge: Harvard University Press, 1965.

Mexico: Splendor of Thirty Centuries. New York: Metropolitan Museum of Art, 1990.

Mullen, Robert J. *Dominican Architecture in Sixteenth Century Oaxaca.* Tempe: Arizona State University, 1975.

Parmenter, Ross. *A Week in Yanhuitlan.* Albuquerque: University of New Mexico Press, 1964.

Phelan, John Leddy. *The Millenial Kingdom of the Franciscans in the New World.* Berkeley: University of California, 1956.

Ricard, Robert. *The Spiritual Conquest of Mexico.* Translated by Lesley B. Simpson. Berkeley: University of California, 1966.

Toussaint, Manuel. *Colonial Art in Mexico.* Translated and edited by Elizabeth W. Weismann. Austin: University of Texas Press, 1967.

Weismann, Elizabeth W. *Mexico in Sculpture.* Cambridge: Harvard University Press, 1950.

Weismann, Elizabeth W. and Judith H. Sandoval. *Art and Time in Mexico.* New York: Harper & Row, 1985.

Spanish Language

Angulo Iñiguez, Diego. *Historia del arte hispanoamericano.* Seville: Universidad de Sevilla, 1945–1950.

Arroyo, Fr. Estéban. *Santo Domingo de Oaxaca.* Oaxaca: 1955.

Artigas, Juan B. *La piel de la arquitectura: murales de S. M. Xoxoteco.* Mexico City: Universidad Autónoma de México (UNAM), 1979.

———. *Capillas abiertas aisladas de México.* Mexico City: UNAM, 1982.

Calders, P. *Acolman: un convento agustino del siglo XVI.* Mexico City: Editorial Atlante SA, 1945.

Curiel, Gustavo. *Tlalmanalco, historia e iconología del conjunto conventual.* Mexico City: UNAM, 1988.

Diaz, Marco. *Arquitectura religiosa en Atlixco.* Mexico City: UNAM, 1974.

Fernandez, Justino. Ed. *Catálogo de construcciones religiosas del Estado de Hidalgo.* 2 vols Mexico City: Secretaria de Hacienda, 1940-42.

Flores Marini, Carlos, et al. "Conventos del siglo dieciseis." *Artes de Mexico,* no. 86/87, 1966.

Gorbea Trueba, José. *Tepeapulco.* Mexico City: Instituto Nacional de Antropología e Historia (INAH), 1957.

———. *Culhuacán.* Mexico City: INAH, 1959.

———. *Yanhuitlan.* Mexico City: INAH, 1962.

Guadalupe Victoria, José. *Arte y arquitectura en la Sierra Alta.* Mexico City: UNAM, 1985.

Islas Garcia, Luis. *Pinturas al fresco del Valle de Oaxaca.* Mexico City: Editorial Clásica, 1946.

Loyzaga, Jorge G., ed. *Catálogo parcial de monumentos religiosos coloniales del Estado de Morelos.* Mexico City: Universidad Iberoamericana, 1973.

Macazaga Ordoño, Cesar. *Nombres geográficos de México.* Mexico City: Editorial Innovación SA, 1979.

MacGregor, Luis. *Actopan.* Mexico City: INAH, 1955.

Martínez Marín, Carlos. *Tetela del Volcán: su historia y convento.* Mexico City: UNAM, 1968.

Maza, Francisco de la. *La ciudad de Cholula y sus iglesias.* Mexico City: UNAM, 1959.

Obregón, Gonzalo. *Pintura colonial en Mexico.* Mexico City: UNAM, 1965.

———. *Atlixco: la ciudad y sus monumentos.* Mexico City: INAH, 1981.

Reyes Valerio, Constantino. *Arte indocristiano.* Mexico City: INAH, 1978.

———. *El pintor de conventos.* Mexico City: INAH, 1989.

Romero de Terreros, Manuel. *Atlatlahucan.* Mexico City: INAH, 1965.

Salas Cuesta, Marcela. *La iglesia y el convento de Huejotzingo.* Mexico City: UNAM 1982.

Santamaria T. Angel. *Catedral de Cuernavaca.* Mexico City: Comisión de Arte Sacro, 1985.

———. *Teposcolula, Coixtlahuaca, Yanhuitlan.* Mexico City: Comisión de Arte Sacro, 1979.

Toussaint, Antonio. *Templo agustino de Ixmiquilpan.* Mexico City: Comisión de Arte Sacro, 1981.

Toussaint, Manuel. *Paseos coloniales.* Mexico City: Editorial Porrua, 1983.

Tovar de Teresa, Guillermo. *Pintura y escultura del renacimiento en Mexico.* Mexico City: INAH, 1979.

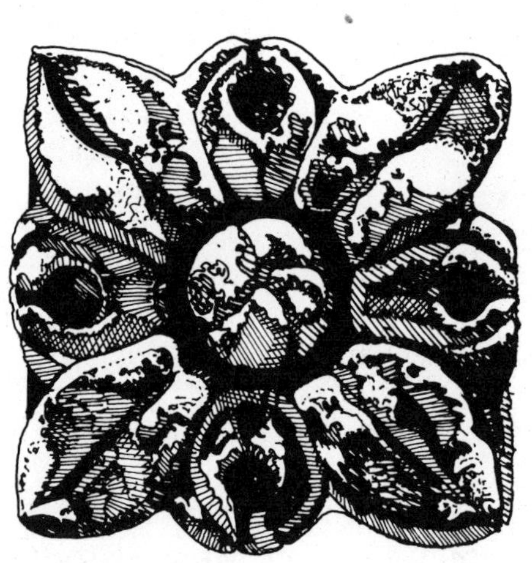

INDEX

A

B

C

D

E

F

G

T

U

V

W

X

Y

Z

RICHARD PERRY, artist and writer, has long been interested in hispanic art and architecture. He is a native of England, where he studied Spanish, art and the history of architecture. After working in advertising, he emigrated to the U.S.A, graduating from New York University with a B.A. in Latin-American Studies. He visited Mexico for the first time in 1966, attending the University of the Americas, where he became fascinated with prehispanic as well as Spanish colonial architecture. After moving to California, he studied archaeology at the University of California, Santa Barbara. He and his wife Rosalind live in Santa Barbara, where they jointly own and operate a small publishing company. Together, they have traveled extensively in Mexico, and recently collaborated on *Maya Missions*, a guide to the colonial churches of Yucatan.

MEXICO'S FORTRESS MONASTERIES is the second in a series of guides to the colonial buildings of Mexico, from Espadaña Press. The first in the series, MAYA MISSIONS, explored the churches and monasteries of Yucatan. We welcome your comments and inquiries. Additional copies of our guides can be ordered direct from the publisher:

MAYA MISSIONS	paperback: $12.95
MEXICO'S FORTRESS MONASTERIES	paperback: $19.95

Add $2.00 shipping and handling for 1 book; 50c for each additional copy.

ESPADAÑA PRESS
P.O. Box 31067, Santa Barbara, California 93130